The Courts of International Trade

The Courts of International Trade

Judicial Specialization, Expertise, and Bureaucratic Policy-Making

Isaac Unah

Ann Arbor

THE UNIVERSITY OF MICHIGAN PRESS

Copyright © by the University of Michigan 1998
All rights reserved
Published in the United States of America by
The University of Michigan Press
Manufactured in the United States of America
⊗ Printed on acid-free paper

2001   2000   1999   1998   4   3   2   1

A CIP catalog record for this book is available from the British Library.

Library of Congress Cataloging-in-Publication Data

Unah, Isaac.
    The courts of international trade : judicial specialization,
expertise, and bureaucratic policy-making / Isaac Unah.
        p.   cm.
    Includes bibliographical references and index.
    ISBN 0-472-10922-7 (cloth : acid-free paper)
    1. Foreign trade regulation—United States.   2. Commercial
courts—United States.   3. Administrative agencies—United States.
4. United States—Commercial policy.   I. Title.
KF1976 .U53   1998
343.73'087—dc21   98-8993
                                                                        CIP

To my parents, Mma-urom and James Unah
and the living memory of my brother, Igiri James Unah

Contents

Figures

Tables

Acknowledgments

This book had its genesis at SUNY, Stony Brook, where I completed my doctoral work and conducted a great deal of the research presented here. Hence, it is only fitting that I start there to acknowledge the several terrific individuals and institutions that supported me during the course of writing this book. Any attempt to list every individual who contributed to my intellectual development at Stony Brook would be futile. But I do especially want to thank two preceptors, Jeffrey A. Segal and Wendy L. Hansen, for their truly constructive support, encouragement, and friendship over the years. I credit them for helping to develop my interest in and knowledge of the U.S. judicial system and its myriad connections to public policy. I also thank Mark Schneider and Paul E. Teske, who, along with Segal and Hansen, read and made numerous constructive comments on earlier drafts of individual chapters. Several colleagues in the law and courts subfield offered helpful comments and critiques on various sections for which I am grateful: Larry Baum of Ohio State, Lynn Mather of Dartmouth, Kevin T. McGuire of UNC at Chapel Hill, Martin Shapiro of UC at Berkeley, and Stephen Wasby of SUNY at Albany.

Several colleagues in our political science department here at Chapel Hill offered much needed encouragement: David Lowery, Stuart Macdonald, Tim McKeown, George Rabinowitz, Donald Searing, Marco Steenbergen, and Mike Munger, who is now at Duke. I owe a substantial debt of gratitude to Charles T. Myers and the entire Team Y of the University of Michigan Press, who brought this book to its present form.

The judges of the Court of Appeals for the Federal Circuit and of the Court of International Trade were gracious enough to respond to my short survey of their party identification. But I am especially grateful to Judge Giles S. Rich of the Federal Circuit for sharing with me his wisdom on judicial appointments.

Many of the arguments made here have been presented in various forms at professional meetings of the Midwest Political Science Association and the American Political Science Association, and at colloquia at UNC at Chapel Hill, SUNY at Stony Brook, the University of Kentucky, and Washington University at St. Louis. I thank various participants in these meetings for helping to straighten my thinking on many of the arguments.

Some portions of the analysis appearing in chapter 7 are adapted from Wendy L. Hansen, Renée J. Johnson, and Isaac Unah, "Specialized Courts, Bureaucratic Agencies, and the Politics of U.S. Trade Policy," *American Journal of Political Science* 39, no. 3 (1995): 529–57; reprinted by permission of the University of Wisconsin Press. I thank Wendy L. Hansen and Renée Johnson for letting me use material from our coauthored paper in that chapter. Portions of chapter 8 are adapted from my article "Specialized Courts of Appeals' Review of Bureaucratic Actions and the Politics of Protectionism," *Political Research Quarterly* 50, no. 4 (1997): 851–78; reprinted by permission of the University of Utah, Copyright Holder.

I am ever grateful for research grants from the Office of the Dean of Social Sciences, UNC–Chapel Hill; the University of North Carolina Research Council; and the W. B. Turner Fellowship Program at SUNY–Stony Brook. I want also to acknowledge a number of research assistants who helped in the data-gathering effort: Heoung-Jae Bae, John Fish, Karen Fox, Stuart Koziöl, Susan De Natale, Renée Johnson, John Boklak and David Schwartz. Finally, I thank my wife, Seanid, for her love and unflagging support throughout this project, and for offering many useful comments on the manuscript.

Key Abbreviations

ABA	American Bar Association
AD	Antidumping
CCPA	Court of Customs and Patent Appeals
CIT	Court of International Trade
CVD	Countervailing Duty
DOC	Department of Commerce
FTA	Free Trade Agreement
GATT	General Agreement on Tariff and Trade
ITA	International Trade Administration
ITC	International Trade Commission
NAFTA	North American Free Trade Agreement
SIC	Standard Industrial Classification
SSA	Social Security Administration
TRAC	Trade Remedy Assistance Center
USTR	United States Trade Representative

Part 1

Specialized Courts and Bureaucracies in U.S. Trade Politics

CHAPTER 1

Specializing the Federal Judiciary through Tribunals of Limited Subject- Matter Jurisdiction

If the advocates must be specialists, can we wholly ignore the need for some specialization in the judicial systems?
Chief Justice Warren Burger[1]

The very need for economy and expertness that led to the development of administrative agencies led to a demand for the same qualities on the part of courts sitting in judgement of these agencies.
Felix Frankfurter and James M. Landis (1928)

The United States Constitution grants Congress the unlimited power to "regulate Commerce with foreign Nations." However, the actual regulating of international commercial activity is handled by independent regulatory agencies and by different organizational units within the executive branch. Several reasons have prompted Congress to delegate much of its power to regulate commerce with foreign nations. Surely among these is the generic reelection imperative. Other important reasons include the complex and seemingly intractable nature of contemporary regulatory policy, the lack of concrete subject matter expertise by congressional lawmakers, and the perennial need for programmatic efficiency in American government. For these reasons, much congressional responsibility for trade regulation in the United States has been shifted over to the president and the executive branch. The shift has not been instantaneous; neither has it always been initiated by Congress.

Throughout the twentieth century, American presidents have requested periodically from Congress additional powers to deal more aggressively with economic matters, such as international trade, that intersect with the constitutionally mandated powers of the president over foreign policy and international relations.[2] In most instances, Congress has

3

happily granted such requests, if only in order to provide the president with sufficient flexibility to act on behalf of the national interest. But for good reason, delegation of congressional powers to the president often raises important constitutional concerns due to the apparent asymmetry in the relationship between Congress and the president, which makes it difficult for Congress to adequately monitor the president and his constituents within the executive branch. The ensuing distrust and tension in the American system of government and in many similar democratic systems create the need to impose reasonable checks upon the exercise of governmental power. That is where the courts come in. In the United States, courts occupy the pivotal position of providing legal guidance ex post to, as well as inspiring discipline in, the executive branch and independent regulatory agencies, such as the International Trade Commission (hereafter ITC or Commission). How courts pursue those interrelated objectives is the subject of the research reported here.

The primary objective of this book is to explicate the nature of the interaction between federal regulatory agencies and federal courts in the process of public policy implementation. Specifically, the study seeks to extend and redirect our empirical attention concerning the political control of bureaucracy by focusing on the issue of judicial oversight of administration in the special context of judicial specialization and expertise. Generally speaking, this is a book about specialized courts, bureaucratic agencies, and U.S. trade politics, and about how the three are interlinked to produce a coherent and stable policy system. In this opening chapter, I implore your indulgence while I explain why and how an empirical study of the interrelationship among these three aspects of American government is both necessary and important.

In American society, bureaucracy is largely understood as the messenger and distributor of government policies and largesse. It remains at the very center of American life because it is the essence of our government. As a result, we have developed certain expectations and stereotypes of this much-maligned institution. We expect bureaucracy to be efficient and accountable. Yet our belief system, shaped by numerous personal encounters with bureaucracy and by mostly adverse mass media accounts, compels us to suspect bureaucracy as being anything but efficient and accountable. The way a bureaucracy performs its tasks typically shapes the type of relationships it develops with its clientele and with citizens and officials in other entities of government. That is what makes bureaucracy the underlying theme of politics in our time.

Ever since definitive social movements erupted in the turbulent 1960s, forcing greater political demands upon government, American bureaucracy has been increasingly scrutinized and evaluated, oftentimes with unrepentant belligerence. The result is the commonly held view that bureaucracy is insensitive and unresponsive to the needs of citizens. And as one informed observer of American bureaucracy, Morris Fiorina (1981, 47), pointed out, the bureaucracy is widely recognized as "a convenient lightning rod for public frustration and a convenient whipping boy" for politicians and the mass publics whenever they are occasioned to criticize government. Today, it is the rule rather than the exception for candidates campaigning for political office to criticize government bureaucracy as the paramount source and symbol of our national ailments, which critics claim can be resolved only by reining in the bureaucracy, closely monitoring its behavior, and most importantly, holding it absolutely accountable. Ronald Reagan expressed these sentiments most succinctly during his 1980 presidential campaign when he observed that "government is the problem, not the solution."

There is a general recognition even by bureaucracies themselves that accountability is of utmost importance to the proper functioning of any government; it is central to effective policy implementation in any democratic state. Accountability in government rests squarely within the corridors of the bureaucracy. It comes as no surprise, therefore, that in the empirical political science literature the interaction between politicians and bureaucratic agencies has received a great deal of attention among public policy and organizational theorists concerned about government performance. The focus is typically on the responsiveness and adaptability of bureaucratic actors and institutions to external political demands. Indeed, this scholarly interest harks back to the era of technical reform and professionalism early on in the twentieth century, when intrepid reformers sought to build the technical expertise of those who were responsible for delivering policy to the American people (Knott and Miller 1987; Wilson 1989).

In the structure of American government, bureaucratic agencies operate in an environment of constant conflict, where a complex nexus of institutional constraints molds the behavior and performance of agencies in certain predefined policy directions. The sheer number and scope of analyses of institutional conflict pitting bureaucratic agencies against various actors in the external political environment speak to the fascination of this area to researchers. In this vein, many would agree that the interaction between Congress and bureaucracy is the most studied phenomenon in American politics, largely because the institutional structure of Congress bears directly and profoundly upon the goals, resources, and operating strategies of bureaucratic agencies (McCubbins and Sullivan 1987; Weingast and Moran 1983; Weingast 1984; McCubbins and Schwartz 1984; Miller and Moe 1983; Wood and Waterman 1994; Wilson 1989).

Other important players in the political system, such as public and private interest groups, have also been given a fair amount of attention in their relationships with bureaucratic agencies, typically with strong connection to politicians. Here researchers often focus on the conflicting loyalties of politicians and the difficult trade-offs they must make between interest-group policy representations and voter preferences in the absence of an acceptable mechanism whereby the neglected or insufficiently represented group can be properly compensated (J. Berry 1977; Peltzman 1976; Denzau and Munger 1986; Gormley 1979; Mitchell 1990; Sabatier 1988).

As the individual presiding over a nationwide constituency, the president exercises sizable influence on the bureaucracy as well. And this influence is clearly reflected in the amount of attention that scholars have paid to presidents regarding their ability and effort to persuade the federal bureaucracy to carry out presidential mandates in the context of systemic budgetary and programmatic constraints (e.g., Aberbach and Rockman 1976; Moe 1982; Waterman 1989; Nathan 1986; Eisner and Meier 1990).

But while disproportionate attention has been paid to the institutions of control located within the legislative and executive branches of government, a disturbing imbalance exists regarding the level of empirical attention given to judicial influence on American public policy. After all, in Chief Justice John Marshall's aphorism, it remains the duty of the courts to say what the law is. Relatively little serious empirical effort has focused on understanding the interactions between courts and administrative agencies, particularly at levels below the U.S. Supreme Court where most court action actually takes place. Assuming that the volume of empirical research can serve as a yardstick of the level of scholarly interest that a given area commands, it seems that the interconnection between bureaucratic politics and judicial oversight has sparked remarkably little interest among scholars who study public policy, administration, and judicial politics. Many of the best-known efforts on this subject matter have been in the form of critical case studies and historical analyses with little or no quantitative applications (e.g., Shapiro 1968; Melnick 1983; Horowitz 1977; Dilulio 1987). Although case studies are valuable in furnishing detailed empirical information about a given policy area or regulatory agency, case studies do exhibit inherent deficiencies. Even the most carefully executed case study is inductive and lacks external validity, making it difficult to generalize case study findings to other policy, bureaucratic, or judicial settings.

Strengthening the need for the study reported here is a further important realization that most studies of judicial review of administrative action have centered on generalist courts. Judicial review as used in this book is the power of courts to evaluate and declare an act of Congress, the president, and administrative agencies null and void. Generalist courts are the traditional courts in American society, the kind that we ordinarily think about when the word *court* is heard, for example, the U.S. Supreme Court, the District of Columbia circuit, the numbered circuits, and local federal district courts. They are the courts whose judges collectively are believed to possess no substantive expertise in any particular policy jurisdiction. *Expertise* is used throughout this book to mean the substantive proficiency that judges display in reviewing complex and seemingly intractable decisions of administrative agencies.

It is most unfortunate that, by focusing mostly on generalist courts, researchers have largely neglected to discuss specialized courts—not because specialized courts are unimportant or uninteresting, but because they fall outside the traditional mainstream of the American court system and because scholars have failed to identify the political value of these courts. For the purposes of this work, *specialized courts* are defined narrowly as courts that possess limited subject matter jurisdiction and are staffed by permanent judges who have substantive expertise in the area. Specialized courts staffed by temporary judges also exist, but those are not the focus of this research. Historically, specialized courts are thought to serve only policy-neutral objectives, such as developing expertise to address complex policy issues and deflecting civil cases from the generalist courts (Frankfurter and Landis 1928, chap. 4; Currie and Goodman 1975). But as we shall discover, specialized courts make very important substantive contributions to our civil justice system and thus command much more than policy-neutral effects. For example, among other potential policy effects, specialized-court decisions have been shown to exert phenomenal impact upon the leniency of patent validity standards (Baum 1977) and upon the extent of trade protectionism present in the United States (Hansen, Johnson, and Unah 1995).

Here is a specific instance of the potential impact of a specialized court on the living standard of American citizens. In 1993, a court case asked a deceptively simple question: Is the Nissan Pathfinder a car or a truck? The Nissan Pathfinder at issue was a two-door, multipurpose all-terrain vehicle, also known as a sports utility vehicle. Under the harmonized tariff schedule of the United States, a *car* is defined as a vehicle used primarily for transporting persons, while a *truck* is a vehicle used primarily for transporting goods. The federal government argued that the Pathfinder was, and should be classified as, a truck because "certain segments of the automotive manufacturing industry, including persons within Nissan, view the [Pathfinder] as a 'truck'" (*Marubeni America Corp. v. United States* 1993).[3] In other words, barring any other objective evidence, the Pathfinder was a truck because it fit the common industry meaning of the term *truck*. The

Pathfinder is a fairly expensive vehicle. If the court agreed with the government, the vehicle would be subject to a higher tariff rate and correspondingly rendered even more expensive for American consumers. Assuming that the market for Pathfinders is elastic in the United States, that is, sales react directly to changes in car prices, then a higher tariff has potential to cause job losses in the U.S. auto industry in the long run.

Thus, how the court addressed this question was of interest not only to the parties directly involved in the case (Nissan and the U.S. Customs Service), but also to consumers, manufacturers throughout the entire American auto industry and its unions, and politicians in Washington. Moreover, how the court addressed the question was of importance to the U.S. economy as a whole. On May 14, 1993, Judge Jane Restani of the U.S. Court of International Trade issued her opinion on the case. According to Judge Restani, the basic structural components of the vehicle, as discussed during oral argument, suggested that the Pathfinder was a car. Also, the sample of the subject merchandise, which was available to the court throughout the trial, practically shouted to the consumer, "I am a car, not a truck." The government had lost; and its wishes to impose a higher import duty on multipurpose, all-terrain vehicles evaporated. Despite the economic and social contributions such as these made by specialized courts, when researchers and politicians discuss these courts, the coverage is usually perfunctory and dismissive and tends to focus theoretically on the perceived dangers of judicial specialization.

Several important questions remain about the nature and contributions of specialized courts. Particularly unresolved are issues concerning the interaction between specialized courts and bureaucratic agencies. How important is bureaucratic structure in the ways that specialized courts respond to administrative task decisions, given that both specialized courts and bureaucratic agencies have expertise in a given policy area; what are the substantive policy implications of courts with narrow subject matter jurisdiction and expertise; how are specialized-court judges selected; what are the core characteristics of specialized courts that distinguish them from generalist courts; what are the virtues and vices of judicial specialization for the U.S. system of justice and the administrative state; and finally, what factors condition the voting behavior of specialized-court judges in their difficult task of reviewing and monitoring regulatory agency actions? These are the key questions that this book addresses, using as a laboratory two specialized courts with exclusive jurisdiction over litigation involving U.S. international trade policy. They are the U.S. Court of International Trade located in New York City and the U.S. Court of Appeals for the Federal Circuit (hereafter Federal Circuit) located in Washington, D.C.

Some critics of specialized courts, such as Professor Martin Shapiro, believe that scholars are reluctant to study specialized courts because they perceive these courts as unnecessary in our political system. The argument goes that from a functional perspective, the objectives served by special-ized courts overlap considerably with those served by administrative agen-cies, and that there is no genuine distinction between specialist judges and bureaucrats. According to Shapiro (1968, 52), "the particular virtue of the judge is ignorance." From the standpoint of judicial specialization, this contention implies that judges who serve in specialized courts have exper-tise, which suggests that they have a narrow view of their policy area and of the law. It further suggests that specialized judges are functionally indis-tinguishable from bureaucrats who also have expertise and a narrow pol-icy focus. Overall, therefore, specialized courts create what amounts to redundancy and inefficiency in the policy process, and so they are rela-tively unnecessary: "To the extent that [judges] specialize, they lose the one quality that clearly distinguishes them from administrative lawmakers. Once they lose that quality there seems to be relatively little reason to have two separate specialists, one labeled judge and the other bureaucrat, mak-ing policy in the same field" (Shapiro 1968, 53).

Why Study Specialized Courts?

Shapiro is correct when he argues that specialized-court judges and bureau-crats are similar on the dimension of expertise and that specialized courts add a measure of redundancy to the system of policy implementation. But redundancy is not, and need not be, synonymous with inefficiency. Rather, redundancy is an effective built-in safeguard for our complex political sys-tem; it adds reliability and predictability to what would otherwise be a cost-lier and surely more chaotic system (Landau 1969).

Furthermore, I reject Shapiro's argument about the irrelevance of specialized courts as a claim that is dated. Instead, I argue here that spe-cialized courts make numerous policy as well as policy-neutral contribu-tions to civil justice and to the delivery of public policy in American soci-ety. For example, as examined in greater detail in chapter 5, specialized courts develop expertise to adjudicate cases in policy areas of special com-plexity, such as international trade, intellectual property, taxes, and nuclear energy. To this list some would assuredly like to include environ-mental policy, where Congress continues to debate complex new rules in response to new forms of environmental degradation caused by advance-ments in technology. In addition, specialized courts contribute tremen-dously toward improving overall judicial capacity by deflecting civil cases from generalist courts. During this era of burgeoning civil and criminal dockets in the courts, where the energy and pecuniary resources of courts and court personnel are being stretched to the limit (Miner 1993; Posner 1983), specialized courts have become invaluable. Most important, specialized courts, whether willingly or unwillingly, have a strong impact in shaping the direction of policy in their subject matter jurisdiction. It is therefore quite necessary and important that we begin to take these courts more seriously, to learn and appreciate how they operate in order to take full advantage of their contributions, and to enrich future debates should it become necessary to establish more specialized courts to alleviate the burdens of civil case volume that grip the present system.

Other compelling reasons exist why political scientists and legal scholars should study specialized courts. We can use these courts as venues to validate behavioral and legal theories of decision making that have heretofore been developed and tested only in generalist court settings, thereby expanding our knowledge repertoire. We can anticipate new insights and new conclusions that would challenge, or at the very least modify, conventional wisdom. Take for example the seemingly straightforward idea of judicial deference. For decades political scientists and legal scholars have maintained that *courts* as a whole give extraordinary deference to bureaucratic agencies' interpretation of statutes in accordance with Supreme Court precedents. No doubt this is a desirable conclusion, as the Rehnquist Court has repeatedly emphasized. But empirical examination of a dual system of expertise, that is, a system where a court and the bureaucratic agency being reviewed both possess considerable expertise over a single policy area, may well lead us to tame our inferences and compel us to reconsider judicial review more holistically in a manner that accurately reflects the dissemination of civil justice in society as a whole, and not just within the mainstream of American judicial politics.

In almost all functional units of modern government, expertise is increasingly an indispensable commodity in public policy formation. The following examples will demonstrate this point. In Congress, the basic structure of decision making is the committee system. And as Jones, Baumgartner, and Talbert (1993) point out, the need to protect committee turf and programs has led to each committee claiming issue monopoly and hence relative expertise over the particular issues under its control. The growing influence of policy think tanks and of different configurations of sophisticated interest groups in framing policy debates in the United States (Berry 1977; Caldiera and Wright 1995; Gray and Lowery 1996) speak to the value of expertise in influencing governments. The tendency for a powerful corporation employing in-house lawyers with considerable advocacy experience in the corporation's area of business to hire even more specialized law firms to represent the corporation in court also attests to the importance of expertise and specialization (McGuire 1995). Moreover, government bureaucrats are hired to deliver public policy in modern political systems because of their relative knowledge and expertise in economics, chemistry, engineering, policy analysis, and law, which allow them to take active control of a policy agenda. Indeed, bureaucratic expertise is especially crucial when the policy domain is characterized by high levels of technical complexity (Allison 1971; Rourke 1984; Khademian 1992; Eisner 1991).

In recent years, political discourse on the expertise of government officials has included consideration of judges' expertise (Baum 1994a; Meador 1983; Revesz 1990). Do specialized judges make better (i.e., more judicious) policy decisions than do generalist judges by virtue of their knowledge of the subject matter; if so, do the resulting benefits outweigh the perceived dangers of specialization; is government making full use of the talents of specialist judges? In European democracies these queries have been largely settled in the affirmative and so specialized courts are widely and effectively used to settle both civil and criminal disputes (Shapiro 1981, chap. 2).[4] The United States, though still lagging behind, appears to be catching up with this trend, albeit incrementally. Historically, popular support for the creation of specialized courts has been discouraging, but recent debates over specialized courts have resulted in a slow shift toward more specialization of the judicial function through subject matter concentration. According to Justice Sandra Day O'Connor, there is "no doubt that when a judge has a particular expertise in an area or field of law, that the judge can prepare for hearings with less time and can resolve issues more quickly and perhaps better."[5] That shift toward more specialization in the judiciary is clearly manifested in the creation or expansion of several specialized courts over the past two decades, including constitutional courts such as the Court of International Trade and the Federal Circuit.

The subject matter concept is also enjoying limited application as an institutional device in some large intermediate circuits for avoiding or eliminating intracircuit conflict. In the Fifth Circuit, for example, there is an "oil and gas" panel that handles all appeals dealing with that subject matter. Granted, the oil and gas panel of the Fifth Circuit came into being because of unusual circumstances. It was created to overcome the frequent problem of judges recusing themselves from these types of appeals to avoid the appearance of impropriety. But other examples of subject matter specialization exist. Virtually all federal administrative agencies employ administrative law judges (ALJs), who can rightly be classified as specialty judges; their job is to settle legal disputes in their respective agencies and to make policy recommendations to agency leaders. In recent years the number of administrative law judges in the federal government has grown phenomenally, with some agencies having as many as 750 ALJs.[6] To achieve a greater understanding of our judicial system and to discover the value of expertise in judicial policy-making, it is important to study various aspects of specialized courts and to compare them with those of generalist courts.

Finally, the scant scholarly attention paid to specialized courts and their policy role may suggest to many that these courts are new to the U.S. judicial landscape. But as former Supreme Court Justice Felix Frankfurter and his collaborator James M. Landis suggest, nothing could be further from the truth. Writing about seventy years ago, Frankfurter and Landis observed, "An important phase in the history of the federal judiciary deals with the movement for the establishment of tribunals whose business was to be limited to litigation arising from a restricted field of legislative control" (1928, 147). As the administrative state began to take hold with the infusion of meritocracy and expertise, there was concomitantly a need to establish specialized courts to oversee these bureaucratic experts. Thus, courts with limited subject matter jurisdiction have existed in the United States for well over a century, interpreting and applying the law in a number of policy areas of special complexity. For example, the Court of International Trade started as an obscure but important tribunal in 1890. Yet the court has been the subject of precious little systematic empirical research by either economists or political scientists who study administered protection. Table 1 presents examples of specialized courts along with their selected characteristics. These courts are ordained by Congress under either its Article 1 (legislative) powers or Article 3 (constitutional) powers to perform ministerial or judicial functions. The primary difference between the two types of courts rests in the extent of the constitutional privileges and protections they enjoy. Article 3 specialized courts have greater levels of constitutional protection than Article 1 courts. Judges in Article 3 courts enjoy lifetime employment and guarantees against salary reduction for any reason; Article 1 judges do not have such protections. Some of the functional features unique to specialized courts are discussed later in chapter 5.

Organization of the Study

The presentation of material in this book is subdivided into three incremental parts. Part 1 examines the character and dynamics of specialized courts and regulatory agencies. Chapter 1 has detailed why specialized courts are worthy of careful study and has set the stage for many of the arguments to follow. Chapter 2 chronicles the history of the specialized

TABLE 1. Specialized Courts and Selected Characteristics

Court	Year Established	Number of Judges	Judicial Status	Article of Creation	Area(s) of Concentration
Bankruptcy Court	1984	326	Trial	Article 1	Bankruptcy cases
U.S. Court of Appeals for the Federal Circuit	[1909] 1982	12	Appellate	Article 3	International trade, patents and trademarks, federal claims; federal employment decisions; veterans affairs; customs regulations and classIfications
U.S. Court of Federal Claims	[1855] 1982	16	Trial	Article 1	Monetary and land claims against the federal government
U.S. Court of International Trade	[1890] 1980	9	Trial	Article 3	International trade, customs regulations and classifications
U.S. Court of Military Appeals	1950	5	Trial	Article 1	Decisions of military courts martial
U.S. Court of Veterans Appeals	1988	7	Trial	Article 1	Military veterans matters
U.S. Tax Court	1924	19	Trial	Article 3	Federal taxes

Source: Baum 1990, 37; Epstein et al. 1994; Revesz 1990; Administrative Office of the United States Courts 1994; Redden 1982.

Note: The year designated in brackets is the year of original creation. A specialized court is one that has a limited subject matter jurisdiction and is staffed by permanent rather than temporary or rotating judges. Under this definition, the Foreign Intelligence Surveillance Court (FISC) is not a specialized court even though it concentrates on a single policy area. The FISC was established in 1978 under Article 3 and is staffed by seven district court judges all selected from different circuits. FISC judges are assigned on a monthly, rotating basis. The FISC has jurisdiction over domestic electronic surveillance for foreign intelligence-gathering purposes. The Railroad Reorganization Court (RRC), established in 1973, falls in the same definitional category as the FISC. The RRC hears cases about the transfer of assets from solvent to insolvent railroads and has five temporary judges selected from the district courts and the courts of appeals. The RRC is an Article 3 court.

courts of international trade and examines the selection of judges to these courts. Here I analyze the official requirements for the selection of specialized-court judges and the unofficial roles played by patronage, partisanship, interest groups, and qualification in the selection process. I make an attempt to empirically evaluate the criticism often leveled at specialized courts that their judges hold lower qualifications on average than generalist court judges do because of the level of scrutiny they receive in the selection process. Chapter 3 delves more deeply into the policy issue of international trade. It gives a political history and the functions and decisional strategies of the two most important venues of U.S. trade policy implementation—the ITC and the International Trade Administration (ITA) of the Department of Commerce (DOC)—and examines how trade cases flow through these administrative agencies to the courts. In explaining the functions and decisional strategies of these agencies, the chapter also explores common problems or irregularities in agency decision making that prompt the need for external checks on agency conduct.

Part 2 focuses on the theoretical underpinnings of the study. Chapter 4 discusses possible mechanisms of judicial control of bureaucracy and reviews the literature on how the president, Congress, and interest groups each try to control or influence federal bureaucracies to achieve their desired policy objectives. In chapter 5, I rely on administrative, legal, and behavioral approaches to develop a unified theory, and I generate hypotheses of how specialized courts, as legal institutions with certain unique characteristics, may exert influence on the bureaucracy. I refine the explanation of these hypotheses in chapter 6 and discuss the data and techniques used in testing them. I rely on both primary and secondary data, which describe economic and political characteristics of industries, as well as on court data derived by content analysis of trade court opinions. Because the dependent variables I seek to explain have binary outcomes, I use mostly nonlinear estimation techniques (probit and logit) to analyze the data.

While some of the earlier chapters do contain some specific discussion of data analysis and results, for example, chapter 2, it is the chapters in Part 3 that consider the core findings and implications of this work. Chapter 7 discusses results of the analysis I performed on the Court of International Trade, examines how this court differs in its decisional trends from generalist courts at the trial level, and identifies the core variables conditioning decision making in specialized trial courts such as the Court of International Trade. Similarly, chapter 8 addresses these issues as they pertain to the specialized courts of appeals, using the Federal Circuit as an example. Chapter 9 summarizes the findings and considers their implications.

CHAPTER 2

Specialized Courts of International Trade and the Selection of Judges

The United States Court of International Trade and the Court of Appeals for the Federal Circuit are the two lower federal courts with exclusive subject matter jurisdiction, as opposed to regional jurisdiction, over American trade policy. The United States Supreme Court, however, remains the final arbiter of all trade disputes.

In recent years, a phenomenal development has taken place in American trade politics. Until the pivotal year of 1979, Congress had expressed relatively little formal interest in fully "judicializing" American trade politics and remedies. But starting with the enactment of the Trade Agreements Act of 1979, which authorized judicial review of "any factual findings or legal conclusions" of agency determinations, Congress has brought the courts into the administration of nearly every aspect of American trade laws. Generally speaking, there is now in place in the United States a comprehensive system for judicial review of civil actions concerning all aspects of import transactions. In fact, presently, a commentator would be negligent to remark upon U.S. trade policy without acknowledging the extensive role of the courts in this area. As Peter D. Ehrenhaft, former special counsel for tariff affairs in the Department of the Treasury, noted, this recent development "demonstrates our long-standing faith in the power of legal machinery" (1981, 598).

By increasing judicial involvement in trade implementation, Congress has sought to directly limit administrative discretion and strengthen the hands of agency clientele such as big business, labor unions, private citizens, and even foreign-owned and foreign-based companies that may have grievances with U.S. regulatory agencies. Recent news accounts suggest that the United States has made some significant gains in its aggressive effort to expand access to American-made goods abroad. By bringing the courts into the oftentimes pugnacious politics of protectionism and encouraging copious judicial review, the government hopes to gain credibility here and abroad as a real fair trader, sincerely committed to leveling the playing field.

Two basic objectives will be explored in this chapter. The first is to introduce the United States trade courts by chronicling their gradual evolution and legitimation, starting from the late nineteenth century, when these courts occupied an obscure position in American trade politics, to the present, when they hold a relatively prominent position in the U.S. trade system. To understand policy change that emanates from judicial review, it oftentimes is necessary to understand how the judges who make the policy decisions are selected and the factors that contribute to their selection. Decades of empirical research on judicial selection to the Supreme Court (Segal 1987; Segal, Cameron, and Cover 1992), courts of appeals (Howard 1981; Slotnick 1984), and district courts (Goldman 1991; Stidham and Carp 1987) suggest that the various participants in the judicial selection process, and especially the type of judges actually selected, have critical impact upon politicized judicial outcomes. A second objective of this chapter therefore will be to explain how judges are selected to specialized courts and what are the key explanatory factors underlying such selection, drawing from the extensive body of research on appointment to generalist courts.

The U.S. Court of International Trade

International trade has always been an important part of the U.S. economy, indeed right from the beginning of the republic. When lawmakers assembled in May 1789 for the first session of Congress, tariff and trade were recognized as the foundation of the economy, and they quickly became the earliest and most pressing issues tackled by the nascent Congress. International trade was considered important enough that serious concerns were raised by many that the government was not giving trade the attention it deserved and that, as a consequence, other nations would not regard the United States "as a serious trading partner as it was still tinkering with its constitution instead of organizing its government" (Farber and Sherry 1990, 132). Thus, one of the first key pieces of legislation enacted by the First Congress was a tariff bill to help the government discharge its debt and protect manufactures.[1] But as Judge Jane Restani of the Court of International Trade pointed out in an essay explaining the historical role of judicial review in the relationship between Congress and the executive branch, it was not long after this bill was enacted that U.S. courts became involved in resolving disputes between the federal government and citizens over tariffs (Restani 1988, 1076). But that involvement did not follow a structured or a systematic institutional framework. Individual problems were handled as they arose, and there was no specific court or tribunal to adjudicate tariff and customs disputes. Judicial review was conducted in the federal courts of general jurisdiction.

An institutional framework was introduced when Congress passed the Customs Administration Act of 1890, the first significant legislation to directly affect the ongoing collection of customs duties and the first key action toward the historical evolution of U.S. trade courts. This act created the Board of General Appraisers, a nine-member, quasi-judicial administrative unit within the Department of the Treasury, which would eventually become the United States Court of International Trade. The board served a clearly delineated purpose. Its primary function was to "examine and decide" cases involving decisions of the United States Customs Service concerning protests against tariffs levied upon imported merchandise. Gradually, the number and types of decisions related to importation grew, and the board soon assumed more of a judicial character than an administrative one. Meanwhile, the board's title became a source of confusion for many about whether it was an administrative body or a court. Indeed, one Senate report stated at the time, "Some foreign countries refused to honor commissions to take testimony issued by the Board [because] it bears the name of a board and not the title of a court."[2] Consequently, the board was dissolved in 1926, and all its functions were transferred to the United States Customs Court by the Act of May 28, 1926.

These changes were more symbolic than substantive, though, because they pertained largely to the nomenclature. The board was renamed the Customs Court, but its jurisdiction and functions remained practically unchanged, and board members officially became judges of the new court. The gradual evolution of the trade courts continued when Congress took another important step thirty years later to integrate the Customs Court more firmly into the United States judicial system by bestowing upon it greater institutional recognition. This recognition came in 1956 when Congress revised the jurisdiction and procedures of the Customs Court and declared it an Article 3 court, with the plenary constitutional protections discussed in chapter 1. Politically, the change was one of immense significance because it ensured the court greater permanence within the broader framework of American trade politics.[3] But problems persisted, especially with regard to the court's jurisdiction and power to provide relief to American businesses and other litigants.

In 1980, Congress passed the Customs Court Act, which created the United States Court of International Trade, to implement the broad judicial review powers enacted into law in the Trade Agreements Act a year earlier. The establishment of this court was prompted primarily by jurisdictional confusion in resolving trade disputes and providing remedy. As one House committee report stated, the "primary statutes governing the United States Customs Court [failed to keep] pace with the increasing complexity of modern trade litigation."[4] Under previous law, the Customs Court had had concurrent jurisdiction with the federal district courts in civil actions arising under any act of Congress providing for revenue from imports "except [in] matters within the jurisdiction of the Customs Court" (D. Cohen 1981, 473). As a result, when trade cases were filed in the district courts, judges there would interpret the law to mean that they had first to inquire whether the action could have been challenged and settled in the Customs Court. If their inquiry yielded an affirmative finding, they would ordinarily dismiss the case for lack of subject matter jurisdiction. In essence, due to the antiquated and uncertain nature of the law, many cases were being decided upon jurisdictional grounds rather than upon their merits.

Numerous deleterious consequences followed. For instance, astute lawyers saw opportunities to shop for more favorable forums in which to litigate their cases, creating even more rampant doctrinal confusion in the system. Many businesses, trade associations, and private citizens bringing lawsuits incurred unnecessary expenditures as a result and suffered momentous frustration because their lawsuits kept ricocheting between the Customs Court and district courts, even though these plaintiffs felt strong conviction about the legitimacy and justiciability of their grievances.

These harsh realities increasingly disenchanted the Justice Department and judges of the Customs Court of their desire for uniformity in the trade law. Also disenchanted were members of the customs and international trade bar and an alliance of business, consumer, and trade groups, including the American Importers Association, which represents such retail giants as JCPenney, Sears, Kmart, and others.[5] Fortunately, there was an emerging consensus within this policy community that significant reforms were needed. With the support of several business associations, members of the professional bar and the Justice Department took the initiative and urged Congress to act. Senate Judiciary Committee chair Edward Kennedy (D-Mass.), and subcommittee chair Dennis DeConcini (D-Ark.) sponsored the bill in the Senate to establish the Court of International Trade to correct those anomalies. Peter Rodino (D-N.J.) of the House Judiciary Committee sponsored a similar bill in the House of Representatives.[6] Senator DeConcini's remarks of September 24, 1980, provide the clearest justification for creating the court:

The clarification and expansion of the customs court's jurisdiction is warranted not only because it will eliminate the considerable jurisdictional confusion which now exists, but because of the other important considerations: considerations of judicial economy, and the need to increase the availability of judicial review in the field of international trade in a manner which results in uniformity without sacrificing the expeditious resolution of import-related disputes.[7]

As the senator noted, improving access to judicial review through uniformity (and therefore predictability) in the law was the main objective for creating the court. The question is why Congress chose this route to address these problems and not another. The answer rests on cognitive and institutional grounds. In the judicial context, uniformity can be achieved in one of two ways. First, Congress can try to enact legislation that covers all future contingencies and that is crafted in clear, straightforward language to facilitate judicial review. Second, Congress can concentrate judicial review of trade matters in a single specialty court, thereby blocking opportunities for litigants to shop around for the optimal forum. The more politically feasible and advantageous of these alternatives is clearly the second because trade is a technical area of law that requires expertise. Concentrating judicial review of trade matters in one specialty court recognizes the problem of human cognitive limitations and also raises the possibility for blame avoidance by lawmakers (Weaver 1986; also McCubbins and Schwartz 1984). And so Congress opted for the second option. Theoretically, the establishment of the Court of International Trade ushered into existence the era of decisional uniformity in resolving trade disputes. But more important, it solidified a growing presumption that administered-protection decisions of regulatory agencies are subject to legal challenge.

On the subject of importation, the Court of International Trade is the first court of record with all the powers of law conferred by statute upon any district court of the United States. Thus, in terms of procedure, the court is equivalent to any federal district court. But it is perceived by many as being a notch lower in public status than federal districts courts. It has nine active-duty judges, including a chief judge, each appointed by the president and confirmed by the Senate. In establishing this court, Congress was careful to try to neutralize, at least in principle, the effects of politics and ideology on the court's business. In the initial proposal to redesignate the Customs Court as the Court of International Trade, one stated objective called for removal of a party affiliation requirement that had guided appointments to the Customs Court. But in order to preserve the integrity of judicial review, this requirement survived. Thus, under current statute, no more than five of the nine active-duty judges appointed to the Court of International Trade may be from the same political party.

The chief judge's tenure lasts until the incumbent reaches age 70, after which a new chief judge is designated by the president. Although the chief judge manages the court and tries to instill a sense of collegiality and harmony within it, the paramount function that the incumbent performs is case assignment. Cases are usually assigned on the basis of expertise or in a manner that promotes legal continuity and judicial economy. It is not unusual, therefore, to find a judge being assigned only cases dealing with classification matters or antidumping matters for long periods of time. Apart from the benefits accruing to legal continuity and judicial economy, this method of case assignment constitutes an effective way for judges to develop and amplify their expertise in a particular area. Each case is assigned to one judge, who hears or reviews the arguments and writes an opinion for the court. However, as former chief judge of the court Edward D. Re noted, under extraordinary circumstances the chief judge may designate three judges to hear a case if there is present a valid constitutional question, if the claim challenges a presidential proclamation, or if the issue raised has broad or significant implications for the administration of trade laws (Re 1981, 441). The court has a permanent home in New York City, although with its nationwide jurisdiction, it can hear cases anywhere in the United States and even in foreign countries when necessary.

The Court of Appeals for the Federal Circuit

All cases decided in the Court of International Trade can be appealed to the Court of Appeals for the Federal Circuit. While international trade is the primary focus of business in the Court of International Trade, such is not the case in the Federal Circuit. Congress ostensibly intended to limit the specialization of the Federal Circuit as much as possible while still giving it a distinctive institutional form. That explains why the court is assigned more than one subject matter. In essence, the Federal Circuit is best characterized as a semispecialized court. But to maintain consistency with the literature, the court is here referred to as a specialized court. In the entire federal judicial system, the Federal Circuit is the only constitutional court of appeals with a nationwide, as opposed to a territorial, jurisdiction. It forms the boldest experiment yet in judicial reformation in the American context. Even though the geographic and subject matter jurisdictions of the Federal Circuit give the court a unique institutional character, its status as an intermediate court and its practices and procedures are similar or equivalent to those found in other courts of appeals.

By statute, the Federal Circuit has 12 active-duty judges, including a chief judge. Judges sit in rotating panels of three to hear cases assigned randomly by the clerk of the court to panels whose membership is unknown to the clerk in advance. The chief judge has the managerial task of randomly assigning judges to panels on a rotating basis. This double randomization process of assigning cases ensures equitable distribution of cases to judges, fosters expertise of the judges in all programmatic areas of the court, and facilitates internal cohesion. The court practices intracircuit stare decisis, that is, previous panel decisions take precedence. But by rules of the court, a precedent cannot be overturned by any three-judge panel unless by consideration en banc. Congress authorizes the Federal Circuit to formulate its own rules to better carry out its responsibilities. So when the court held its inaugural session en banc in October 1982, it adopted all the decisions of its predecessor courts as precedent in order to maintain continuity in Federal Circuit law.

Congress established the Federal Circuit by expanding and combining the functions of the erstwhile Court of Customs and Patent Appeals (CCPA) and those of the Court of Claims in the Federal Courts Improvement Act of 1982 (Public Law 97–164). The main legal impetus for the court's creation was the need to reduce intercircuit conflict so as to achieve greater decisional coherence in circuit law, especially in the areas of patent and trademark and international trade (see generally Meador 1992; Markey 1992).

But that was not all. Apart from the manifest goal of minimizing intercircuit conflict, a covert political objective could also be detected. Typically, judicial reform movements to establish or expand the jurisdiction of specialized courts have been promulgated and fueled by what Frank Baumgartner and Brian Jones term the "mobilization of enthusiasm" (1993, 178); that is, action for change is led fervently by corporate interest groups with particularistic stakes in the outcomes of these courts' decisions (as was the case in the now defunct Commerce Court)[8] or by groups such as professional bar associations seeking self-preservation. However, on the road to establishing the Federal Circuit, something somewhat unprecedented in the history of specialized courts transpired. Big-business interest groups were largely united in favor, while key bar associations were split in their support. For example, the American Bar Association (ABA) declined to support creation of the Federal Circuit, fearing that the new court would be a specialized court and citing the dangers of specialization, such as tunnel vision and juristic decadence. Not surprisingly, the Patent and Trademark Bar Association was strongly in favor. The most striking development, though, was that the federal government played an unusually activist role in the court's creation (Meador 1992).

According to an analytical account furnished by Lawrence Baum (1991), the main "interest group" pushing for the establishment of the

Federal Circuit was not big business or the bar; instead, it was the federal government, acting through the Justice Department. According to Baum, the government's activism in creating the Federal Circuit was less out of desire for the "neutral virtues" of a specialized judicial machinery but more a tacit and calculated attempt to control the course of public policy overwhelmingly in the government's favor. Analyzing some of the problems associated with specialized courts, economist and Seventh Circuit judge Richard A. Posner concurs: "Specialists are more likely than generalists to identify with the goals of a government program, since the program is the focus of their career" (1983, 785).

For now it suffices to say that in some respects, anecdotal evidence supports these interpretations. In an interview of lawyers practicing before the Federal Circuit published in the *Almanac of the Federal Judiciary* (1996, 2:1), practitioners commented that "specific judges are inclined to take the government position to the extreme," especially in government contract cases. Similarly, during the 10th anniversary celebration of the Federal Circuit, an appraisal of the court presented by Donald Dunner, a frequent practitioner before the court, also referred to the perception of many that the court has a progovernment bias in nonpatent cases (see Dunner 1992, 300). This appraisal raises the possibility that judges of the Federal Circuit may have been selected primarily from within the federal government and so are inclined to favor the federal government.

Selecting Judges to Specialized Courts

Judicial selection presents each president with an enormous opportunity to stamp a personal imprimatur upon an independent federal judicial machinery and upon judicial policy. According to former Reagan attorney general Edwin Meese III, "No President exercises any power more far-reaching, more likely to influence his legacy, than the selection of federal judges" (quoted in Abraham et al.1990, x). That explains why most American presidents, especially those who took office after the New Deal, take judicial selection seriously, although with considerable individual variation among presidents in the style and intensity with which they handle this important responsibility (Abraham et al. 1990; Goldman 1993; McFeeley 1987). Appointments to specialized courts are at least as important as appointments to other lower federal courts, perhaps more important from the perspective of presidential policy agenda because these appointments allow the president to exert a sizable and enduring impact upon a particular policy arena.

Specialized courts can be likened to bureaucratic agencies as hotbeds of political patronage when it comes to selecting individuals to sit on these courts. Two assumptions commonly made by critics of judicial selection to specialized courts are that because of patronage, specialized-court judges generally have slimmer qualifications than judges in other federal courts of the same level, and that the repetitive nature of the business of a specialized judiciary makes it difficult, according to Richard Posner, "to maintain [or attract] a high quality federal . . . bench" (1983, 780). The patronage and repetitive work arguments are polemical claims with which specialized-court judges would strongly disagree. And indeed, it should be pointed out that systematic empirical evidence has never been furnished to support those claims.

According to the patronage theory as applied to specialized courts, no single senator, even a senator from the president's party, can claim "ownership" of vacancies on these courts because of their nationwide jurisdiction. As narrated by Alexander Hamilton in the *Federalist Papers,* no. 66, the role of the Senate is that of a dispassionate, unpretentious body whose fundamental interest is oriented toward the *merit* of an appointment, nothing more. Under this assumption, the patronage theory centers on the putative absence of that form of political back-scratching termed senatorial courtesy, which governs appointments primarily to district courts (Carp and Stidham 1996, chap.8). Under senatorial courtesy, a senator from the president's political party from the home state where the vacancy exists can forestall or "veto" any nomination that she or he finds objectionable. But because of the presumed ineffectiveness of senatorial courtesy when it comes to vacancies on specialized courts, the president and his lieutenants in the White House and in the Department of Justice are thought to have free rein in picking individuals to these courts, with scant, if any, opposition from senators. Consequently, it is generically thought that the president uses these positions as plums for rewarding patronage or loyal service or for accomplishing constituency obligations. Historically, the concept of patronage connotes mediocrity. Consistent with this connotation, the popular thinking is that the president doles out these "spoils" without paying much attention to such qualities as the judicial temperament, legal competence, and integrity of the appointee.

For the remainder of this chapter, the patronage theory will be analyzed along with other selection factors in light of recent nominations and appointments to the Court of International Trade and the Federal Circuit. Some of the assumptions underlying the theory will be debunked as myths, especially the assumption that no senator can claim ownership to specialized-court vacancies. Examples will be presented showing recent instances in which a senator claimed ownership of vacancies in a specialized court simply because the court was located in that senator's state. But generally speaking, I argue that from the president's perspective, the underlying logic of most contemporary judicial appointments carries a policy-related explanation as opposed to one of mere reward of patronage. First, the president appoints individuals who share his policy or judicial philosophy and who can work to advance that philosophy. Second, in the rare chance that someone is appointed whose philosophy diverges from the appointing president's—say, a member of the opposition party—the appointment is designed specifically to gain legislative support from members of the opposition party for pending presidential programs. According to the longitudinal study of appointments to the federal courts conducted by Barrow, Zuk, and Gryski (1996, 15), presidents are more likely to make cross-party appointments when they are politically vulnerable either because of low public esteem (Nixon and Ford) or because the opposition party controls the Senate, as occurred frequently in recent presidential eras.

I further argue that the patronage theory is context specific, even within the band of specialized courts. It flourishes more in truly specialized courts such as the Court of International Trade than in semispecialized ones such as the Federal Circuit.[9] Other important considerations of judicial selection to specialized courts do exist, including the roles of partisanship, interest groups, and expertise. Before analyzing all these factors, however, it is necessary first to take a close look at the formal criteria for selecting judges to the two specialized courts.

Formal Criteria for Appointment to the Specialized Courts of International Trade

Theoretically, the formal requirements for appointing judges to specialized courts at the federal level are similar to those for selecting judges to other federal courts. Under the United States Constitution, the president has the power to appoint judges, subject to confirmation by a favorable majority vote in the Senate. Augmenting this constitutional requirement, the statutes creating these specialized courts include other specific provisions designed to promote political balance on the courts or to limit the president's power to stamp a personal imprint on the internal machinery or policy direction of the courts.

Under the Customs Court Act of 1980, for example, it is stated that "[t]he President shall appoint, by and with the advice and consent of the Senate, nine judges who shall constitute a court of record to be known as the United States Court of International Trade." In addition to this general provision, there are two requirements: (1) "Not more than five of such judges shall be from the same political party;" and (2) "The President shall designate one of the judges of the Court of International Trade who is less than seventy years of age to serve as chief judge. The chief judge shall continue to serve as chief judge until he reaches the age of seventy and another judge is designated as the chief judge by the President" (Public Law 96–417). In theory, the party provision is meant to elevate the court above politics by weakening the effect of ideology, while the age requirement for the chief judge is designed to limit presidential influence on how the court is administered. As demonstrated by Brown (1982) in the case of executive agencies and suggested by Baldwin (1985, chap. 3) in the case of independent regulatory commissions, the partisanship requirement is grossly ineffective because it can easily be circumvented by a determined president who selects stealth candidates who are not officially of the president's party but actually do share the president's political views.

The formal requirements for appointment to the Federal Circuit, as laid out in the Federal Courts Improvement Act of 1982 (Public Law 97–164), are slightly different in that Congress formally recognized "competence and experience" as factors that determine the quality of the federal judiciary. Lawmakers made a suggestion in the law that the president should select "from a broad range of qualified individuals" when making appointments to the Federal Circuit. Given the historical role of politics in judicial selection, however, it is unrealistic to believe that legislative language calling for qualified judges will actually result in the appointment of judges of higher average qualification than the holdover judges from the predecessor courts. Since the suggestion for the selection of qualified individuals applies to all post-1982 appointments, a test was conducted using the ABA's rating of judicial nominees to determine if there has been a significant improvement in the quality of newly appointed judges to the Federal Circuit compared to holdover judges. The ABA rates nominees as "Well Qualified," "Qualified," or "Not Qualified."[10] Table 2 shows that fewer post-1982 nominees actually received the ABA's top rating than nominees to the Federal Circuit's progenitor courts. Obviously, an ABA rating is only a reasonable approximation of a nominee's qualification, not a full measure. But overall there exists no statistically significant difference between the two groups. It is possible that the post-1982 nominees, most of whom were Republicans, may have been victims of the ABA's supposed liberal bent, an accusation made by Republicans during the Bush administration. Consequently, some of these judges may not have received ratings commensurate with their true qualifications, and therefore some caution is urged in placing too much faith in this particular finding. But on the surface, it does appear that contrary to what the enacting Congress might wish, recent appointees to the Federal Circuit are not commanding greater competence and experience than the holdover judges.

Informal Criteria for Appointment to Specialized Courts

In reality, there are no formal qualifications for federal judges. Indeed, United States citizenship is not required, nor is a law degree. The literature points to a number of informal considerations for appointment, however, including "political participation, professional competence, personal ambition, plus an oft-mentioned pinch of luck" (Howard 1981, 90). Although Howard's appointment factors are derived from his interview of circuit judges, these factors are also germane to specialized courts. To become a federal judge, a nominee must clear several hurdles involving intense scrutiny of his or her intellectual prowess, legal competence, and moral standing by the executive branch (beginning with the White House Office of Legal Counsel and the Department of Justice), the American Bar Association (and the specialized bar, in the case of appointment to a specialized court), and the Senate Judiciary Committee, culminating in the final screening and vote by the Senate. According to a detailed case study of the federal judicial selection process conducted by Harold Chase (1972), politics and ideology are an integral part of every step of the process. But for both the president and the Senate, political patronage seems to be a particularly important factor for appointment to specialized courts.

Political Patronage

To understand what role political patronage plays in judicial appointments, we must first understand what the concept means and what its implications are. If we view patronage appointments literally as the "payment of political reward" (Fenno 1959, 227), then the vast majority of judicial appointments in the United States qualify as patronage appointments. For example, in a study of judicial selection to general jurisdiction courts during the Bush administration, Sheldon Goldman (1991, 104)

TABLE 2. Bivariate Comparison of ABA Rating of Holdover and Post-1982 Appointees to the Federal Circuit, 1964–96

	Holdover Judges[a]	Post-1982 Judges	Total
Exceptionally or well qualified	7 (64%)	4 (36%)	11 (50%)
Qualified	4 (36%)	7 (64%)	11 (50%)
Total	11 (100%)	11 (100%)	22 (100%)

Note: Data are from the American Bar Association. Holdover Judges category excludes ratings for Giles S. Rich and Oscar Davis, who were both appointed prior to 1964. Rating information was unavailable from the ABA for appointments before 1964.

[a]A chi-square test with 1 degree of freedom shows that the ABA rating of holdover judges is not statistically different from that of post-1982 judges ($\chi^2 = .727$), n.s.

reported that about 62 percent of Bush appointees to district courts had a history of party activism. Goldman also reported parallel findings for other presidents going as far back as Lyndon B. Johnson (also McFeeley 1987). Given these findings, we can extrapolate that appointments to specialized courts would display a similar characteristic. If, on the other hand, we view patronage appointments through the lenses of a cynic, as the appointment of lesser-qualified individuals for one reason or another, then one must make a comparative examination of specialist and generalist judges' qualifications for proof. My position is that selection to specialized courts need not subsume low merit. After all, the president has the entire nation rather than a particular state or geographic circuit from which to select the most qualified individual.

Data on individual background characteristics and qualifications of Federal Circuit judges is assembled in appendix A1. Part of the information presented there was used here to construct table 3, which compares the ABA's rating of appointees to the Federal Circuit and to all other courts of appeals for both the Reagan and Bush administrations. The small number of judges appointed to the Federal Circuit by Reagan and Bush prevents a statistical test of the differences in qualification between appointees to the two types of courts. Nevertheless, there is strong evidence that a higher proportion of appointees to the generalist circuit courts *do* receive the ABA's highest rating than of appointees to the Federal Circuit. Only 30 percent of the combined Reagan and Bush appointees to the Federal Circuit were rated "Exceptionally/Well Qualified," compared to 61 percent of appointees to all other circuit courts.

In terms of professional expertise, the background data for Federal Circuit judges suggest that judges come to the court with federal govern-

TABLE 3. Comparing ABA Rating of Reagan and Bush Appointments to the Federal Circuit and Other Circuit Courts of Appeals

| Rating | Reagan Appointments | | Bush Appointments | | Combined Reagan and Bush | |
	Federal Circuit	All Other Circuits	Federal Circuit	All Other Circuits	Federal Circuit	All Other Circuits
Exceptionally or well qualified	1 (25%)	46 (59%)	2 (33%)	24 (64.9%)	3 (30%)	70 (61%)
Qualified	3 (75%)	32 (41%)	4 (67%)	13 (35.1%)	7 (70%)	45 (39%)
Total	4 (100%)	78 (100%)	6 (100%)	37 (100%)	10 (8%)	115 (92%)

Note: Data for the Federal Circuit are from the American Bar Association; average percentages for all other circuits are drawn from Goldman 1993, 293. There are insufficient cases in some cells to permit accurate chi-square tests.

ment prosecutorial experience or expertise in a variety of subject areas of the court or in some related subject area. Also, judges average about 53 years of age when appointed and are tapped primarily from the federal government, particularly the Department of Justice, which may explain why the court tends to favor the federal government.

There is no denying that patronage is an important determinant of appointment to specialized courts. Presidents usually nominate individuals who are visible to them, and senators typically submit for nomination the names of individuals they know either through the party machinery or through campaign work. Between the Court of International Trade and the Federal Circuit, there is strong anecdotal evidence that patronage plays a role, especially with regard to appointments to the Court of International Trade. The projected image of this court is one where individuals selected to it ought to have significant background experience in international trade or some related field, whether as prosecutors, defense attorneys, or law professors. But for the most part, such is not the case. While the judges display a wealth of varied qualifications, most of those selected since 1980 have had no discernible scholarly or prosecutorial experience in international trade before joining the court (see appendix A2), although it should be noted that judges do gain expertise in international trade after being on the bench awhile. That begs the suggestion that political patronage plays a role in these appointments.

An interview of 10 international trade lawyers and several Court of International Trade judges published in *Manhattan Lawyer* by Rifka Rosenswein points to some important critiques about appointments to that court, critiques which are emblematic of selection to other specialized courts. According to Rosenswein,

> Six of the ten international trade lawyers interviewed say the judges eventually learn the ropes, but they worry that administration officials and U.S. senators do not take the same care as they do with other judicial appointments, even though the court's judges are appointed for life and go through the same confirmation process as other federal judges. The court's New York locale means that few U.S. senators take an active role in pushing home-state favorites. (1991, 8)

Because of the court's geographic location and the Republican presidential fortunes of the 1980s, the Court of International Trade was a boon for Republican senator Alfonse D'Amato of New York, who, during the Reagan and Bush regimes, viewed vacancies on the court as his own to fill. According to Paul Windel, chair of Senator D'Amato's judicial screening panel, D'Amato holds this view because, "[t]he court does sit in New

York" (Rosenswein 1991, 8). In 1991, there were eight active-duty judges on the Court of International Trade. Of these, six were native New Yorkers, and three of these six were appointed based upon a personal recommendation by their good friend Senator D'Amato. The three judges were Gregory Carman, a former Republican member of Congress from Nassau County; Nicholas Tsoucalas, a former state Supreme Court justice from Queens; and Dominick DiCarlo, a former Republican State Assembly member from Brooklyn who is now chief judge of the Court of International Trade. Thus, as a result of senatorial courtesy and the Reagan and Bush administrations' practice of actively involving home-state Republican senators in trial court–level appointments (see Abraham et al.1990, 54–55), D'Amato was able to use the Court of International Trade for patronage appointments.

But this patronage practice permeates the Democratic party as well. In his two appointments to the Court of International Trade to date, Democratic president Bill Clinton has also used the court to reward his friends. Donald C. Pogue, a former hospital and health care commissioner in Connecticut, was Clinton's roommate when the two were attending Yale Law School. Pogue was appointed by Clinton in 1995, as was Evan J. Wallach, who was the president's close friend when the two were studying in England. While they do have other qualifications, neither Pogue nor Wallach had sufficient prior experience in international trade to warrant appointment to this specialized court.

There is also a tendency for presidents to use appointments to specialized courts to reward loyal service. The case of the first female judge in the Court of International Trade is illustrative. According to Rosenswein (1991), before becoming a judge, Jane Restani, a registered Independent, was a veteran litigator in the Civil Division of the Justice Department during the presidencies of Jimmy Carter and Ronald Reagan. Although she had no prior experience in international trade, Restani received a call one day from a Justice Department official who asked whether she would be interested in sitting on the Court of International Trade. Being unfamiliar with the court at the time, she requested some time to research the court before giving her response. Afterward, she agreed to serve and was appointed by President Reagan in 1983.

Partisanship or Ideological Compatibility
Judicial selection research points to partisanship or ideological compatibility as being one of the most important determining factors of judicial appointments. For the most part, being active in one's political party is a necessary though not sufficient condition for being nominated and eventually appointed. Political activism serves as a cue to the policy leaning of

a potential judge and is important because with every appointment, the president hopes that the appointee's policy leaning is consistent with the president's policy prerogatives and judicial philosophy.[11] Partisanship is important in another sense. Generally speaking, research on Senate confirmation of judicial nominees conducted in the 1970s through the 1990s by Songer (1979), Segal (1987), Goldman (1991) and Biskupic (1992) suggests that a nominee is significantly more likely to win confirmation, among other factors, when the president's party controls the Senate. That is simply a manifestation of political conflict in which a Republican-controlled Senate makes every conceivable effort to forestall a Democratic president's appointments through closer scrutiny, delays, and rejections.[12]

In the course of this study, a questionnaire was sent to judges of the specialized courts here analyzed asking them to identify their party affiliation (see appendix A3). One response submitted by Judge Giles Sutherland Rich of the Federal Circuit stood out as a testament to the importance of partisanship in judicial selection. At the age of 93 in 1997 as this book went to print, Judge Rich was the oldest and longest-serving active-duty jurist throughout the history of the federal judiciary. He had had widespread experience and had seen many appointments, having been a federal judge for forty years, surpassing the record previously held by Supreme Court Justice Oliver Wendell Holmes. In his response letter, Judge Rich related the circumstances of his appointment and made an observation that goes to the crux of the partisanship matter:

I was a New Yorker until I came to Washington in 1956. I was generally inclined toward FDR until he tried to run for his last term on the theory that he was indispensable, but could never bring myself to register [D]emocratic because New York was being run by Tammany Hall. Fortuitously, I registered [R]epublican when Eisenhower ran and thus made it possible for him to nominate me to be a Federal judge. *You can determine the party affiliation of a judge with about 98% accuracy by looking at the party of the President who appoints him/her.* Presidents don't nominate judges of the party out of power, unless for a couple of elevations to appear nonpartisan. (emphasis added)[13]

Based upon statistics reported in Carp and Stidham 1996 (237), presidents do overwhelmingly appoint partisans to federal judgeships. Between 1963 and 1993, Republican presidents appointed Republicans to the generalist courts of appeals 94 percent of the time, while Democratic presidents appointed Democrats 89 percent of the time. Thus, the statistic cited in Judge Rich's statement is nearly accurate. In the Federal Circuit, judges' responses to my survey attest to a strong relationship between the appointing president's party affiliation and that of the judges. Approximately 93 percent of the appointments made by Republican presidents went to Republican partisans (i.e., 14 out of 15 appointments total). The only exception here was the 1956 Eisenhower appointment of Giles S. Rich, who identified himself as a "nominal" Republican but "really" an Independent. For the Democrats, roughly 78 percent of all appointments by Democratic presidents went to Democrats (i.e., seven out of nine total). The two exceptions, Daniel M. Friedman and Helen W. Nies, were appointed by Jimmy Carter; they both identified themselves as Independents. While partisanship is clearly important, other factors such as the willingness of interest groups to support a particular candidacy can also play a key role.

Interest Groups
One of the dangers typically attributed to specialized courts is that they are susceptible to interest-group pressure for favorable policies (Baum 1977). This pressure may come from a variety of sources, including attuned pro-industry groups, labor unions, and professional bar associations. Also, the pressure may be exerted in different ways, for example, through associations' support for certain judges' nominations or through assistance rendered to a court. In 1984, for instance, Federal Circuit judges openly asked the Federal Circuit bar to "help define our work," a request to which the bar was exhilarated to respond (Middleton 1984).

Since the Federal Circuit hears cases from a variety of subject matter areas, there exist several different trade groups and professional bar associations that can potentially influence who wins a seat on the court, although such influence would be diffuse. The key bar associations include the Patent and Trademark Bar Association, the Customs and International Trade Bar Association, the Government Contracts Bar Association, and the Federal Employee Rights Bar Association. Collectively, these associations form the Federal Circuit Bar Association. Presumably, each association is interested in placing on the court one of its own, preferably an individual whose views are compatible with the dominant views of the association. This presumption is validated by a recent of survey of legal practitioners before the Federal Circuit, which found that "almost every attorney polled was annoyed that his or her own area of specialization was not better represented in the way of the judges."[14]

Of the various professional bar associations cited in the previous paragraph, the patent and trademark bar is perhaps the most aggressive and best organized and so has enjoyed remarkable success relative to others in placing its favored politicians on the Federal Circuit. This aggressive posture harks back to 1956, when the association vigorously pushed for

Giles Sutherland Rich, one of the principal drafters of the Patent Act of 1952, to become judge of the Court of Customs and Patent Appeals (see Bennett 1991, 30). Currently, patent and trademark policy along with government contract policy are the two areas most represented by way of the judges of the Federal Circuit. Unfortunately for international trade policy development, no judge with extensive prior expertise in that area has ever been appointed to the court. It is therefore one area in which representation on the Federal Circuit is urgently needed.

One nomination to the Federal Circuit of an international trade expert came in 1988 when Ronald Reagan nominated former ITC chair Susan W. Liebeler to be judge of the Federal Circuit. Liebeler, a registered Independent from California, had close ties with Republican party leaders such as Attorney General Edwin Meese and National Security Adviser William Clark (Cohodas 1988). She received strong backing from President Reagan in her court nomination. In 1986, when Reagan had appointed Liebeler to the ITC, the president had personally lobbied senators on her behalf, which led opponents to wonder whether Liebeler was really a stalwart Republican in disguise (Arthurs 1986). The ABA rated Liebeler "Qualified," while the Federal Circuit Bar Association rated her "Extremely Well Qualified." The ITC Trial Lawyers Association, whose members principally represent petitioners before the Commission, also supported Liebeler's nomination. But in a stunning twist of fate, the one bar association that mattered most—the Customs and International Trade Bar Association—issued a report that was highly critical of Liebeler, painting her as an ideologue who "consistently rejects the guidance of the Congress" when deciding trade cases (Cohodas 1988, 676). In other words, she consistently ruled against the members of the bar and their domestic clients.

Other intense opposition to Liebeler's nomination came from big businesses (particularly the steel industry) and labor unions[15] that had fallen victim to her streak of free-trade decisions, and from senators and representatives from the import-vulnerable states of Ohio and Pennsylvania. Within this context, the most vociferous opponent was Republican Senator John Heinz of Pennsylvania, who charged that Pennsylvania's steel industry had been hurt by Liebeler's trade decisions and that Liebeler "has demonstrated an ideological approach to trade law and economics that has allowed her to ignore both the law and congressional intent in reaching conclusions that have regularly been at variance with those of most of the other commissioners" (Cohodas 1988, 675). On February 23, 1988, the Senate Judiciary Committee declined to recommend her to the Senate, by a vote of six to seven, and ultimately her nomination failed because of her free-trade views and interest-group opposition, not because she lacked the subject matter competence and experience to sit on the court. The Liebeler confirmation fight suggests that it would be very difficult for anyone with a clearly discernible viewpoint on administered protection to be confirmed to a position on the trade courts.

Conclusion

This chapter has sought to chronicle the gradual evolution of the United States trade courts so as to give the reader the lay of the land in preparation for subsequent analyses of the potential impact of these courts on American trade policy-making. Whatever shape this impact may take, it is important to note that the role of courts in U.S. trade policy-making evolved from a piecemeal effort of Congress to promote fair trade and provide better service and greater court access to American industries and workers suffering from import competition. All indications suggest that these courts are here to stay because they serve a vital policy function.

A second objective was to examine the contours of appointments to the specialized courts. Patronage, partisanship, and organized pressure are among the important factors that influence appointment to these courts. Analysis using the ABA's rating of judges as a crude measure of qualification suggests that judges appointed to specialized courts do generally meet similar qualifications as those appointed to other federal courts. But as suggested by the Federal Circuit example, specialized courts of appeals judges do tend to be rated lower than judges in other circuit courts, which would support critics of specialized courts, such as Richard Posner. Hence, greater scrutiny of qualifications is called for when making appointments to these courts to prevent them from becoming political dumping grounds for underqualified judges. Under the assumption that patronage appointments need not subsume low merit, the evidence presented here pertaining to specialized-court appointments suggests that patronage is indeed an important factor in appointments, especially to the Court of International Trade, where in the 1980s Senator Alfonse D'Amato (R-N.Y.) played an active role in packing the court with New Yorkers.

CHAPTER 3

Bureaucratic Venues and Mechanisms
of U.S. International Trade
Policy Implementation

At different times in the history of the United States, Congress has taken pains to create administrative agencies and to staff these agencies with experts who are responsible for implementing international trade and import policies. Implementation is used throughout this book in the same sense as in Pressman and Wildavsky 1973 and refers to the activities undertaken by bureaucrats to accomplish the goals set in statutes. In the United States, trade policy is implemented by a number of regulatory agencies, but the primary ones are the International Trade Commission (ITC), the International Trade Administration (ITA), which is housed within the Department of Commerce (DOC), the U.S. Customs Service, and the Office of the U.S. Trade Representative (USTR).[1]

Although all these agencies are important in their own unique ways and play different roles in American foreign trade policy implementation, my focus throughout the book is on the DOC and the ITC.[2] These are the two foremost implementers of American trade laws. In analyzing these agencies, I shall concentrate on how rules and procedures are applied in making decisions concerning the antidumping and countervailing duty trade laws. More will be discussed about these laws later in this chapter, but at the outset, a brief conceptual explanation of these laws will be useful.

Generally speaking, dumping is a form of price discrimination, which occurs when countries sell their goods abroad at a price lower than the home market price or at a price below the average cost of production. In other words, the goods are being sold at less than fair value (LTFV). There are several reasons why firms may engage in dumping. For one, firms choose to dump because they are new entrants into a competitive market and desire to build customer loyalty in order to survive. But most often, firms engage in dumping because they want to increase their market share, dominate the market and eventually extinguish the competition, and reap economic profits (Krugman 1987; Prestowitz 1988, 373–417). Several assumptions underlie the practice of dumping. First, the quality of the product is less important to consumers than the price. Second, separate national markets preclude the reimportation of the lower-priced exports. Third, the exporter possesses market power in the home market and therefore can afford to sell at a higher price in the home market to compensate for the lost revenue from selling abroad at below fair market value. Finally, demand is more elastic in the foreign market than in the exporter's home market. In terms of dumping in the United States, this last assumption means that the U.S. market is more sensitive to price than is the exporter's home market (Knoll 1989).

The countervailing duty law is invoked to counteract the subsidy that foreign governments give their industries to help them compete on the world stage. Under international trade laws, subsidizing certain domestic (e.g., nondefense) industries is not permitted. Increasingly, however, nations have come to view subsidization, albeit illegal, as a strategic policy instrument to gain competitive advantage in trade, and this is one of the major causes of contemporary trade disputes. The antidumping and countervailing duty laws form the bulk of international trade conflict since the 1970s and, for reasons to be discussed later, are the most commonly used avenues for American companies seeking U.S. government protection against unfair foreign competition.

This chapter will examine the flow of international trade cases from the regulatory agencies to the courts. The discussion concentrates on the contours of bureaucratic implementation of U.S. foreign trade policy. It begins with broad historical overviews of the ITC and the DOC's ITA and a delineation of the important functions that these two agencies perform in the U.S. trade policy system. Then, a detailed examination is given of the specific investigative procedures employed by these agencies to reach their policy decisions about whether to award import relief to American industries. Within this context, the irregularities or biases that underlie agency application of administrative rules and procedures will be exposed and analyzed. The basic contention in this chapter is that because of these irregularities and biases, judicial review is an essential stabilizing force in the implementation of U.S. trade policy.

Flow of Trade Cases through Administrative Agencies to the Federal Courts

All trade cases appealed to the courts have already undergone administrative scrutiny and so have an administrative history. The litigation process usually begins when an American industry decides to petition the government for protection against foreign import competition. Petitions are filed simultaneously with the DOC and ITC. These two agencies serve different regulatory functions within the trade policy implementation system. The DOC's job is to determine whether there is sufficient evidence to support claims of unfair-trade practices, such as dumping. The ITC's job is to determine whether the industry has suffered material injury or is facing a threat of material injury because of the unfair-trade practices. *Material injury* is defined vaguely in trade law as "harm which is not inconsequential, immaterial, or unimportant."

Agency investigations occur simultaneously and can yield either a negative or an affirmative decision. Each agency starts by conducting a preliminary investigation to determine if the facts of the case warrant a full-scale investigation. The preliminary investigation allows an agency to quickly dispose of frivolous petitions with a negative ruling. An investigation proceeds to the final stage if the claim made in the petition is found worthy of more serious attention. Thus, there are two major steps leading to the decision to grant protection to domestic industries (D. Cohen 1990, 1195). Figure 1 is a flow diagram depicting how cases move through the administrative agencies to the courts. At each administrative decision point, an aggrieved party to the proceedings, that is, either the petitioner or the respondent, can appeal the regulatory decision to the Court of International Trade.

Step 1: Preliminary Investigations

Under the antidumping and countervailing duty laws, both the DOC and the ITC must conduct preliminary investigations, except in countervailing duty cases involving countries that are nonsignatory to the GATT Subsidies Code, in which case only the DOC[3] is involved throughout. The purpose of the investigation is different for each agency. For the DOC, it is to determine whether there is reasonable indication that the claim of dumping or foreign government subsidization can be supported with hard evidence. For the ITC, it is to determine whether there is reasonable indication of injury to the U.S. petitioner. If the ITC reaches a negative finding at this stage (i.e., no reasonable indication of injury exists), the investigation is terminated. At this point, the import-competing U.S. industry may appeal the ruling to the Court of International Trade. If the DOC rules negatively in its preliminary investigation, the case proceeds to the final investigation stage. Under the current trade law, if either the DOC or ITC preliminary decision is affirmative, a preliminary import duty (in the form of a bond) is imposed on the imported goods involved, and the foreign firm accused as the unfair trader may challenge the agency ruling in the Court of International Trade.

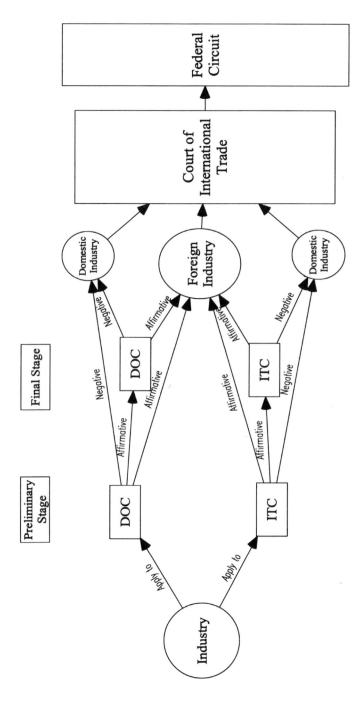

Fig. 1. Decision sequence of trade cases from bureaucratic agencies to the courts

Step 2: Final Investigations

If the DOC rules negatively in its final determination, then the case ends, and the import-competing U.S. industry again may commence a court action. If the DOC rules affirmatively, the ITC conducts its final investigation to determine whether material injury exists due to unfair-trade practices. If the ITC rules negatively, the investigation terminates and the case ends. Once again, import-competing U.S. industries can appeal the ruling to the Court of International Trade. If the ITC rules affirmatively, then the DOC will impose final duties on the imported goods. The key point in the whole investigation process is that only when both agencies rule affirmatively in their respective investigations will protective tariff increases equal to the margin of dumping or subsidization be imposed on the foreign goods and collected by the federal government. When that happens, the foreign firm may once again appeal the finding to the Court of International Trade.[4] Until the Trade Act of 1979, foreign firms were not allowed to appeal agency decisions to U.S. courts.

The time frame for a petition to move from the regulatory agencies to the Court of International Trade varies, depending upon the stage at which the agency's decision is appealed to court, how complicated the case is, and how quickly the agency completes its investigations. It is common for cases to exhibit what can be called the "Ping-Pong effect," that is, the tendency for trade cases to go back and forth between the agencies and the courts, prolonging the time it takes to finalize a particular controversy. But typically, from the time a petition is filed to when a final investigation is completed, it takes from 9 to 14 months for an antidumping case and 7 to 10 months for a countervailing duty case (International Trade Commission 1994, 38).

**Historical Evolution of the International
Trade Commission**

Origin of the ITC

Like most other independent regulatory commissions in the United States, the ITC (until 1974 called the Tariff Commission) has a rich history.[5] This history really starts with the legislative power granted to Congress to levy and collect taxes and regulate trade between the United States and other nations. As indicated in chapter 2, from the late eighteenth century to the mid-nineteenth century, well before the ITC was created, the history of tariff imposition, collection, and adjustment formed the essence of U.S. trade policy (Gourevitch 1991).

During this early period, tariffs, not corporate or individual income taxes, were the predominant and most stable source of federal government revenue (Dobson 1976; B. Yarbrough and R. Yarbrough 1991, 205; Krasner 1976; Bauer, Pool, and Dexter 1963). Indeed, according to John Dobson, until the ratification in 1913 of the 16th Amendment, which mandated the imposition of direct income tax, "tariffs accounted for between 50 and 90 percent of total Federal income" (1976, 1). Congress periodically overhauled tariff rates to adjust revenue levels to meet the fiscal and investment needs of government and business. Tariff and the economy were like conjoined twins, inextricably bound to each other. About this relationship Pietro S. Nivola has observed that in U.S. trade history, "protectionism has always pulsated with growth and contraction in the economy as a whole, and naturally, with the relative vulnerability of domestic industries to international competition . . . [particularly in periods of] business slumps and panics" (1986, 579). Corresponding to this observation, trade politics has always produced internal legislative conflicts because members have different agendas to pursue and diverse interests and political constituencies to placate for the sake of their own careers.

Early on, regionalism and industrialization were two of the most important determinants of whether particular lawmakers advocated high or low tariff rates. Lawmakers from the Cotton Belt in the South advocated low tariffs to maintain high demand for cotton and other agricultural products. Northerners, including lawmakers from New England, New York, and Pennsylvania, on the other hand, sought high tariffs to promote regional industrialization and to ameliorate market-imposed structural difficulties (Goldstein 1993, chap. 2). Due to these differences and diverse regional influences on lawmakers, the process of revenue adjustment was highly conflictual and unsettling to many in Congress. Pressure to increase tariff rates *and* simultaneously encourage domestic export mounted and proved too onerous for some lawmakers, and actually led to significant logrolling (Nivola 1986, 585). Tariff disputes intensified partisan brawls and sectional cleavages between Northerners and Southerners in Congress (Morrison, Commager, and Leuchtenburg 1977, 173–88). These disputes were testament to lawmakers that tariff issues were too convoluted, too complex, to be handled effectively by Congress alone.

Pressure from outside and from within Congress itself grew, calling for lawmakers to delegate the complex and technical matters of tariff formation and administration to an independent, nonpartisan body of experts that would be insulated from the political arena and that would promote "scientific management" of tariff matters (Dobson 1976). In 1916, during the administrative reform era, the 63rd Congress took critical steps toward significant delegation of trade and tariff affairs. The ITC was created during that year in the spirit of reform to help "take the tariff out of politics . . . [by making] a dispassionate and disinterested scrutiny" of tariff issues (Dobson 1976, 86–87). The new independent agency was given "fact-finding" responsibilities, which took much weight off Congress and helped reduce somewhat the internal partisan and regional disputes between lawmakers concerning international trade and tariff policy. The objective of divorcing politics from the administration of tariff policy was largely unsuccessful in the long run, however. Political conflict remains a live issue but one played out in an additional arena, the ITC.

Functions of the ITC

As one would suspect, the Commission's functions were fewer and far less complex in the beginning than they are now. The ITC was delegated broad authority to *investigate* the administrative, fiscal, and economic effects of U.S. customs laws as well as to study tariff relationships between the United States and other countries. The Commission was also required to report its findings to Congress and the president. Over time, the scope and complexity of ITC functions gradually increased. The task of administering trade policy became more difficult, partly in response to an increasingly interdependent and competitive world, as reflected in the introduction of structural changes in financial markets and in the establishment of international regimes such as the General Agreement on Tariff and Trade (GATT).

The Commission changed from being primarily a fact-finding independent regulatory agency to being a bipartisan, quasi-judicial body charged with the responsibility to make rules and administer trade remedy laws subject to limited judicial review. But in response to the renewed political salience of foreign trade to the U.S. economy and to presidential and congressional election politics since the 1970s, Congress was no longer willing to rely nearly exclusively on bureaucratic implementation. Hence, in the Trade Act of 1974, Congress provided greater opportunities for American industries, (and now) unions, and workers to seek judicial review of final agency determinations, but it stopped short of permitting the courts to specify remedies. In the Trade Agreements Act of 1979, Congress went further and broadened the scope of judicial review of agency trade decisions by giving foreign producers the prerogative to appeal their cases to American courts and by calling for interlocutory judicial review (Barringer and Dunn 1979, 33–35; Horgan 1988). What this meant was that interested parties to a trade dispute no longer had to wait until a final determination was issued by the agencies before seeking redress in court;

preliminary determinations, which are good predictors of final rulings, could now be contested in court. Overtly, judicial review was expanded to ensure greater fairness, accountability, and representation of the broader public interest (Farish 1984; Vance 1981). Covertly, it was expanded to relieve Congress of intense interest-group pressure for product-specific protectionist legislation.

Increasingly, the core of the Commission's workload involves investigating claims of material injury to domestic industries, alleged to have been caused by foreign dumping or subsidization. The jurisdiction for determining the existence of dumping or subsidization does not rest with the ITC. The DOC has that responsibility. But in addition to determining injury, the ITC also takes action to counteract the selling of U.S. trade secrets as well as infringements upon intellectual property rights, such as copyright, patent, and trademark, registered to U.S. citizens and corporations.

The ITC is comprised of six commissioners, each appointed by the president and confirmed by the Senate to a term of nine years. Thus, there is an inherent overlap in appointments. No more than three commissioners can be from the same political party at any given time. But the president has the option to appoint Independents or members of a third party. The partisan requirement is weak; therefore, it can easily be circumvented. The obvious intent of lawmakers regarding the party requirement was to neutralize the effect of any one political ideology on the Commission's rulings. But empirical analyses by several political scientists (e.g., Hansen 1990) and economists (e.g., Baldwin 1985; Moore 1992) show that commissioners are not impervious to the vicissitudes of ideological politics. While ideology is not the only factor that can influence commissioners' decisions, it does consistently have a significant effect. For example, in his analysis of political voting patterns on ITC import injury cases from 1949 to 1983, Baldwin concluded that "Republican commissioners always voted in a more protectionist manner than their Democratic or Independent counterparts" (1985, 92). Commission decisions are made on a collegial, though not consensual, basis. At least a tie vote is required before the Commission can rule in favor of the petitioner who seeks governmental assistance.

Historical Evolution of the International Trade Administration

Origin of the ITA

The International Trade Administration (until 1980 called the Industry and Trade Administration) is an executive-level agency that resides within the Department of Commerce. This agency focuses on helping U.S. companies export their goods and services and on strengthening the nation's international trade posture. The agency also participates in formulating and implementing U.S. foreign trade and economic policies by working closely with the ITC, the USTR, and other trade-related agencies within the executive branch. The ITA was formed within the DOC in 1980 when Congress transferred the administering authority over trade from the Treasury Department to the Commerce Department, following a presidential directive from Jimmy Carter (Executive Order 12188) to consolidate the federal government's nonagricultural trade functions under a single agency. Prior to this consolidation, import trade functions were dispersed arbitrarily among several executive departments, including the Departments of Commerce, Labor, Agriculture, State, and the Treasury. As a result, the implementation of important trade functions was seriously marred by disagreements and brawls over turf. Frequently, U.S. trading partners would play U.S. agencies against one another to extract trade concessions, leading to disjointed and erratic trade policies.

The transfer of responsibility for import trade administration from Treasury to Commerce was meant to eliminate this problem, especially against the backdrop of a burgeoning U.S. trade deficit, troubles in financial markets, and intense public outcry for immediate legislative action. As an added dimension, the Treasury Department meanwhile was perceived as having too much invested in maintaining amicable foreign economic relations with U.S. trading partners to risk being tough on them when these foreign trading partners engaged in unfair-trade practices against U.S. producers. According to I. M. Destler, the trade committees in Congress approved the transfer of the administering authority after "judging Treasury to be insufficiently aggressive in enforcing the unfair-trade statutes" (1992, 117).

Sections of the ITA and Their Functions

The ITA is composed of four relatively mutually dependent sections. The first is the international economic policy section, which focuses on identifying and broadening U.S. trade and investment options abroad. The international economic policy section also coordinates the United States's participation in bilateral trade agreements, such as the Free Trade Agreement (FTA) with Canada, and in multilateral trade agreements, such as the General Agreement on Tariff and Trade (GATT) and the North American Free Trade Agreement (NAFTA).

The second ITA section is the trade development section, which focuses on providing major U.S. industries with a point of contact in the

DOC. This section specializes in assisting U.S. industries with important foreign trade problems concerning access. It provides U.S. industries with information that would enable them to take full advantage of emerging trade opportunities abroad, such as bidding for international contracts. In addition, this section collects and analyzes intelligence on foreign industries and trade policy.

The third section is the U.S. and foreign commercial service section, which operates through a global network of trade specialists in American and foreign cities to promote export awareness and to stimulate the exportation of U.S. goods and services. One specific method that the section employs to stimulate interest in exporting is holding trade fairs and exhibitions in the United States and abroad to promote awareness of U.S. industries.

The last section of the ITA is the import administration section, and it is the most important for this study. Of all the sections of the ITA, the import administration section has had the most rapidly growing responsibility in the implementation of U.S. foreign trade policy, at least throughout most of the 1980s. As a testament to the increasing responsibility of the import administration section to U.S. trade policy in general, it is noteworthy that, compared to other sections of the agency whose budget allocations either fluctuated or remained flat, the import administration section commanded the most rapid and steadily rising budget allocation throughout most of the 1980s, as indicated in figure 2.[6] This growth is partly explained by the extraordinary rise in the number of industry petitions, and hence investigations, spurred by recent changes in trade laws that make it easier for industry to obtain regulatory relief (Nivola 1993, 24).

The import administration section is charged with administering U.S. industry trade petitions involving alleged dumping or subsidization of imports in violation of trade laws. Thus, in the two-step investigation process described earlier, it is the import administration section that conducts the investigation for the DOC.

Bureaucratic agencies such as the DOC and ITC are given widespread discretion to make rules and to use them to implement congressional legislation. But as any federal judge would attest, this grant of discretion is not unlimited. Judicial review to settle grievances so as to bring agencies in line with congressional intent is an important way of limiting agency discretion. Generally speaking, court cases may target any aspect of agency decision making. In trade policy, however, the procedure or methodology used by bureaucrats to reach their final rulings and their reliance upon discretion are the two most common targets of litigation.

When new laws or amendments are enacted, they often generate unin-

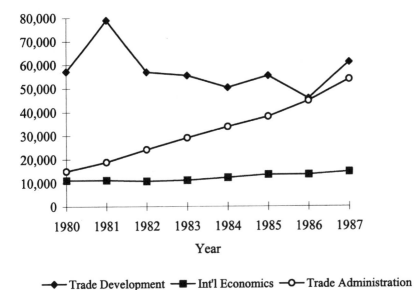

80,000
70,000
60,000
50,000
40,000
30,000
20,000
10,000
0

1980 1981 1982 1983 1984 1985 1986 1987

Year

—◆— Trade Development —■— Int'l Economics —○— Trade Administration

Fig. 2. Budget of the ITA of the Department of Commerce by division (in thousands of dollars)

tended consequences. One of these by-products is the fresh opportunity for litigation due to a rearrangement of existing benefits and coalitions. Some scholars have carefully assayed a series of recent amendments to U.S. trade laws and have concluded that these laws are systematically biased in favor of domestic industries (Barringer and Dunn 1979; Boltuck and Litan 1991; Hansen and Prusa 1993a, 1993b; Murray 1991). The biases have indeed spurred a flood of court cases in recent years. But even though it is the laws that are biased, the administering authorities and their implementation of the laws form the target of most of these lawsuits.

Unfair-Trade and Import Relief Rules and Implementation Procedures

Most aspects of U.S. trade policy can be categorized under two broad policy instruments. These are the fair-trade rules and the unfair-trade rules. Both types of rules operate under the guidelines of GATT. Section 201 of U.S. trade law (sometimes called the *escape clause*) is an example of a fair-trade rule. Trade need not be unfair for the United States or other signatories to GATT to invoke the escape clause to safeguard a domestic industry from economic distress. *Fairness* here means that GATT approves of a given state action, and as such the action is not subject to formal retaliation by third parties. Fair-trade rules, such as the escape clause, allow a country to take unilateral action to protect its industries temporarily if such industries are being harmed by past concessions made in multilateral trade agreements. Under section 201, the ITC determines what harm has occurred to U.S. industries and issues a recommendation for a remedy to the president, who may accept the recommendation or reject it for "policy reasons." The president makes the final decision and may also propose an alternate remedy best suitable to national interest. Under the escape clause, relief can take many forms, including tariffs, quotas, orderly marketing agreements, or adjustment assistance (above and beyond unemployment compensation) for workers in the industry. But whatever the president decides, Congress must be notified to consider the president's proposed policy initiative.

Under fair-trade rules of GATT, other countries are free to retaliate against unilateral acts of protectionism. As a result, U.S. presidents often act with considerable restraint in this area. In recent years, presidents have relied on their authority under the escape clause to keep U.S. markets open (Goldstein 1993, 197) by either giving relief to only a handful of industries out of several meritorious cases or, in some cases, ordering a negotiated settlement instead of imposing tariffs on the foreign traders. It is not surprising, therefore, that over the years, industry use of the escape clause law to seek import relief has been sparse indeed (Destler 1992, 140–41; Baldwin 1985).

Several other cognate reasons exist as well to explain the prevailing industry disinclination to utilize the escape clause mechanism. First, the test for injury is very tough. Under the escape clause, injury must be "serious" and imports must be a "substantial cause" (not less than any other cause) of the injury. Second, to prevent escalation of trade disputes, relief under the escape clause is only temporary; it is terminated upon indications that the domestic industry's economic outlook has improved. Third, relief under the escape clause is politically transparent in that it attracts popular attention and can be subject to intense scrutiny and criticism by free-trade advocates in Congress and the press who believe in the theory that a country's prosperity is related to its level of openness to international trade (McKeown 1984). Consequently, presidents would normally consider all other alternatives before opting for an escape clause relief. Finally, when presidents do use the escape clause to assist American industries, the relief is often anemic, oftentimes in an effort to tender the criticism that would otherwise emerge that such assistance is inconsistent with stated government objectives to advance free trade (Finger, Hall, and Nelson 1982). The growth in recent years of bilateral negotiations, such as voluntary export restraints (VERs), is a direct consequence of the government's effort to minimize reliance upon the escape clause law (Coleman and Yoffie 1990; Nivola 1993).

Unfair-trade laws bear fewer punitive restraints than fair-trade laws do and so are more popular among U.S. industries as a recourse for seeking governmental protection. Unfair-trade laws fall under Title VII of the Trade Act and include the antidumping law (section 731), countervailing duty law (section 701), and unfair practices in import trade law (section 337). As an indication of the relative popularity of the unfair-trade laws, between 1980 and 1990, there were 534 countervailing duty and 635 antidumping investigations (including steel) initiated by the trade agencies. These figures do not include 751 review investigations of antidumping and countervailing duty orders and suspensions. The fair-trade law enjoyed strikingly less popularity, with only 20 escape clause investigations initiated from 1980 to 1990 (Nivola 1993, 24; see also Destler 1992, 166).

An important fact in the popularity of the unfair-trade laws is that the government can continue to provide relief for as long as the conditions that necessitated the relief in the first place persist or until an administrative review deems such relief terminated. Another reason these laws are popular is that the injury test is easier to meet under them than under the fair-trade (i.e., escape clause) standard. The agency simply has to find a "reasonable indication" that a U.S. industry is being harmed or is being threatened with harm to raise the possibility of relief being granted. Moreover, there is less uncertainty under the unfair-trade laws because the president has no veto power over agency decisions. Unfair-trade laws give more power to the bureaucratic agencies than to the president, which makes judicial review all the more critical.

The question is why these laws were adopted in the first place. Throughout most of the post–World War II period, following adoption of the GATT charter in 1947 to help rejuvenate Western economies, the practices of dumping and unfair subsidization have been strongly discouraged by GATT. There was a realization among member states that if, for example, unrestricted subsidization were permitted internationally, it would seriously disrupt world commerce and create global inefficiency by skewing production power away from the most efficient countries, those that have abundant resources to produce the export product most cheaply and competitively for consumers. Members further reasoned along the lines of most economists that the most effective way to enhance global efficiency, stem market distortions, and enhance the rebuilding effort was to encourage nations to maintain a trade policy conditioned upon the classical theory of comparative advantage—the idea that because nations are different in terms of production resource endowment as well as in economic preferences and tastes, they should engage in open trade to take advantage of these differences (Krugman 1987; McKeown 1984).

The DOC and Dumping Investigations

When U.S. industries file dumping petitions, usually after assessing their probability of obtaining a successful outcome, the responsibility of the DOC is to investigate the foreign firm for possible violation of antidumping laws. As explained earlier, the process is itself convoluted but the mechanics are even more technical. The DOC determines the existence of dumping by comparing product prices in the United States with (1) the average home market price of the foreign producer, or (2) the average price of the product in a third country, if the agency judges the producer's home market prices to be inadequate. If data are inadequate or unavailable in the home market or in a third country, then the agency is mandated by law to compare U.S. market prices with (3) a "constructed value"[7] of the commodity allegedly traded unfairly.

Constructed value serves as proxy for home market value and is defined as the average production cost per unit of the imported commodity (plus 10 percent of the cost for general administration expenses and 8 percent for profit). The DOC determines constructed value by using accounting standards of the country in question (see Horlick and Oliver 1989, 19; and generally Boltuck and Litan 1991, 23–56). If the foreign market value (usually considered by DOC as the fair price) is found to be higher than the market value for the same or like products in the United States, then dumping exists and the agency issues a ruling to that effect against the foreign producer. Upon successful demonstration to the ITC of the existence of injury (or threat thereof), the target country is officially assessed a tax in the form of an antidumping duty, which is equal to the margin of dumping. Algebraically, dumping margin (DM) can be expressed as

$$DM = \frac{(P_{FM} - P_{USM})}{P_{USM}}$$

where P_{FM} denotes average price of the good in the exporter's home market, and P_{USM} is the unit price of similar or like products in the United States. The purpose of this tax is to relieve the domestic industry of the damaging effects of price discrimination since, theoretically, a duty on imports has the indirect effect of making foreign goods more expensive in the United States, thereby reducing the quantities sold in the United States. A duty on imports also has the effect of increasing the price that domestic producers can charge for their products and, ceteris paribus, their profitability (see appendix B1 for a partial equilibrium analysis of the distributive effects of import duties on various sectors of an economy).

Irregularities and Biases in DOC Dumping Determination

The process of determining the existence of dumping and of calculating dumping margin was made deliberately complicated and obscure by Congress so that it can escape careful public scrutiny. Presumably, by keeping an inquisitive public at a distance and making it difficult for them to judge the propriety of trade policies, politicians can better manage blame from conflicting trade policy outcomes via excuses and justifications (Weaver 1986; McGraw 1991). But an unavoidable consequence of this obscurity is that regulators in the bureaucracy are often forced into making discretionary judgments, which quite often are arbitrary or biased, in order to accomplish the universal goal set out in the laws.

One contentious and well-litigated practice of the DOC concerns the determination of foreign market value with which U.S. import prices are compared to determine dumping. In this instance, the agency usually disregards the foreign producer's home market sales that are below the cost of production.[8] That is, P_{FM} in the foregoing equation is overestimated, causing the constructed average home market price to be artificially high. Therein lies an important bias in favor of import-competing U.S. industry petitioners. The consequence is that the DOC is significantly more likely to find foreign market prices higher than prices in the United States (i.e., to find that an incidence of dumping exists).

According to many informed observers, this practice is unfair and is inconsistent with the guiding article 2.6 of the Antidumping Code of GATT, which requires fairness when making price comparisons for the purpose of calculating dumping (Boltuck and Litan 1991, 203; Gillen 1991). Not only does this practice unnecessarily penalize foreign producers for selling goods at low prices in their home markets, but it also penalizes U.S. consumers who stand to benefit substantially from a negative finding through lower consumer prices if the GATT provision were correctly construed and the process fairly implemented.

Other procedural biases exist as well. The DOC typically averages foreign market prices of the product in question over a period of six months and compares this value with U.S. import prices for individual sales of the product or like products to determine dumping margin. A second procedural bias is that the agency simply refuses to take an average of U.S. market prices of the U.S.-made product or its substitute before comparing this value with the average foreign market price (or foreign market value). Rather, in gathering information to perform such comparisons, the DOC usually ignores those unit prices in the U.S. market that are above the foreign market value and considers only those that are below the foreign market average (Murray 1991). Once again the result is a dumping margin that is inflated and significantly tilted against foreign competitors and in favor of U.S. producers. What is the justification for this practice? According to Boltuck and Litan (1991, 14), the DOC feels that the practice guards against "spot" or "rifle shot" dumping. Ironically, the agency overlooks the fact that U.S. producers *do* sell products in different U.S. markets at different prices in response to local demand and supply conditions.

One final disconcerting aspect of DOC investigation procedure concerns the use of "best information available," which is usually the information alleged by domestic petitioners in their case briefs. The DOC usually ignores data submissions by foreign respondents who are targets of pending dumping investigation if the agency perceives such data as inadequate, or if the data are not submitted in a timely fashion and in English, or if the data are not in a specified computer-readable format. From these enumerated conditions, it is apparent that the hurdles the foreign defendant must clear are numerous. If any of the conditions is not satisfied, the DOC will use the best information available (BIA), thus giving domestic petitioners considerable advantage. The requirement is onerous to foreign traders, as they have only 30 days to assemble the data they need to defend themselves before regulators. In this context, the DOC uses BIA as a credible threat (backed by legal precedent) to obtain prompt compliance with its requests. Once the agency has made a determination to use BIA in the context of "noncompliance," there is no turning back, even if the foreign firm eventually submits the required data before the investigation is completed. Since judicial review is based upon the administrative record, late data submissions are often ignored by the courts even though such data may be, from a practical standpoint, the best information available before the investigation is finished and a final decision is rendered. In the case of *Olympic Adhesives Inc. v United States* (1989), which involved administrative review of antidumping actions concerning animal glue and inedible gelatin from Sweden, Judge Kenton Musgrave of the Court of International Trade approved of this regulatory practice.

As the foregoing discussion shows, the process of estimating the average cost of production and of determining the margin of dumping is technical and difficult, requiring the DOC to make several arbitrary and discretionary judgments along the way. Given that, an important question is whether the method used by the DOC to determine the foreign market value significantly influences the subsequent margin of dumping. For one, Tracy Murray's investigation of the dumping practices of the DOC led to a conclusion that "the constructed value method was almost twice as likely to result in an affirmative dumping determination than were third-country sales" (1991, 45). The discussion thus far suggests that the process of determining dumping is not neutral. In many instances arbitrary decisions are made that have negative consequences for aggrieved parties. These facts merge to create an impetus for those unfavorably affected by agency rulings to seek their day in court.

Irregularities and Biases in DOC Countervailing Duty Determination

Whereas dumping duties are meant to counteract the effects of price discrimination by a foreign firm, the statutory purpose of countervailing duties is to offset the benefits of a bounty or grant provided by a foreign government to its industries to strengthen their production and exportation. Business leaders in the United States always believe that their firms can survive any head-to-head competition that is based upon fair-trade principles but that they cannot compete with a foreign government's treasury. They therefore find foreign government subsidization intolerable and are willing to fight it in the U.S. trade agencies.

Like the procedure for determining dumping margins, the process of determining countervailing duties is also obscure, perhaps even more so. This obscurity is due in part to a long-term disagreement over what actually constitutes a countervailable subsidy; thus a key question in any discussion of subsidy determination is "What is a countervailable subsidy?" GATT and Congress both share part of the blame for much of the disagreement over the meaning of *subsidy*. Neither GATT (in the Subsidies Code) nor the U.S. Congress (in the governing statute) provided any meaningful definition of *subsidy* (Jackson 1991, chap. 11). In the case of *Zenith Radio Corp. v. United States* (1978), the U.S. Supreme Court was asked to settle this critical issue and to answer a clearly difficult question that GATT economists, lawmakers in Congress and their army of congressional aides, and federal bureaucrats in Washington could not answer. The Court was of little help in fashioning a definition. Following traditional protocols of jurisprudence, the Supreme Court deferred to the bureaucracy, ruling that it was up to the secretary of the treasury to determine the class or kind of subsidies that may be countervailable. The issue remains controversial.

The difficulty surrounding the determination of countervailable subsidies involves the need to differentiate between the effects of domestic subsidies (e.g., good roads, educational infrastructure, and national defense) that have direct social and economic values for a country and the effects of export subsidies that directly enhance the competitive position of particular domestic industries in foreign markets. The economic and social benefit of both kinds of subsidy are largely inseparable and differ only in intensity and concentration, which explains why this issue is hard to resolve.

One instinctive requirement of national sovereignty is the ability for nations to promote legitimate government policies that benefit their citizens. Given that, it is oftentimes difficult to determine just where a government crosses the line to behave in a manner that is contrary to its commitment to the GATT requirement barring nations from taking actions such as domestic subsidization that can potentially distort trade. But when clear evidence of illegal subsidization emerges, foreign governments have every reason to be concerned, because such subsidization creates an externality (i.e., third-party effect) that can have a deleterious impact upon their own economies.

Sometime during the early 1980s, the DOC adopted what is known as the *general availability criterion,* under which the agency screens out socially beneficial foreign government subsidies that are not limited to certain establishments only but are available to all industries in the economy. Such socially benign subsidies are, of course, not subject to countervailing duties. One functional difficulty with the general availability criterion, which the DOC neglected to address until forced to do so by the Court of International Trade in 1985, is that generally available benefits may in fact accrue disproportionately to one particular industry, giving that industry an unfair competitive advantage in the world market.

In 1985, in the case of *Cabot Corp. v. United States,* American producers of carbon black feedstock charged that their Mexican counterparts were being unfairly subsidized by low energy prices in Mexico. Although low energy prices were generally available to other industries, these Mexican producers of carbon black used a disproportionate amount of the available energy resources. The Court of International Trade ruled against the DOC and ordered the agency to recognize the functional distinction between generally available subsidies used heavily by more than one industry and generally available subsidies whose benefits accrue disproportionately to one particular industry. In 1988, Congress agreed with the court and incorporated this feature into the Omnibus Trade and Competitive Act because the DOC's standard would have subjected many U.S. firms to countervailing duty cases from other countries.

The DOC currently countervails three classes of subsidies that are deemed to have direct and significant effects on U.S. markets: (1) upstream (or indirect) subsidies, which are subsidies for raw materials that are nongeneral in nature and therefore favor a particular industry or firm; (2) export subsidies, which are subsidies that single out for preferential treatment those goods that are exported, as opposed to those that are sold in the producer's home market; and (3) production subsidies, which are subsidies such as research and development grants, loan guarantees, government loans with below-market interest rates, and forgiveness of past loans by the government (Knoll 1989). The margin of countervailing duty is usually equal to the amount of the subsidy or an amount sufficient to counteract the negative effect of the subsidy on U.S. competitors.

The ITC and Material Injury Determination

Unlike the DOC's responsibility, which involves separate investigations for antidumping and countervailing duty petitions and the use of different methodologies to determine the existence of dumping and subsidization, the ITC's investigatory responsibility is theoretically indistinguishable for both dumping and subsidization claims. That is partly because the ITC investigates only the domestic industry. Any problems, irregularities, or biases that the ITC encounters or introduces into its investigation are germane to both dumping and countervailing duty determinations. The procedure for investigating injury is theoretically straightforward but complex in practice. A theoretical tact will be followed in explaining how the ITC investigates injury.

There are three important and interrelated steps that the ITC takes in its effort to determine whether a domestic petitioner has suffered injury, after which point duties may be levied. The Commission determines (1) what the product is; (2) whether there is injury to the domestic industry; and (3) whether the injury (if any) was caused by imports.

Determining what the product in question is sounds simple enough, but in reality, it often is not. The difficulty lies in the fact that in most injury claims, the investigated product is part of a continuum of characteristically similar products. In the investigation of minivans from Japan, for example, the Commission noted that "the dividing lines between minivans and other types of vehicles are not completely clear, in part due to the fact that the minivan was designed as a 'hybrid' vehicle."[9] According to U.S. law, the product that the domestic petitioner alleges to have been disadvantaged by import penetration must be "like" the imported product. If not "like," then it must be "similar in characteristics and uses with the article subject to investigation."[10]

Given this statutory requirement, the Commission typically relies upon one or more of the following to determine similarity between the domestic and imported products: the physical characteristics and end uses of the products, the substitutability of the products, similarities in the channels of distribution, consumer and producer perceptions of the products, characteristics of manufacturing facilities and employee attributes (e.g., the type of education or training they require), and in rare circumstances, the price of the products.[11]

Assessing existence of injury to U.S. producers is the crux of the ITC's administrative responsibility. In carrying out this task, the agency typically considers the volume of imports of the merchandise that is alleged to have been dumped. In 1984, Congress responded to political pressure from import-competing industries that expressed dissatisfaction with the amount of relief being received, and it mandated the ITC to cumulate the volume of exports from two or more countries of "like" products if such imports competed with each other and with a U.S.-made product. The rule makes no exception even in cases where a particular country's volume of export, standing alone, is insignificant and therefore insufficient to cause material harm to U.S. industry. As explained in the subsequent section on injury causation, this rule clearly increases the likelihood that the ITC will find the volume of imports large enough to conclude that material injury or retardation of a domestic industry exists.

The next important consideration in the determination of injury is the effect of imports on prices of like products made in the United States. The Commission determines whether there is significant price underselling of the U.S.-made product by the imported merchandise and whether the lower-priced import restricts the ability of U.S. producers to raise their prices, which they otherwise would have done. Economic logic suggests that the volume of imports is inversely related to domestic prices. So if the volume of import is high enough, the Commission is likely to find that U.S. producers are unable to raise prices and earn reasonable profit to sustain themselves in the marketplace and thus hold the foreign importers accountable.

Finally, the Commission determines the impact of imports on the affected industry. In this respect, U.S. law requires the ITC to consider "all relevant" economic factors that may have a bearing upon the status of the industry. These factors include actual or potential decline in output, sales, market share, profit, return on investment, and capacity utilization. Also considered are the actual or potential negative effects on cash flow, inventories, employment (e.g., plant closings), wages, investment and growth, and the ability to raise capital.

These three factors—volume of imports, their effect on prices, and their impact on the affected industry—constitute the traditional approach to injury determination that the Commission has adopted, although not all commissioners over the years have accepted it as the most practical approach (Knoll 1989; Barringer and Dunn 1979). In examining these factors, the Commission typically uses the previous three years in the industry's history as a point of reference with which to compare the current status of the industry. If the volume of imports is significantly high and its effect on domestic prices and on the industry is negative, then the Commission concludes that there is injury to the domestic industry. That is not the end of the matter, however. The Commission must conduct an injury causation test to link the injury to imports.

In 1984, Congress authorized the ITC to consider imports of the product under investigation from all countries competing in the United States. A cumulation proviso such as this has the effect of raising substantially the likelihood that the ITC will find injury by reason of imports. Indeed, according to the analysis of the intervention effect of cumulation conducted by Hansen and Prusa (1996), cumulation increases the chances of an affirmative determination by 20 to 30 percent and has actually changed the ITC's decision from negative to positive in one-third of all cumulated cases.

To tie injury to imports, the Commission usually must do three things. First, it must establish that there is substantial price underselling. That is, does the foreign import undersell the domestically manufactured good on the basis of price? To answer this question, the Commission compares the average price of the import with that of the domestically manufactured product. If the average price of the import is lower, the ITC takes this finding as evidence of price underselling and as evidence of injury by reason of the imported product. Usually no serious consideration is given to quality differences between imported goods and U.S.-made goods if there is overlap in competition between them.

Second, the ITC examines lost sales by the domestic industry (see Jameson 1986, 532). Lost sales occur when a U.S. consumer purchases an imported product rather than a domestically produced good solely because the imported merchandise costs less. To gather information on lost sales, the agency has a practice of making telephone contacts with customers who have defected as alleged by the petitioning industry. Customers are queried about what they purchased and, more important, its origin (whether foreign or domestic product). If the product is foreign, they are further asked whether their purchasing decision was based solely on price differences, assuming the U.S.-made product was available at the time of the purchase. If a majority of those interviewed answered these questions in the affirmative, the ITC concludes that lost sales do exist due to imports and that these imports have caused injury to the domestic industry.

Third, the ITC analyzes the import trend. Correlating import penetration of the U.S. market with the profit figures of the U.S. competitor provides partial indication that imports are indeed responsible for the material injury suffered by the domestic industry. More specifically, a negative correlation between imports and domestic industry profit provides useful ammunition for the ITC to hold foreign competitors liable for the depressed condition of the domestic industry. Once this critical connection between imports and injury has been established and the DOC finds that dumping or subsidization has occurred, duties are imposed on the foreign producer as a way to return both sides to a level playing field.

Problems in ITC Determination of Material Injury

The process of injury determination by the ITC has its own flaws, too. Some are avoidable because they are generated unintentionally by the agency for reasons having to do with administrative expediency. Others are statutory and so unavoidable but are flaws nonetheless that have been challenged in court from time to time. These perceived flaws are addressed in this section.

Like most other independent regulatory commissions in the federal system, the ITC usually conducts open hearings, similar to those found in the courts, to gather evidence and build a strong record to support an administrative ruling. In the interest of due process, the agency has discretion to allow limited discovery of information by legal counsel from both sides. It should come as no surprise that given the importance of discovery to the outcome of a case and the mercurial tendencies of administrative discretion, the Commission has been sued several times for arbitrariness in allowing the discovery of "sensitive information" in some cases and not permitting discovery at all in others (see e.g., *Roquette Freres v. United States* 1983).

Also, U.S. trade law mandates the ITC to determine injury "by reason of imports" before quantitative restrictions can be imposed on a foreign competitor, but the law is unclear on what *imports* means in this context. Does the term refer to that portion of imports traded unfairly (i.e., dumped or subsidized), or does it speak to the entire volume of import from one country or cumulatively from many countries? Obviously, the latter is more restrictive on trade than the former. The problem is therefore one of statutory construction to determine the proper legislative purpose. There is disagreement within the Commission over what constitutes the most accurate interpretation of the concept "imports." But more often than not, the commissioners have adhered to the more expansive, all-imports conceptualization.[12]

This interpretation is inconsistent with congressional intent and with GATT antidumping and subsidies codes, both of which advocate procedural fairness and an expansive international trade posture. According to a House of Representatives bill reported in the 98th Congress, the expressed purpose of cumulation, for example, is to "eliminate inconsistencies in Commission practice and to ensure that the injury test adequately addresses simultaneous *unfair* imports from different countries" (emphasis added).[13] A textual interpretation of this statement would suggest that only the unfair portion of imports of any particular good, not the entire volume, ought to be countervailed. GATT rules add immeasurable credence to this view. Article 6(1) of the GATT Subsidies Code specifically requires nations to conduct "an objective examination of the volume of *subsidized* imports" (emphasis added). The failure of the Commission to correctly read the intent of Congress has resulted in several lawsuits challenging the ITC on administrative and constitutional due process grounds.[14]

Under certain circumstances where imports compete with each other and with domestic products, and where such imports are subject to investigation, the ITC often cross-cumulates unfair imports to determine injury. Cross-cumulation is a practice in which the agency aggregates unfairly dumped imports and unfairly subsidized imports in the course of a single investigation to facilitate an injury decision. Trade laws do not require cross-cumulation, however, and so it is an uncommon ITC practice (K. Berry 1989, 657; Mock 1986, 459–60). The problem is that when the agency does use cross-cumulation, it has done so inconsistently, often in response to political pressure. These and other problems that plague trade policy implementation call for effective decentralized mechanisms of oversight. If international trade policy implementation is to proceed with minimum irregularities, judicial review offers *the* key ingredient to achieve and sustain this objective.

Conclusion

Delivering international trade policy to the American people is largely a bifurcated responsibility shared by the ITC and the DOC. The objective of this chapter thus was to delineate what these two agencies are, what their functions are, and how they go about performing those functions. To weed out frivolous industry petitions to maintain systemic stability, both agencies are required to conduct a preliminary investigation; they must determine first if there is reasonable indication of the validity of the allegations raised in the cases filed before they can launch a final and more detailed investigation. The DOC's job is to determine the existence of unfair-trade practices, while the ITC's is to determine the existence of injury pursuant to such unfair practices. Both agencies must rule affirmatively before final import duties can be imposed on the foreign traders.

In addition to the inherent indeterminacies in the trade laws, the process of conducting investigation to make these various determinations is obscure and complex. It is a great source of frustration for the implementing authorities, which often leads to agency decisions that are either arbitrary or outrightly erroneous. In consequence, an undeserving party might be favored while one more deserving of regulatory protection might be injured in the process. The need for continued agency monitoring to ensure procedural fairness and broader representation therefore becomes essential. It is because of arbitrariness and the potential for abuse of bureaucratic discretion that mechanisms of political and judicial oversight are built into the system of trade policy implementation. Specialized courts are especially well equipped to search for, detect, and correct such transgressions by virtue of their expertise. Chapter 4 addresses this issue of political and judicial oversight, focusing particularly on the political branches. A more detailed examination of judicial influence on bureaucracy is reserved for chapter 5.

Part 2

Theoretical and Methodological Underpinnings

CHAPTER 4

Judicial and Political Mechanisms of Control over Bureaucracy

It is harder to *run* a Constitution than to frame one. . . .
Woodrow Wilson (1887)

In our democratic system, "judges see bureaucrats at a distance and through the lenses of conventional stereotypes." So writes James Q. Wilson in his book *Bureaucracy: What Government Agencies Do and Why They Do It.* "From a distance, a government agency is a machine designed to achieve a goal. The judge's job is to start the machine, change the goal, or both" (J. Wilson 1989, 292). The mechanisms that judges and political superiors of the bureaucracy have at their disposal to start this metaphorical "machine" and change its goals are numerous, and they form the focus of this chapter. I begin by examining the mechanisms available to the courts to "tame" the bureaucracy and showing why courts matter in the policy-making process. Then I turn my attention to a discussion of the mechanisms of congressional and presidential control of bureaucracy. I conclude by noting that ultimately the kinds of decisions agencies make and the policies they produce are a result of bargaining and compromises between regulatory agencies and key external actors and forces within the policy system. These external actors and forces determine the extent to which administrative policies are stable, coherent, and predictable.

Limitations and Mechanisms of Judicial Influence

Although the U.S. Constitution makes no explicit prescription for policy delivery by federal bureaucracies, decision making in today's government takes place mostly within bureaucratic institutions. In trade policy, Congress has enacted about 200 statutes pertaining to the administration and enforcement of customs and international trade laws of the United States (Bennett 1991, 337). Because the enforcement of these statutes is actually carried out largely by the Department of Commerce and the International Trade Commission, it is not an exaggeration to assert that the United States would have had an unsophisticated and unremarkable trade policy were it not for the decisions and activities of these agencies. But because of the potential for bureaucratic drift, that is, the tendency for agencies to produce policies that deviate from those preferred by lawmakers who originally delegated power (Epstein and O'Halloran 1994, 699), bureaucratic actions cannot go unchecked.

Of the three constitutional stations of power (Congress, president, and courts), courts are institutionally the most limited in their ability to exert influence on policy implementation. This limitation comes straight from our constitutional heritage. While judges do have the ability to start the bureaucratic machine and change bureaucratic goals, oftentimes with an activist posture (Dilulio 1987; Harriman and Straussman 1983), there is one sobering fact: government bureaucracies do not owe their immediate existence to courts as they do to the president or Congress. So bureaucracies can simply ignore court decisions altogether or refuse to acquiesce to some aspects of adverse court rulings.

Occasionally, nonacquiescence is a systemwide problem. We witnessed such behaviors in the Southern states during the 1950s and 1960s, when local Southern magistrates, police, and education officials ignored or actively opposed enforcement of the Supreme Court's decision in *Brown v. Board of Education* (1954) to end school segregation (Giles and Walker 1975; Rosenberg 1991). But most often, nonacquiescence is agency specific. In their analysis of nonacquiescence of federal administrative agencies, Samuel Estreicher and Richard L. Revesz characterized agency nonacquiescence to court decisions as a "pervasive and longstanding" problem (1989, 683). For instance, in an effort to reduce the number of benefit recipients during Ronald Reagan's first term in office, the Social Security Administration (SSA) gained notoriety for its repeated refusal to make court-ordered procedural changes requiring proof of change in medical condition before benefits could be terminated.[1]

Generally speaking, the inability of courts to force compliance with their own decisions is their major source of institutional weakness. But does that mean courts are impotent in their ability to affect the internal operation of bureaucracy? No. Nonacquiescence is only a problem to the extent it is tolerated by courts and to the extent that third parties fail to pressure courts to demand agency compliance with their rulings. The explosion in civil litigation in the United States since the 1970s is only one indication that courts do get results. At the very least, courts are able to bring important issues to the forefront of public consciousness and agenda. With resolve, courts are not ineffectual. That being said, it must be emphasized that courts are clearly constrained in the legal process. Courts cannot initiate legal action against a bureaucracy. Rather, they must await legal controversies to be brought to them for a resolution before they may act, and even so, court actions are narrowly circumscribed by legal rules and are constrained in the amount of remedy they can provide. Most important, as Alexander Hamilton pointed out in the *Federalist Papers,* No. 78, courts are limited because they have neither the power of the purse strings nor the power to force others to comply with their decisions.

In light of these seemingly daunting institutional weaknesses, a key questions is: How can courts exercise effective influence over policy implementation? Fortunately, the Constitution does reward courts with the power of *judgment,* which is characterized by finality. The ability to render judgment is a discretionary matter. And it is the chief source of the institutional power that courts possess to exert influence upon the parameters of bureaucratic policy-making. Court rulings are an important mechanism of judicial influence over agency action. Through their rulings, courts can impose tangible ex post costs on a bureaucracy by rearranging its priorities and modifying its rules and practices that the courts deem unreasonable. When agencies fail to comply, courts can levy fines on them or hold agency personnel in contempt or both. As James Q. Wilson (1989) and William T. Gormley (1989) both have indicated, courts can also impose procedural requirements that can strain agency budgets and personnel and significantly undermine an agency's ability to control its own programs and turf.

Another possible mechanism of influence available to courts is the ability to undermine the reputation, respectability, and subsequent bargaining position of bureaucracies through adverse decisions. Such decisions represent a potential threat to the longevity of administrative programs because adverse decisions are a sign of serious agency slippage or bureaucratic drift. In this context, an agency may suffer a reduction in prestige and bargaining position with key political actors and supporters.

But even in the face of such sanctions and their potentially disruptive consequences, compliance is never automatic nor complete. The level of compliance typically depends upon the presence of certain resources such as the clarity and firmness with which courts communicate their rulings to agencies and upon the net utility for the agency in complying (Pacelle and Baum 1992; Spriggs 1996). But the mere fact that courts are capable of imposing extreme punishment on an agency for its malfeasance signifies that a pragmatic agency will try to avoid clashes with judicial authorities.

Political Control

For more than a century, public policy scholars, starting most notably with Woodrow Wilson ([1887] 1978), have devoted a great deal of effort in search of ways to analyze and understand the behavior of unelected public officials and the mechanisms that elected officials employ to manage their policy directives so as to meet programmatic goals and satisfy the desires of an inattentive and disorganized public. These efforts led scholars to a small set of principles, or theoretical perspectives, some dynamic and robust and others somewhat rigid, that they used as a guide in understanding the politics of public policy formation and implementation. They employed these principles with the understanding that innumerable difficulties are involved in the analyses of (asymmetric) control relationships between elected politicians and unelected bureaucrats.

Three main theoretical perspectives form the basis of most of the inquiries into the political control of bureaucratic action: politics and administration dichotomy, external control focusing on regulated interest groups (pluralism), and agency or institutional theory.

Politics and Administration Dichotomy

The drive to separate politics from the delivery of public policy started vigorously at the turn of the twentieth century in response to the growth of machine politics and the political graft, corruption, and inefficiency that machine politics generated. The focus of politics and administration dichotomy was on enhancing the "neutral competence," or independence and greater professionalism, of those public officials charged with implementing public policy programs (Heclo 1978; Knott and Miller 1987; Rourke 1992).

In this context, the earliest systematic attempts to analyze political control over administration took a very optimistic view of bureaucrats and strongly emphasized the position of structural reformers who advocated the celebrated efficiency and rationality of the Weberian model of an "ideal-type" bureaucracy. Early studies in this genre that provided much of the foundation for later theoretical developments include those of Woodrow Wilson ([1887] 1978), Goodnow (1900), DeWitt (1915), White (1927), and of course Max Weber (1946), all of which emphasized a technical rather than a political approach to government. Later in the 1940s and in the 1950s, several scholars began to recognize politics as an integral part of governance; they include administrative scholars such as Waldo (1948), Simon (1957), and Kaufman (1956). Due to the hierarchically organized structure of governmental organizations in the United States, the supporters of politics and administration dichotomy reasoned that separating politics from administration would facilitate political control over policy implementation by making communication easier and uncorrupted.

In the epoch of bureaucratic analyses, politics and administration dichotomy was indeed a magnificent piece of political theory, formulated and implemented by political reformers and entrepreneurs to whom several important regimes in American politics, such as the New Deal and the current administrative state, may be credited. The dichotomy stressed the received expertise and instrumental (i.e., adaptive) rationality of bureaucrats. Its power was derived from the assumption that by allowing public administrators to operate with relative autonomy and freedom from constant direct oversight and control by elected officials, their neutrality and competence in administering public policies would be enhanced (Waterman 1989, 1–26; Heclo 1978, 80–98). However, contrary to early popular belief, this view is somewhat naive and is an inadequate framework for examining influence over agency behavior.

Upon reevaluation of the early literature on politics and administration dichotomy, it seems an exaggeration to refer to the early works as studies of political control over bureaucratic behavior, since the goal of the dichotomy that early scholars studied was to increase the professionalism, power, and independence of bureaucrats relative to those of their political overseers. The increased power and independence of bureaucrats ostensibly hindered the effectiveness of politicians to control the bureaucracy, in spite of a hierarchically organized governmental structure. According to some analysts, both efficiency and neutrality actually suffered under the dichotomy theory (Knott and Miller 1987).

The strength of a theory can be judged on the basis of its resilience and internal capacity to adapt to changing political conditions, and the ability of a theory to meet these criteria is based upon the tenability of the theory's assumptions. One of the biggest difficulties with the principle of politics and administration dichotomy is that it unwittingly assumed away the potential for bureaucrats to exhibit mixed motives and divided loyalties. The theory shows no appreciation for the importance of judicial review or of political factors such as interest group contestation and interagency conflicts. All these factors are important in the process of defining and redefining organizational rules for proper program management and agency performance (Aberbach and Rockman 1976; Nathan 1986). Furthermore, politics and administration dichotomy downplayed the fact that bureaucrats are not what Martin Shapiro (1968, 52) calls "political eunuchs" who are positioned simply to guard the ideal in policy decisions made by congressional lawmakers or by the president. Instead, as contemporary policy scholars recognize, bureaucrats have their own interests, preferences, and motivations, which may or may not be compatible with those of elected policymakers and which they pursue within the constraints imposed by the political system (Arnold 1987; Fiorina 1981).

Pluralism

The politics and administration dichotomy began to crumble in the 1940s because of its failure to recognize the importance of politics in agency decisions and the compatibility of these decisions with the policy goals of democratic overseers. Emphasis on the dichotomy started to decline in the early 1940s following the classic work of E. E. Schattsneider (1935); the decline accelerated with later works by Bernstein (1955), Truman (1959), and Lowi (1964), along with the study of free-trade politics by Bauer, Pool, and Dexter (1963). A common theme stressed by these revisionists was the critical roles played by pluralist political interests in shaping public policy. Lowi (1964, 680) gives the best conceptual characterization of the pluralist view as one that "stresses conflict and conflict resolution through bargaining among groups and coalitions organized around shared interests." But it was Schattsneider whose cogent description of the pluralist theory has captured the most scholarly attention in contemporary political thought.

Schattsneider examined the sources of the biggest legislative disaster in United States history in the arena of international trade: the Smoot-Hawley trade bill enacted in 1930 in response to depressed economic and political forces. Policymakers in Congress failed to look beyond particularistic benefits for their constituents as they drafted this important bill. Consequently, the Smoot-Hawley bill increased average tariff rates on all imported goods to an all-time high of 60 percent in 1932 and propelled the country further into the Great Depression, as 25 key U.S. trading partners swiftly retaliated against this unilateral imposition of tariffs (Nivola 1986, 583; Destler 1986; cf. Eichengreen 1988, 92–114). Schattsneider attributed the lopsided nature of the Smoot-Hawley bill to unbalanced interest-group pressures. He concluded, "Although . . . theoretically the interests supporting and opposed to [tariff] legislation are . . . approximately equal, the pressures upon Congress are extremely unbalanced. That is to say, the pressures supporting the tariff are made overwhelming by the fact that the opposition is negligible" (1935, 285).

The pressures from the opposition may have been "negligible" because the opposition was unable to organize effectively. In his refinement of the pluralist view, Mancur Olson (1965) noted that the efficacy of any group's efforts to organize and secure benefits from the political process depends upon the group's strength, which in turn depends on its ability to minimize transaction costs by controlling the free-rider problem through a mixture of discrete sets of selective incentives.

Lowi's 1969 study puts the focus on interest-group strengths into a perspective that considers mass public attitudes and the government's effort to regulate interest-group activity. He observed that contemporary interest-group activism comprises a "new public philosophy" in which a strong sense of consensus emerges among citizens. There is a general belief, according to Lowi, that organized interests are adequately representative of the distribution and intensity of citizen concerns and that consequently, the proper role of government should be limited to facilitating the bargaining and contestation of these competing interests through wider access to government.[2] What that suggests is that society is relatively uninterested in regulation and that bureaucrats should be given greater autonomy and flexibility to respond to "appropriate" client-specific conditions. The self-correcting mechanism that would result from interest-group competition and the stability it would engender seem to correlate well with the neoclassical economic concept of equilibrium in the marketplace, the basis of the economic theory of regulation advanced by the Chicago school (Stigler 1971; Peltzman 1976; Becker 1983).

The traditional interest-group view is that regulation is supplied in response to public outcry over negative externalities (or market failures), inefficiencies, and inequities in the marketplace (see Bentley 1908, then compare recent works such as Rhoads 1985; Wolf 1988; Robyn 1987; Mitchell and Munger 1991). However, the Chicago school, led by George Stigler, challenged and to a certain extent succeeded in changing the conventional wisdom. Stigler (1971) argued that "as a rule, regulation is acquired by industry and is designed and operated primarily for its benefit" (3). This argument gave rise to the so-called capture theory. Before Stigler's article appeared on the scene, Bernstein (1955, 74–102) had emphasized a similar position, that bureaucrats were "captives" of interest groups. In particular, Bernstein argued that all regulatory agencies go through what he identifies as a "life-cycle" in which capture by regulated groups was the culminating phase.[3]

Regulatory capture represented a rather strong indictment of the utility maximizing "regulator."[4] The regulator is portrayed as someone who is passive and callous to public welfare and as one whose motivation for public service is tainted by narrow self-interest. For example, legislators are motivated by reelection while bureaucrats are motivated by the power to control their own programs and turf. In both instances, the support of a powerful interest group is crucial. By this account, the regulator is highly susceptible to regulatory manipulation and capture by any industry or labor group that has adequate political resources to utilize the state to seek monopoly profit unavailable through competitive market arrangements, even if it may result in substantial deadweight (social) costs. In his review of James Q. Wilson's 1980 book on the politics of regulation, Kenneth Shepsle (1982, 219) describes this characterization superbly: "Regulators, rather, are seen to be engaged in dancing with a producer version of the proverbial 800-pound gorilla. When it dances, you dance; when it stops, you stop!"

But neither Stigler nor Bernstein recognized the capacity or the incentive for bureaucrats and policymakers to make compromises that consider general public interest. Becker (1983, 1985), Peltzman (1976), Denzau and Munger (1986), and others have provided formal refinements of the capture formulation, refinements that emphasize the trade-offs (including the compensation of losers through redistribution) that regulators, particularly lawmakers, must make between public welfare and their career interests so that everyone with a stake can be accommodated. By emphasizing the power of producer groups, capture theory clearly places enormous emphasis on the demand side of policy regulation and precious little on policy change emanating from the supply side or, more appropriately, the political side of regulation (Derthick and Quirk 1985; Noll and Owen 1983). The consequence of this imbalance is compelling. As Salamon and Siegfried (1977), Gormley (1979), Meier (1985), and J. Wilson (1980) all observe, the phenomenon that emerges is an elaborate system of independent policy subsystems that are manifested in neat, cozy, triangular relationships involving relevant congressional subcommittees, bureaucrats, and established organized interests, all engaged in a profitable partnership. These relationships are popularly known as *iron triangles*. One possibility that may be disquieting to the advocates of capture theory is that no one particular iron triangle may be able to dominate any given policy area because of the existence of a broader network of advocacy coalitions (Sabatier 1988). So, while economists emphasized how these cozy triangles flourished, the potential for political dynamics to induce outcomes in these structures was assumed to be largely irrelevant.

As proof that political dynamics do matter, we need to recognize that it was diffuse interests such as consumer coalitions and professional groups, outside the normal flow of iron-triangle politics, that introduced the *idea* and laid the foundation for the successful deregulation of the airline, trucking, and telecommunications industries (Derthick and Quirk 1985; Robyn 1987; Teske 1991). Capture theory could not explain such an "unexpected" turn of events. Indeed, the proponents of capture theory agree that the theory is unable to explain or predict developments such as deregulation or the occasional triumph of a diffuse public over organized coalitions (Peltzman 1989, 14–17).

In short, while regulatory capture is an appealing and concise theory, it does not present an accurate picture of policy regulation in the United States; it neglects the role of institutions, the precursors of political strategy and conflict, both of which are necessary to bring structure and predictability to bureaucratic performance. As Friedman (1962), Lindbloom (1977), and Shepsle (1979) all attest, no policy analysis cast in economic terms would be complete without identifying a systematic connection to politics. Political scientists have recognized that capture theory falls into a category of incomplete theories of regulation. In particular, it makes no room for what North (1990, 182) describes as "humanly devised constraints that shape human interaction." Also, the role of policy entrepreneurs who may possess the requisite resources and motivation to identify profitable ideas and galvanize a policy coalition to bring such ideas to fruition is entirely ignored (Baumgartner and Jones 1993; Quirk 1990; Schneider and Teske 1995).

Agency Theory

Emphasis has therefore shifted to agency theory in the effort to understand politics and its importance to the analysis of external influence on bureaucratic behavior. Agency relationships exist when one organizational unit of government depends upon another for information or decisions. Therefore, agency theory argues in favor of an institutional view of control over bureaucracy (Moe 1984; Pratt and Zechauser 1985; Waterman 1989, 1–26). The theory contends that democratic overseers of bureaucracy have bargaining advantages that, if properly utilized, can lead an agency to engage in activities that produce socially superior results (Miller and Moe 1983; Moe 1984; Bendor, Taylor, and Van Gaalen 1985). Advantages such as the capacity to determine the incentive structure (Miller and Moe 1983; Fiorina 1981) limit the available policy choices of bureaucrats (Eavey and Miller 1984; Ferejohn and Shipan 1990) and minimize transaction costs through institutional design (North 1990; McCubbins and Page 1987; Eggertsson 1990), making it possible for democratic superiors, including the courts, to exert effective influence upon bureaucratic behavior.

The use of agency theory in political analyses originated from studies of nonmarket (i.e., hierarchical) production arrangements by economists, focusing on uncertainty, conflict, bargaining, and contracting in market-oriented organizations (see, e.g., Coase 1937; Alchian 1950; Alchian and Demsetz 1972; Williamson 1975). The underlying assumption of this framework is that no enacted contract is ever complete; that is, contracts never accommodate all possible contingencies. A complete contract in this sense would mean that contractors operate under full information. However, in most practical situations, particularly those that occur within the context of a dynamic political environment, complete contracts are virtually impossible due to asymmetrical resources. Because agency theory assumes that resource asymmetries exist in contractual relationships (Holmstrom 1979; Fama 1980; Niskanen 1971), the theory is best applied to hierarchical settings, which are characterized by asymmetrical resources typically in the form of information, expertise, or authority.

Thus political scientists have used this theory to analyze a variety of political and legal relationships, ranging from an analysis of intergovernmental relations and the impact of federal grants on state and local spending and taxing (Chubb 1985) to an examination of the transmission of legal authority in the federal court system (Caldeira 1985; Songer, Segal, and Cameron 1994). Given the hierarchically organized structure of government institutions in the United States, this framework fits the public bureaucracy context well.

Much of the recent work on institutional analysis based on agency theory has been done by congressional scholars and rational choice theorists, using conceptual and game-theoretic methodologies (e.g., Ferejohn and Shipan 1990; McCubbins, Noll, and Weingast 1987, 1989). Although early empirical literature on the control of bureaucracy showed politicians in Congress to be passive and thus to have a great deal of difficulty observing and controlling bureaucratic outputs (Niskanen 1971; Downs 1967), more recent analyses show these conclusions to be largely inaccurate (e.g., McCubbins and Sullivan 1987). These analyses have shown, for example, that legislative and executive overseers of the bureaucracy have a number of centralized as well as decentralized mechanisms at their disposal for controlling, or at least actively influencing, agency behavior (e.g., Fiorina 1981; Neustadt 1990).

Congress
Congressional overseers have several centralized mechanisms with which to control bureaucratic behavior. Centralized mechanisms are those over which Congress has direct and immediate control. They can be completely changed or merely fine-tuned to achieve congressional objectives. Under these centralized mechanisms, congressional overseers can threaten active intervention via direct oversight, hearings, and evaluation (Calvert, Moran, and Weingast 1987; Weingast 1984); they can "stack the deck" with a number of specific administrative procedures designed to constrain agency behavior and move it toward certain collectively beneficial results (McCubbins, Noll, and Weingast 1987, 1989; Epstein and O'Halloran 1994). Politicians in Congress can also use their authority to define

bureaucracy's "strategic advantages" toward their own objectives by introducing greater uncertainty into the relationship to reduce the probability of agency deception and to allow lawmakers to anticipate the bureaucracy's behavior actively and take prompt action (Bawn 1995; Bendor, Taylor, and Van Gaalen 1985). The effectiveness of centralized mechanisms of control such as these has led some scholars to the conclusion that Congress dominates the bureaucracy because "Congress gives us the kind of bureaucracy it wants" (Fiorina 1981, 333; cf. Moe 1987).

Legislators also have available to them decentralized mechanisms of control. These are the control mechanisms to which congressional access is indirect and incremental. Assuming that the public is attentive and desirous of having an impact upon the policy process, overseers in Congress can easily resort to the efficiency and effectiveness of constituency feedback (McCubbins and Schwartz 1984). Furthermore, Congress can use pecuniary tools should direct oversight and evaluation prove ineffective. Some have argued that the appropriations process can be used as a tool to reward or punish an agency for its behavior, thereby forcing the agency to perform its tasks while anticipating congressional reaction (Ogul 1981). Although the appropriation process may be useful in controlling the behavior of certain types of historically low-profile agencies such as the Federal Emergency Management Agency (FEMA), the use of threat of reductions in an agency's appropriations to induce compliance with policy objectives is generally ineffective. That is because, as Davis, Dempster, and A. Wildavsky (1966) and A. Wildavsky (1984) have shown, the budgeting process is too conservative and incremental for appropriations to be effective as a control weapon.

If all these decentralized mechanisms of control prove ineffective or unsatisfactory, then Congress can play its last and most potent card, which is to delegate greater authority to the *courts* to review agency decisions based upon the evidentiary record and according to law. Granted, Congress cannot hope to achieve complete compliance with legislative mandates even from such delegation, but Congress can improve its lot considerably with it. Although there is controversy over how much federal deference judges should accord administrators (see Farber and Frickey 1993; Cannon 1991; Barshefsky and Firth 1988) and over how far judges should delve into floor speeches and legislative history to decide cases (Scalia 1989; Shepsle 1992), textual evidence from judicial opinions themselves, as well as case-study evidence furnished by a variety of legal scholars and social scientists, suggests that judges do typically base their decisions on precedent, committee records, and prelegislation material to discern legislative intent (Vance 1981; Rodgers 1979; Farber and Frickey 1993; Melnick 1983; Katzmann 1988). That gives the enacting legislature some hope of achieving further compliance with its law. Furthermore, it explains why Congress has continually opened agency choices to judicial review, suggesting that judicial review may indeed be the key to the effectiveness of decentralized oversight and enforcement.

By exercising judgment and bringing finality to many agency decisions, an independent judiciary is clearly important to the politics of Congress and to the enforcement of congressional policies. According to Landes and Posner (1975, 879), "the independent judiciary facilitates rather than, as conventionally believed, limits the practice of interest group politics [of Congress]." The reason is that, much like private contracts, legislative covenants are not self-enforcing (Williamson 1975). The active presence of an independent judiciary ensures that enforcement will take place. If, as argued in chapter 3, we accept that irregularities or biases can interfere in agency decision making because of potential conflict between the goals and motivations of bureaucrats and lawmakers (McCubbins and Page 1987; Wood and Waterman 1991), then the judiciary ensures that, through the norm of maintaining stability and continuity in legal interpretation (via reliance upon stare decisis and legislative history), the will of the enacting legislature will likely prevail, at least, until a subsequent legislature changes the law (Landes and Posner 1975). Hence, from the perspective of Congress, judicial review is an effective, albeit indirect, way of keeping bureaucratic behavior from serious derailment.

The idea that courts keep congressional intent alive has led some to argue that the practice of judicial decision making based upon intent and legislative history amounts to a silent but "profitable partnership" between Congress and courts at the expense of the executive branch (Melnick 1985). The executive branch suffers a net loss since judicial review detracts from its authority and discretion; Congress achieves a net gain in the form of assurances that the purpose of the current legislation will prevail; and finally, the courts win pecuniary rewards in the form of higher budgetary appropriations and salary increases for judges, based upon their performance (Landes and Posner 1975, 875–902).

Although overwhelming evidence shows that Congress is able to control bureaucratic behavior, various studies in international trade have reported mixed results on the ability of Congress to control the behavior of the ITC, largely because of the agency's status as an independent regulatory body. Some researchers, including Baldwin (1985), Takacs (1981), and Shughart and Tollison (1985), claim that because of institutional requirements that were designed to raise the ITC above politics, Congress does not sway the policy choices of regulators in this agency. These studies have certain methodological weaknesses, however. Either they examined a very limited set of laws or failed to use as controls subcommittee- or committee-level variables that may directly capture the oversight powers of relevant trade committees such as House Ways and Means or Senate Finance. Together, these two committees have nearly exclusive jurisdictional powers over trade policy and, one would suspect, are capable of exercising substantial influence over the ITC. Given that most congressional decision making takes place in committees (Smith and Deering 1984; Fenno 1973), any systematic attempt to uncover congressional influence on agency behavior ought to be concentrated there (Cook and Wood 1989).

Recent empirical studies that have incorporated committee-level measures with some success are those of Hansen (1990), in her cross-sectional analysis of the demand and supply of antidumping and countervailing duty regulation in the United States, and Moore (1992) and Anderson (1993) in their examinations of voting behavior of commissioners of the ITC in antidumping cases. By systematically accounting for the influence of congressional committees, using locational decisions of petitioning industries' production facilities in committee members' districts, these researchers concluded that "petitions involving the constituencies of Senate trade subcommittees are systematically favored" (Moore 1992, 465) and that "Congress does have influence over its agency's decisions" (Hansen 1990, 35).

In sum, the literature on congressional control and influence is vast, and much of it provides compelling evidence that Congress (in many instances, aided by an independent judiciary) is quite capable of exerting, and in fact does exert, substantial influence on the performance of administrative agencies.

President
While much work on political control over bureaucracy has focused on Congress, it must be emphasized that bureaucrats have multiple principals, including the president. Indeed, the president shoulders the weight of his entire administration and is held accountable, even for the performance of bureaucrats, if the public disapproves of the way the incumbent is handling his job as president. Some researchers have empirically validated this claim (Mueller 1970; Ostrom and Simon 1988). Clearly, the president has a strong incentive to see to it that his policy directives are followed. Empirical evidence suggests that the president's influence on bureaucracy is concrete and highly quantifiable (Moe 1982; Wood and Waterman 1991).

How can the president influence bureaucracy effectively? Several studies point to the fact that the president, too, has a number of strategies to choose from in influencing bureaucratic choices. For example, the pres-

ident can employ passive strategies such as the persuasiveness of the insti-
tutionalized presidency and the aura of the Office of the President (Heclo
1978; Neustadt 1990; Nathan 1986). Furthermore, as a distracted Richard
Nixon attempted unsuccessfully in the 1970s and a more focused and
determined Ronald Reagan actually succeeded in doing in the 1980s, the
president can reorganize agencies through executive orders so as to meet
presidential policy goals. Such reorganization is possible because federal
agencies are fairly fungible organizations; they rarely resist successfully a
determined president's effort at reorganization.

In one study of political control of bureaucracy conducted by B. Dan
Wood and Richard W. Waterman (1991), the authors examined reorganization and other activities in many agencies and across several presidential
administrations. One of these was the May 1981 Reagan reorganization of
the Office of Surface Mining and the strategic allocation of the agency's
resources. The office was established within the Department of the Interior
in 1977 to implement the Surface Mining Control and Reclamation Act of
1977. According to Wood and Waterman, the president introduced structural changes in enforcement policies, for example, eliminating field
enforcement offices, centralizing decision-making authority, and stripping
field enforcement officers of their discretionary authority to issue citations
of violation and cessation orders. These changes led to outcomes that were
generally consistent with Reagan's probusiness stance on the environment.
Specifically, there was evidence of a dramatic decline in the number of cessation orders issued by the agency throughout most of Reagan's two terms
in the White House (816–18).

In addition to reorganization and resource allocation (via the Office
of Management and Budget [OMB]), a president can use the authority to
make professional appointments to and remove uncooperative bureaucrats from agencies to obtain compliance with policy goals. A number of
studies focusing on a variety of federal agencies conclude that agency performance and policy outcomes vary systematically across presidential
regimes with respect to the hiring and firing of agency leaders (Wood and
Waterman 1991; Moe 1982, 1985; Wood and Anderson 1993). But while
the power of the president actually to remove recalcitrant agency heads
from the administration is unlimited, such is not the case with regard to
independent regulatory commissioners. Presidents cannot unilaterally
remove independent regulatory commissioners from office without congressional approval.[5] Given this limitation, it is difficult for a president to
use the firing power to achieve policy goals in an independent regulatory
commission since commissioners are substantially more insulated from
presidential power and political influence than are leaders of executive-
level agencies.

In international trade policy, researchers such as R. Baldwin (1985) and Wendy Takacs (1981) have maintained the complete insulation and independence of the ITC from direct presidential influence. Wendy Hansen's 1990 cross-sectional study of the demand and supply of trade regulation in the United States also found insignificant presidential influence on the ITC (measured in terms of party identification) and essentially confirmed the insulation hypothesis. The fact that researchers have found insignificant presidential impact on ITC behavior is puzzling, especially in light of the fact that ever since the enactment of the Trade Expansion Act of 1962, Congress has continually expanded the powers of the president to engineer international trade policy, presumably in a way consistent with the liberal ideology historically advocated by American presidents and most members of Congress (Goldstein 1986; Pastor 1983; Destler 1992). It is possible that past studies employed inadequate measures in their attempt to uncover presidential influence.

On the other hand, empirical evidence suggests that the president does have significant influence on the trade agencies located within the executive branch, such as the DOC, which are directly under the president's control. It is widely understood that trade policy is foreign policy (Cooper 1987) and that trade policy is an important part of most major foreign policy and national security questions that any president in the contemporary era must confront (Keohane and Nye 1989; Yankelovich and Destler 1994). Given that, along with the fact that the DOC is responsible for developing and implementing a variety of foreign trade strategies for the president, it is logical to expect the president to exercise substantial control over this agency (Boltuck and Litan 1991). For example, Hansen and Park (1995) recently tested a combined statist and pluralist model of trade policy formation by the DOC. Among their findings is that foreign security concerns of the president play a significant role in the agency's decisional trends.

But generally speaking, when it comes to trade authority, the president is in a weaker position relative to Congress, and in no small measure because of judicial review. Some have interpreted the delegation of congressional authority to the president as merely symbolic and as a systematic attempt by Congress to protect itself from onerous interest-group pressures and the indelible specter of Smoot-Hawley (Destler 1986). Yet it is also possible that congressional delegation of authority to the president is genuinely meant to encourage the making of good public policy (Kelman 1990, 201). Presumably the president's experience in the international domain would allow for the necessary adjustments that would sharpen the contours of U.S. trade policy. Are these two interpretations of congressional delegation of trade policy at odds? Not necessarily.

The reason is that both interpretations are consistent with the increasing role of the courts in trade policy-making. Congress uses judicial review as a strategic policy instrument. Consider that congressional delegation enhances executive branch power and leads to more flagrant political decisions, which in turn spark court actions by adversely affected groups. Courts undermine the effectiveness of presidential influence on agency decisions in a way that favors Congress, since courts usually take a hard look at congressional records and legislative material to construct the intent of any given statute when reviewing agency choices. Furthermore, courts facilitate the making of meaningful public policy by ensuring that administrators are evenhanded in their enforcement policies, are subject to accountable standards of performance, and are behaving in a manner that is consistent with legislative purpose.

Conclusion

As the literature review in this chapter clearly indicates, no specific government entity can claim to hold all the cards to control bureaucratic behavior. Each of the stations of power I have examined has its own unique mechanisms with which to influence bureaucratic behavior. Indeed, it is through negotiation and compromise between bureaucrats and these external actors that optimal policies and decisions can be formulated.

In a rather peculiar way, this chapter has brought to light the dearth of empirical research into judicial review of bureaucratic actions. Only recently have serious attempts been made to accommodate courts directly in agency control studies, and these attempts have occurred largely in game-theoretic models of the Supreme Court (Ferejohn and Shipan 1990; McCubbins, Noll, and Weingast 1987, 1989; Spiller and Gely 1992). Granted, game-theoretic models offer plenty of rigor and intuition for those who understand the esoteric language of game theory. But the most notable drawback is that these models are hardly amenable to empirical testing with hard data, and this disadvantage raises issues of flexibility and inference in the minds of many scholars.

Studies in public law and public administration that deal with this issue have somehow focused on purely normative questions, such as the suitability of active court involvement in overseeing the substance of bureaucratic choices (Horowitz 1977; Glazer 1978; Graglia 1982; Shapiro 1988), rather than on addressing objective issues about institutional processes, distribution of resources and incentives, the motivation of judges, their contributions to policy, and the overall political implications of judicial oversight. These are important concerns that demand more attention in political control studies. Concerted efforts to study this area can further our understanding of the formation and distribution of incentive structures by Congress and the variation in policy output by bureaucracy and allow us ultimately to develop a better theoretical understanding of how the American democratic process really works and why it is, according to Woodrow Wilson ([1887] 1978), harder to *run* a constitution than to frame one. In chapter 5, I discuss the theoretical approach to my study. Relying on the judicial politics, law, and public policy literatures, I develop a unifying theory of judicial review and influence over bureaucracy to gain a better understanding of the role of specialized courts in American society. This theory is meant to apply to trial and appellate courts below the Supreme Court.

CHAPTER 5

Judicial Review, Specialization, and Influence on Bureaucratic Action

> It is emphatically the province and duty of the judicial department to say what the law is.
>
> *Chief Justice John Marshall (1803)*

The above aphorism, quoted from *Marbury v. Madison,* underscores the enormous power of judges to shape public policy and the lives of citizens of the United States. Judicial review has been debated extensively by legal practitioners, who typically concentrate on assessing the morality of judicial decisions and the legal soundness of such decisions. Social scientists interested in the topic, on the other hand, have focused on analyzing the social and political impact of judicial review and the decisional trends that emerge when judges adjudicate questions that directly concern federalism and presidential, congressional, and bureaucratic behavior. In this context, scholars find it interesting to ask questions as to why judges decide cases in a certain way, what kinds of variables within legal institutions and the larger political environment mold the thoughts of judges when they review regulatory controversies, and how effective are judicial decisions.

The answers to these questions as reflected in the critical articulations of legal and political science theories mirror accurately Justice Antonin Scalia's observation that "the law does not move in a straight line" (1989, 521). In other words, there is a dynamic quality to legal institutions manifest in the answers to these questions. Over the years, a number of theoretical issues, which I shall discuss in this chapter, have dominated scholarly attention on how federal judges use their authority to check and constrain bureaucratic behavior and the actions of politicians. Sometimes federal courts are predisposed to take a more activist posture, as earlier in this century when federal judges overturned a significant number of legislative enactments that gave "excessive" power to the executive branch to regulate the economic lives of American citizens (see, e.g., *Schechter Poultry Corp. v. United States* [1935]; Wolfe 1994, 150–53; Abraham 1988, 11–15).

At other times judges are more restrained, opting to pay homage to the Madisonian ideal of separate branches that share power, thereby leaving bureaucrats wide leeway to use their expertise to determine the parameters of policy implementation.

Scalia's observation that law does not move in a straight line underscores the dynamic nature of courts, which is the result of ideological fluctuations caused by turnover in judges. Robert Dahl (1957) has argued that at the Supreme Court level, a new justice is appointed on average every 22 months. For lower federal courts the time interval is even shorter because of dramatic increases in the number of new judgeships within the past 50 years (Carp and Rowland 1983, 57–58; Bond 1980), making such fluctuations a crucial factor in any analysis of policy change emanating from the judicial branch. Behavioralists such as C. Herman Pritchett, Glendon Schubert, Jeffrey A. Segal, Harold J. Spaeth, and a host of other past and present judicial scholars have argued in one form or another that our understanding of the role of courts in policy-making is predicated upon our making a connection to this ideological fluctuation. Therefore, as pointed out in chapter 2 on the selection of specialized-court judges, careful a priori consideration of such fluctuation and of various case-specific, environmental, and legalistic factors may be the best way to fully predict and understand the decisional trends of courts and their impact on policy implementation.

In this chapter, after giving a brief overview of the key issues concerning judicial review in the contemporary era, I discuss the theoretical approaches that scholars have used to develop an understanding of the judiciary's policy-making relationship with the bureaucracy, under the assumption that courts and bureaucracies have dissimilar characteristics and motivations. With this background, I turn my attention to specialized courts to explain the core attributes that differentiate specialized courts from generalist courts. I discuss the general significance of judicial specialization in the U.S. justice system and speculate on why specialization in a legal context ought to be given serious attention by political scientists interested in the workings of political institutions. Finally, I explain two competing models of judicial behavior, which I then use to model policy-making in specialized courts.

Overview of Contemporary Judicial Review

The contemporary era of judicial review is one that emphasizes deference to administrative agencies. But to give a comparative context, any serious discussion of the contemporary era must necessarily start with its prelude, the Lochner Era (1905–36), which was ushered in with the U.S. Supreme

Court decision upholding the right to contract in *Lochner v. New York* (1905). During this long period, scholarly emphasis was on the activism of courts in economic matters. Federal courts, led by the Supreme Court, were distrustful of economic regulation and sought to curtail the power of both state and federal governments to regulate how industries conducted business. Courts demonstrated their power by striking down ambitious state and federal laws that limited corporate behavior, particularly in the realm of contract law, for example, laws governing minimum wage and the number of hours in the workday. In this sense, the Lochner Era witnessed an aggressive effort by courts to constrain a fledgling administrative state by granting minimal judicial deference to administrative agencies. This effort culminated in the Supreme Court's decisions in the so-called New Deal cases, for example, *Schechter Poultry Corp. v. United States* (1935) and *Carter v. Carter Coal Co.* (1936). In these cases, the Court invalidated efforts by the National Recovery Administration to cartelize industries (*Schechter Poultry*) and to regulate labor relations (*Carter*) as unconstitutional delegation of legislative authority to the executive branch and as illegal attempts to regulate business activity.

Toward the end of the Great Depression, a new judicial era (the contemporary era of judicial review) that emphasized judicial deference was ushered in, as the federal government actively sought to use the administrative state to address the untold economic and social miseries brought on by the depression. The era follows President Franklin D. Roosevelt's memorable struggle with the Supreme Court over his plan to improve the economy and his campaign to "pack" the Court (with his ideological allies) and minimize judicial opposition to his economic proposals. The president won this struggle largely due to personnel changes in the Court (Segal and Spaeth 1993, 95–97; Caldeira 1987) and especially because Justice Owen J. Roberts unexpectedly switched from opposing New Deal programs to supporting them, starting with his vote in the case of *West Coast Hotel Co. v. Parish* (1937).

Scholarly emphasis then shifted in 1937 to judicial restraint, following the Supreme Court's decision in *West Coast Hotel,* when the federal courts dramatically shifted course and moved to give greater judicial deference to agency interpretation of statutes, leading to a more active regulation of business by state and federal officials.

Although the politics of administration has the largest impact on whether regulation is active or passive, courts have periodically intervened to demand a more or a less forceful regulation of business activity. From the 1960s to the 1980s, there was a clear shift in the policy focus of federal regulation. New ideas emerged from zealous social reformers and critics such as Ralph Nader of Public Citizen, Peter Drucker of New

York University, and Alfred Kahn of Cornell, and from environmental groups such as the Sierra Club, to improve service delivery in the private sector as well as to address consumer safety concerns about products of the industrial system (Derthick and Quirk 1985; Pertschuk 1982). The combined strength of these new developments, aided by strong public outcry over product safety, pollution, and other market failures, shifted the focus of public debates gradually from economic to social and environmental regulations during the 1970s and 1980s (J. Berry 1977; J. Wilson 1980). Partly because of this shift, many cite that period as one of the most interesting eras in judicial behavior (e.g., Rosenberg 1991, chap. 10). Reformers sought to constitutionalize social and environmental regulation by using the courts, just as civil rights revolutionaries did in the 1950s and 1960s.

With little precedent to rely on, the social reformers used their own creativity and imagination to obtain moderate to significant success through the courts. Part of that success relates to the long-term reaction of judges to social litigation. Over time, judges became bolder and more willing to support reform advocates after realizing that politicians were not doing enough to protect American citizens from harm. Judges did not simply defer to bureaucrats and legislators as they had done for many years. Rather, they participated actively, for example, in issuing tough new rules to guide environmental regulation (Melnick 1983), reorganizing prisons (Dilulio 1987), and determining budgetary allocations for education (Harriman and Straussman 1983, 343). It was clear that courts were addressing administrative actions more forcefully than in previous times. Judge David Bazelon of the court of appeals duly attests to this bolder approach in *Environmental Defense Fund v. Ruckelshaus* (1971, 597):

> We stand on the threshold of a new era in the history of the long and fruitful collaboration of the administrative agencies and reviewing courts. For many years, courts have treated administrative policy decisions with great deference, confining judicial attention primarily to matters of procedure. On matters of substance, the courts regularly upheld agency action, with a nod in the direction of the "substantial evidence" test, and a bow to the mysteries of administrative expertise. Courts occasionally asserted, but less often exercised, the power to set aside agency action on the ground that an impermissible factor had entered into the decision, or a crucial factor had not been considered. Gradually, however, that power has come into more frequent use, and with it, the requirement that administrators articulate the factors on which they base their decisions.

From the perspective of this work, one of the more memorable events of this period was the call for more specialized justice in various substantive areas of public policy to better handle the complexities of modern regulations. Some expressed a strong desire for an environmental court whose judges would possess the requisite expertise to evaluate and oversee environmental policy-making (Whitney 1973a, 1973b). Others proposed expanding the power and jurisdiction of existing specialized courts, such as the Court of Customs (Gerhart 1977; Jordan 1981, 747–48), to better handle international trade litigation. Where the need was strong and the opposition could be overcome, some of these calls were answered.

Theoretical Traditions

Analyses of judicial review have emphasized two crucial issues concerning the theoretical linkages between agencies and their judicial overseers. I discuss these issues in the context of judicial specialization, relating them to the theoretical underpinnings of specialized courts, upon which I elaborate later in the chapter when I examine the core characteristics of specialized courts. I want first to set the stage for a more in-depth discussion of these two crucial issues.

The first issue of judicial review of bureaucratic action concerns *judicial legitimacy* (Gambitta, May, and Foster 1981; Halpern and Lamb 1982; Horowitz 1977). Put simply, are judges equipped with the right tools to examine substantive policy decisions of bureaucrats? Bureaucrats typically have a great deal of expertise in their policy jurisdiction. And as Francis E. Rourke (1984, 15) and Graham T. Allison (1971) both noted in their explication of the bureaucratic model, expertise is the basic foundation of bureaucratic power and autonomy. Moreover, as I discussed in chapter 4, the dichotomy of politics and administration that early on helped shape our perception of government was premised largely upon bureaucratic expertise and professionalism. Contrary to career bureaucrats, who can be characterized as experts, judges typically are generalists, whose strongest virtue lies in their "ignorance" (Shapiro 1968, 52). In a judicial context, ignorance (or the lack of subject matter expertise) enables judges to view legal conflicts with wider conceptual lenses and gives their decisions a measure of generality. Since bureaucratic activities and judicial responses to them generally occur within the context of policy implementation, the question of whether judges are equipped with the right tools to decide substantive policy controversies is appropriately one of legislative delegation and accountability.

On this difficult and normative question of judicial legitimacy, I argue that, when necessary, judges in generalist courts should devote the time and energy to examine substantive decisions of bureaucrats because of the dysfunctions of bureaucratic agencies, such as their tendency to act inflexibly and to lose sight of their goals (Bardach and Kagan 1982; Knott and Miller 1987, 166–88). Furthermore, I argue that with regard to judicial policy-making, questions of legitimacy are largely irrelevant when it comes to specialized courts; specialist judges are better suited than generalist judges to address substantive questions of policy because they have expertise.

The second theoretical issue of contemporary judicial review harks back to Alexander Hamilton's conceptualization of the judiciary as "the least dangerous branch" of government (*Federalist Papers,* no 78). The issue here concerns *judicial effectiveness* in overseeing bureaucratic choices. Does judicial review have a clear impact on the ways in which bureaucrats implement policy? Judicial effectiveness is a theme that runs through several important works in political science and is usually formulated in terms of compliance and impact in the sequential interaction between agencies and courts (Giles and Walker 1975; Meier 1985; Johnson and Canon 1984; Riker and Weingast 1988; Strover and Brown 1975; Wasby 1981).

Regarding judicial effectiveness, my view is that judges do possess crucial information and expertise. Granted, some judges possess more information and expertise than others. I seek to know whether the extent of information and expertise possessed by judges makes a significant difference in judicial behavior. I argue that judicial expertise leads to greater judicial efficiency and more deeply considered policies than does judicial nonexpertise, particularly in areas of special complexity. But first I address in more detail the question of judicial legitimacy in the context of specialization.

Judicial Legitimacy

The question of judicial legitimacy arises because of the active involvement of judges in policy-making and implementation, a situation that has occurred with increasing frequency in recent times. The question surfaces whenever judges assume responsibility for public controversies and address not only due process questions but also substantive questions as to the correctness of bureaucratic choices. Harvard Law Professor Abram Cheyes (1976, 1281) describes this state of judicial review:

> Over the past two decades, courts have assumed responsibility for desegregating school systems, reapportioning legislatures, regulating

employment practices of major companies, supervising land use planning in municipalities, directing credit practices of banks and credit card companies, monitoring environmental quality and even managing mental institutions and prison systems. What has happened is much more than a doctrinal shift. It adds up to a radical transformation of the role and functions of the judiciary in American life.

Presumably such active judicial response has been caused by the growth of bureaucratic power and the intractability of administrative discretion (see chap 4; also Stewart 1975). According to David Rosenbloom (1981, 25–51), in a political milieu of growing bureaucratic power and unresponsiveness, judges feel a fundamental need to assert individual rights and foster greater representation of diverse interests in the administrative state.

As a theoretical concept, legitimacy typically evokes the idea that society recognizes and accepts the formal authority of government officials to affect policy. In this regard, the legitimacy of judges to question the substance of bureaucratic policy implementation can be linked appropriately to public opinion and public approval of the judicial branch. In the past, the judiciary has fared well on this dimension. When public esteem for the judiciary is compared to public esteem for the legislative and executive branches of government, the judiciary has consistently come out strongly ahead (Sarat 1977, 439; Caldeira 1986; Marshall 1989, 140).[1] Still, this does not adequately address our vexing legitimacy questions, which are: Do courts have the right tools to change the substantive policy decisions of bureaucrats? If indeed courts do not possess the right tools, is there strong public outcry against particular court decisions?

Generally speaking, legal scholars who oppose activist judicial review (i.e., the consideration by judges whether government decisions lead to "good" outcomes for society) have complained bitterly that judges do not have the requisite tools to address substantive policy (Horowitz 1977, 33–36) and caution that judges should apply their power sparingly (Cramton 1976; Elhauge 1991). They argue that judges are encroaching upon constitutional and statutory boundaries of judicial review, ignoring the canons of statutory interpretation, which require them to examine agency choices against arbitrariness using the narrow conventions of interpreting the rule of law (Glazer 1975; Graglia 1982; Horowitz 1977; Katzmann 1988, 15; Koch 1986). Opponents of active judicial review anchor their argument to the separation-of-powers doctrine and to the democratic process. Lino Graglia (1982, 156), for example, contends that activist judicial control of agency behavior is totally undemocratic and that it is unthinkable that the framers of a charter of representative self-government could have meant to grant judges the power of final decision on questions of public policy without setting it forth in unmistakable terms in the Constitution. The argument is convincing and Graglia does not stand alone. In a series of essays in the 1970s, Nathan Glazer (1975; 1978) charged that the modern judiciary has arrogated too much power and has become "imperialistic" in its examination of, and impositions on, a wide range of social policy issues, without sound constitutional justification. Early on, Emmette Redford (1969, 71) argued similarly that because the selection of federal judges is not sanctioned by popular elections, any effort by judges to make substantive policy would be grossly undermined and would be ineffectual (also Rapkin 1989, 6).

But this debate surrounding judicial legitimacy is more ideological than it is substantive. To see how, we need only to examine the structure of our political system. As discussed in chapter 2, federal judges, including those in specialized courts, are not popularly elected but appointed by politicians, presumably on the basis of partisan or ideological compatibility and professional experience. Bureaucrats are also not elected but appointed. Yet critics are more accommodating of bureaucratic policy-making, even though the Constitution never mentioned bureaucrats or even envisioned them in such a capacity. Although judges are different from bureaucrats in that judges have lifetime tenure and are less subject to exacting standards of accountability than are bureaucrats, judicial decisions deemed unacceptable can be overturned or amended by legislation. Thus, if we examine judicial legitimacy from an electoral standpoint, we see that judges are clearly no less legitimate policy-makers than are bureaucrats who are granted broad discretion to make rules and decide important policy questions that affect Americans daily.

The concern over judicial legitimacy therefore seems seriously misguided. Henry Abraham echoed this sentiment when he stated that "the debate over the legitimacy of judicial review is now an academic exercise" (1988, 7). Indeed, while lower federal judges do have a tendency to seek the power and prestige of higher judicial office (Ball 1987; Baum 1994b, 752), their life tenure in government service strongly suggests that they may have lower career pressures than do bureaucrats; that may make judges even more responsive to public needs than bureaucrats, who have limited and unprotected tenure in government and are much more apt to seek to further their careers outside government (Gormley 1979, 666; Gormley, Hoadley, and Williams 1983; J. Wilson 1980).

The incursion of judges into the substantive decisions of bureaucrats is necessary for other reasons. There are often logical problems with bureaucratic decisions, caused either by too much flexibility or by a lack of flexibility, that oftentimes lead to arbitrary and capricious decisions as bureaucrats attempt to cope with the tensions created by a clash of their institutional needs for autonomy and flexibility on the one hand and external political pressures for accountability on the other (Bendor, Taylor, and Van Gaalen 1985; Riker and Weingast 1988; Scholz and Wei 1986). Judicial review is also needed to constrain politicians in Washington to honor their obligations to citizens instead of favoring parochial groups at the expense of the public. As long as these problems persist in American politics, activist judicial review will remain viable and may further dilute the power of the bureaucracy in American politics (Rourke 1992, 539–46).

Empirical evidence suggests that bureaucratic decisions are being increasingly subjected to judicial review. A study by Graham K. Wilson (1985, 86) shows that all but one of the 24 health standards issued by the Occupational Safety and Health Administration (OSHA) were challenged in court as of 1985. Stanfield (1986, 2764) reported that over 80 percent of the approximately 300 regulations issued by the Environmental Protection Agency (EPA) each year end up in court. The seeming institutionalization of litigation in American government is perhaps best demonstrated by McIntosh (1983), who found support for the proposition that litigation against bureaucracies and other government institutions is seen by many Americans as an alternative to traditional forms of political participation such as voting and paying taxes. Across the United States, judges continue to take a hard look at these legal controversies and to define substantive solutions, which may or may not be compatible with the implementation capabilities of bureaucrats (Melnick 1983). Significantly, we observe no widespread public discontent and no crisis of confidence with the judiciary, which could be interpreted as tacit approval of judges' qualifications to make substantive decisions.

The argument in favor of judges deciding procedural and substantive questions can be made even more strongly for judges in specialized courts. These judges are repositories of both technical and legal knowledge within the narrow jurisdiction of their courts. That, more than any other factor, makes specialist judges well qualified to examine the substance of bureaucratic decisions. From a public policy standpoint, their specialization makes such an examination and the possible redirection of bureaucratic decisions meaningful because specialist judges have a keen understanding of the background of legal controversies and bureaucratic practices. In addition, specialist judges are more likely to be up-to-date on changes in statutes than are generalist judges. These attributes are particularly important in deciding technical issues where these specialist judges can generate unique insights into legal controversies and apply their expertise. In technologically complex policy areas such as patent rights, and in technical areas such as international trade and taxes, specialized judges, because of their expertise, may produce better, more satisfying outcomes for litigants than generalist judges can.

For example, in one patent infringement case early in this century, Judge Learned Hand of the Court of Appeals for the Second Circuit, well known for his legal acumen, expressed serious frustration over the technicality of the patent issues he was asked to judge. He advocated the use of specialists in adjudication for reasons that are similar to those enumerated here. In his published opinion, Judge Hand wrote:

> I cannot stop without calling attention to the extraordinary condition of the law which makes it possible for a man without any knowledge of even the rudiments of chemistry to pass upon such questions as these. . . . How long we shall continue to blunder along without the aid of unpartisan and authoritative scientific assistance in the administration of justice, no one knows; but all fair persons not conventionalized by provincial legal habits of mind ought, I should think, unite to effect some such advance. (*Parke-Davis & Co. v. H.K. Mulford Co.*, 1911)

Because of their expertise, specialized court judges are able to make meaningful contributions to public policy. Commenting on the incremental shift toward specialization in judicial systems, Judge Richard Posner of the Seventh Circuit noted that "a person who does only one job may perform better than an abler person who divides his time among several jobs, none of which he learns to do really well" (1983, 780). Therefore, the normative question of judicial legitimacy, of whether judges should question and redress inappropriate substantive decisions of bureaucrats, is less important in an environment where judges specialize. Such judges have the right tools, knowledge, information, and expertise, to make meaningful and informed decisions.

Judicial Effectiveness

The capacity of judges to check bureaucratic action and make effective policy pronouncements has been of concern to many observers. The question of judicial effectiveness can be asked quite straightforwardly: Is judicial review an effective check on bureaucratic behavior? I argued in chapter 4 that judicial review is key to the effectiveness of decentralized enforcement of legislation. Critics such as R. Shep Melnick (1983, 383–87) and Donald Horowitz (1977, 33–56), however, claim that judicial review is ineffective because it creates a vacuum whereby judges, lacking in adequate knowledge of the characteristics and limitations of bureaucracies, issue policy standards that are so sweeping and ambitious that bureaucrats are unable to implement them.

Others complain that courts are guilty of complicity in the maladies of the administrative state. They argue that there is simply too much judicial deference to administrative agencies for there to be effective and adequate judicial remedies for those aggrieved by bureaucratic dysfunctions (Lowi 1969; Shapiro 1968; Rosenbloom 1981). In support of this view, Martin Shapiro, for example, concluded that courts do not provide much of a check on agency actions. Rather, they merely provide "symbolic assurance" to citizens that their government seeks justice (1968, 13–15). According to Shapiro, "at least during the last twenty years the federal courts system has devoted the vast bulk of its energies to simply giving legal approval to agency decisions" (1968, 264). Similarly, Theodore Lowi (1969, 298) concluded that courts have been ineffective in controlling agency actions despite their vigilance. According to Lowi, courts have willingly sanctioned the congressional abdication of power to bureaucrats.

Recent studies conducted primarily at the Supreme Court (Sheehan 1992; Crowley 1987; Spaeth and Teger 1982) and circuit court (Willison 1986) levels have tended to add credence to the deference (and therefore judicial ineffectiveness) hypothesis. These studies point to a considerable degree of deference to administrative agencies' interpretation of statutes. These various works reported that the federal courts grant more weight to a federal agency's side of the story than to the opponent's when making final decisions on the merits (cf. Spiller and Gely 1992).

The standard test for deference is "reasonableness" of agency decision in light of the governing statute. Consistent with this test, for example, Supreme Court Justice Thurgood Marshall stated in *Zenith Radio Corp. v. United States* (1978)[2] that "when faced with a problem of statutory construction, this Court shows great deference to the interpretation given the statute by the officers or agency charged with its administration" (quoting *Udall v. Tallman*, 1965). In other words, judges are not supposed to substitute their own interpretation for that of the agency. Insofar as judges determine that an agency action is within reasonable bounds of the statute, they must defer to the views of administrators. This standard was reinforced by the Court's decision in *Chevron, U.S.A. Inc. v. National Resources Defense Council* (1984, 842):

If the intent of Congress is clear, that is the end of the matter; for the courts as well as the agency, must give effect to the unambiguously expressed intent of Congress. If, however, the court determines that Congress has not directly addressed the precise question at issue, the court does not simply impose its own construction on the statute, as would be necessary in the absence of an administrative interpretation. [Here] the question for the court is whether the agency's answer is based on a permissible construction of the statute.

Providing empirical confirmation for this practice, various studies have examined time periods of about eight to ten years and have reported a 70 to 73 percent success rate of administrative agencies in the Supreme Court (Crowley 1987; Spaeth and Teger 1982). Reginald Sheehan, who examined the success rate of different parties at the Supreme Court for a much longer period (1953–88), found a higher rate of deference (76.9 percent) to federal agencies (1992, 488). Willison (1986, 326) reported a similarly high rate of deference for the Supreme Court (70 percent) and for the D.C. Circuit Court of Appeals (66 percent), with reasonable variation in success rate across agencies. Why do administrative agencies tend to do so well in court? And does this high rate of deference undermine the effectiveness of judicial review generally?

The high success rate of administrative agencies may be attributed to the resources peculiar to them, such as their frequent player status, experienced legal representation, and special position as part of the federal government, which may make the high cost of case preparation and legal research less visible and less overwhelming (Galanter 1974; cf. Sheehan, Mishler, and Songer 1992). It is also possible that the high rate of deference to administrative agencies reflects the complex and technical nature of the issues that come before the courts, issues that judges may believe agencies with expertise in the area are uniquely qualified to judge.

Due to the infrequency of interaction between specific administrative agencies and the generalist courts that review their actions, bureaucratic uncertainty plays an important role in the outcomes of judicial review in generalist court contexts. Therefore, even though the rate of deference to agencies is high, there is the potential that judges are actually imposing real constraints, albeit indirect, on administrative behavior. The presence of judges is a safety factor for the reliability of the implementation system because it compels agencies to anticipate court reaction to their policy choices. Thus, in the context of bureaucratic implementation, the courts loom large with latent influences on agencies.

So while the reportedly high rates of judicial deference to administrative agencies may give pause to the advocates of agency delegation (e.g., Mashaw 1985) and may, on the surface, suggest that judicial review is ineffective, I would hasten to caution against making such generalized conclusions, especially in the absence of ample empirical evidence. It must also be emphasized that there may be considerable variation in the rates of judicial deference across administrative agencies due to differences in the institutional structures of courts themselves. For example, researchers have only recently begun to examine the level of deference accorded administrative agencies by specialized courts.

Judicial Specialization, Institutional Arrangements, and Influence on Agencies

Specialized courts have expertise just as bureaucratic agencies do. From this perspective, specialized courts and bureaucratic agencies have similar institutional characteristics.The expertise of specialized courts is drawn from their unidimensional policy focus, which sets them apart from their generalist counterparts. In addition, because of the frequency of interaction between specialized courts and their agencies, uncertainty plays a less important role in this context than it does in the relationship between generalist courts and bureaucracies. Expertise and uncertainty are the two institutional characteristics that may define the types of policy outcomes in judicial review.

Political scientists who study the interdependence of Congress and bureaucracy have long shown that institutional arrangements, or the rules of practices and procedures, are crucial to the nature of public policy outcomes (Shepsle 1979, 1989; Moe 1985, 1989; Wood and Anderson 1993). Institutionalists such as Shepsle define this institutional theory as an attempt "to explain the characteristics of social outcomes on the basis not only of agency preferences and optimizing behavior, but also on the basis of institutional features" (Shepsle 1989, 135). These institutional features would include organizational mission, preferences, and decisional strategies. Typically, institutional features vary from one governmental organization to another. And under the logic of this institutional theory, organizations with similar institutional arrangements tend to behave alike, especially where the decisional strategies are alike.

With regard to the interaction between administrative agencies and specialized courts, the type of decisional strategy adopted by an agency, or forced upon it by congressional legislation, may determine how successful the agency is in court. The adversarial, case-by-case adjudicatory format of American courts facilitates for judges the tasks of case management and evaluation. Correspondingly, it is natural for courts to review those regulatory decisions that are made on the basis of an adversarial-styled, adjudicatory format, where agencies have assembled a detailed evidentiary record and petitioners have an ample opportunity for discovery of material information at each party's disposal. The judge's task of examining and evaluating the agency record is dramatically enhanced when the steps of an investigation are clearly documented (Pierce, Shapiro, and Verkuil 1992).

In this regard, independent regulatory commissions are more court-like than are executive branch agencies, which are typically headed by a single bureaucrat. Commissioners are collegial and hear cases en banc. They follow a majority-rule decision criterion, and their decisions are typically based upon the record established during investigations and public hearings. As discussed in chapter 3, the ITC, for example, uses public hearings as a routine part of its decision process. The commissioners make their decision in conference after considering, arguing, and counterarguing the facts and evidence of each case among themselves to determine the "truth." Given the parallelism of independent regulatory commission decisional style with that of real courts, it is expected that regulatory commission decisions are more likely to be upheld by courts than decisions of executive-level agencies such as the DOC.

As indicated earlier, one of the continually debated issues in judicial review concerns the effectiveness of courts. Although empirical research points to a considerable degree of deference to agencies by courts, it is hard to tell whether judicial review is generally ineffective, as some have argued. The fact that courts generally do have a significant amount of control over administrative *processes* and can hold agencies in contempt indicates that they do have the tools to exert effective influence on the implementation process (Baum 1982). Only scant evidence exists to directly support claims of judicial ineffectiveness. Empirical support supplied by scholars such as Melnick (1983) and Rapkin (1989), using critical case studies of environmental and social welfare policies, is limited and inconclusive and has raised other issues. For instance, we do not know whether differences in institutional structures of courts themselves have an important bearing on the level of judicial deference accorded administrative agencies.

By virtue of their expertise and information symmetry with the bureaucracies whose decisions they review, specialized courts can tell us something new about judicial review; they can inform us that expertise makes a considerable difference in the outcomes of judicial review. I argue that specialized courts give considerably *less* deference to administrative agencies than do generalist courts and suggest that specialization permits these courts to play a remarkably effective, substantive role in policy implementation by shifting outcomes one way or the other. In other words, specialized courts exercise far more than merely neutral effects on public policy.

An empirical study of this type must examine trends in specialized courts, taking into account the unique features of these courts. Thus, I next take a detailed look at specialized courts, focusing on their core functional characteristics and their potential importance in the U.S. civil justice system. Then I discuss two competing models of judicial decision making and suggest how they can be unified and used to study specialized-court decision making.

Core Characteristics of Specialized Courts

Specialized courts are thought historically to serve only policy-neutral objectives in the civil justice system (Frankfurter and Landis 1928, chap. 4; Currie and Goodman 1975). Some of these objectives include developing expertise to better address the complex and technical questions of public policy and fostering overall judicial capacity by reducing case congestion in the generalist courts. The claim of policy neutrality is based directly on certain core attributes of specialized courts, which differentiate them from generalist courts. These characteristics also define the particular virtues of judicial specialization that are discussed subsequently. The core attributes of specialized courts include (1) development and virtues of judicial expertise, (2) concentration of judicial activity in one court, (3) complexity and salience of the policy jurisdiction, and (4) homogeneity of cases. These attributes allow specialized courts to have a significant substantive impact on the public policy process.

Under the assumption that these courts are not afflicted by a crisis of volume as the generalist courts are, it is possible that in this era of increasing litigiousness, mixed with limited judicial resources (Litan 1989; Grossman et al. 1981), specialized courts may make better, more informed decisions than generalist courts, particularly in complex policy areas (Jordan 1981, 747). Also, I argue that judicial specialization and the expertise of judges lead to greater efficiency in the dissemination of justice in the specialty court setting.

Development and Virtues of Judicial Expertise
Expertise of judges is engendered by the special judicial setting. The narrow jurisdiction of specialized courts means that judges can gain expertise rapidly in the policy area they oversee since these judges are repeatedly presented with cases posing similar questions of law and fact. Moreover, specialized courts facilitate for their judges the development of further specialization within a specialization. This means that judges have opportunity to develop expertise in a general policy area, say, international trade, and to also develop further expertise in a subarea of international trade, say, antidumping law or customs law. The expertise of specialized-court judges may therefore in fact be quite comparable to, and at times greater than, that of bureaucrats.

In the Court of International Trade, my discussion with court staff about judges' expertise indicates, for instance, that Chief Judge Edward D. Re, in addition to having expertise in overall trade matters when he sat on the court, specialized in product classification cases from the U.S. Customs Service and decided most of his cases in that area. Also Judge Jane Restani specializes in antidumping cases, particularly those involving cumulation of imports by the DOC and the ITC.

The question is: Whence came expertise? Certainly expertise comes from prior professional experience. But then, even experienced lawyers in a particular field of law, upon ascending to the bench, must go through a process of socialization where they learn the ropes procedurally and substantively about being a judge. Thus, judicial expertise is an attribute that is never acquired automatically once a judge ascends to the court; it is developed incrementally, and there is always a measure of uncertainty associated with its development. A key insight from organization theory is that because of constraints on learning, organizations think and learn by actually doing things in order to assemble the skills necessary to solve the stream of problems they encounter (M. Cohen, March, and Olsen 1972; Kingdon 1984). They consciously adapt their behavior as they accumulate experience (Lindbloom 1959). The development of expertise in specialized courts is analogous to this process. Although many judges in specialized courts do have prior experience before they join the court, they must learn to become specialists while on the bench, through repeated access and adaptation to related case stimuli.

One important virtue of judicial expertise is that it leads to greater efficiency in the dissemination of justice, benefiting individual litigants as well as the legal system. Judges who concentrate their decision making and who therefore specialize in a given policy area are reservoirs of knowledge about that area. They have a deep understanding of the critical background and aspects of legal controversies arising in the area. They are able to monitor agency practices closely. They have an acute familiarity with the history and purpose of the law at issue because they keep track of amendments to existing laws and anticipate the type of litigation those amendments might engender in the future. Finally, because of their expertise, specialized-court judges have a good grasp of how to resolve such controversies in the most efficient, meaningful, and equitable way possible. That cannot be said of generalist judges. The problems associated with their lack of subject matter expertise, such as superficial understanding of the substantive issue, excessive delegation to law clerks, and delays in preparing for arguments and in writing opinions, are exacerbated by the rise in judicial workload.

Legal practitioners such as Posner (1983), Meador (1983), and others have lamented the growing reliance of generalist judges on law clerks and staff attorneys, which they have attributed to increased case volume. "The ratio of authorized legal assistance to circuit judges is about four to one [in 1983]; as recently as 1969 it was one to one" (Posner 1983, 767). These legal assistants are not merely gofers. The high ratio of legal assistants to a judge suggests that there is a growing reliance of judges on legal aides to conduct legal research and draft opinions for judges. In Posner's view, "it seems inevitable that as the ratio of law clerks to judges grows, more and more of the initial opinion-drafting responsibility will be delegated to law clerks, increasingly transforming the judge from a draftsman to an editor" (768). The problems of coordination and supervision also multiply relative to the number of assistants a judge supervises, which distracts judges from their functional responsibilities.

Unlike judges in generalist courts, specialist judges do not need a large number of legal assistants who spend time conducting research and analyzing information that judges rely upon for their decisions. In the Court of International Trade, for example, active-duty judges are assigned two law clerks and a secretary; senior judges presumably have a reduced workload and so are given a choice of either two law clerks or one law clerk and one secretary. With continued access to cases that concern the same general area, the specialist judge can be up-to-date on changes in statutes and bureaucratic practices and can adjudicate cases meaningfully and expeditiously, with substantial savings in time and money for litigants. According to Judge Nicholas Tsoucalas of the U.S. Court of International Trade, specialized-court judges have more time than generalist judges do to review cases and write opinions. When asked to compare his 18-year experience as a generalist state court judge with his experience as a federal judge on the Court of International Trade, Judge Tsoucalas responded that in the Court of International trade "you're able to read, you're able to write, and you're able to dictate to your secretary" (see Rosenswein 1991, 8). In addition to the resource gains derived from expeditious judicial action on cases, litigants can appreciate the privilege of having a judge to decide their case who is knowledgeable about the procedural and substantive nuances of the controversy. This expertise may actually bolster positive perceptions that litigants may hold of the justice system and improve their identification with it, no matter what the outcome of their dispute may be.

Citizens' perceptions of the legal process strongly affect their evaluation of it. Research on legal culture, self-interest, and the legitimacy of political authority by Sarat (1977), Tyler (1990), Sears and Funk (1990), and others shows that whether or not legal decisions favor particular litigants, the contesting parties are more likely to accept the legitimacy of decisions and accord them a high degree of credibility if they believe that these decisions were rendered fairly and by judges who have a great deal of substantive knowledge about the policy area (see also Brenner 1984; for an analysis of such behavior that moves beyond mere self-interest in economic systems, see Kreps 1990; for social systems, see Granovetter 1985). Moreover, those who study responses to Supreme Court authority using legitimacy theory argue that while the Supreme Court's authority is imperfect, it is more likely to be accepted by the interpreting (lower courts), implementing (bureaucracies), and consuming (litigants and citizens) populations if, among other factors, the opinion writer is perceived to be keenly knowledgeable about the subject matter (see Canon 1991, 437–40; Pacelle and Baum 1992; Rodgers and Bullock 1976).

Generalizing these conclusions to lower courts, it would seem reasonable that a basic benefit to direct parties before a specialized court is that their cases are decided expeditiously and meaningfully by specialist judges. Reasonable litigants will appreciate this aspect of their legal experience irrespective of whether the specific outcome of the controversy favors them.

In addition to generating resource benefits to direct parties and public admiration for the judiciary, there are other special virtues associated with specialized courts that also accrue to the entire justice system. Specialized courts deflect cases from the civil dockets of generalist courts, enabling generalist courts to manage their residual civil and criminal dockets better than they would be able to otherwise. A disturbing problem in the U.S. justice system is the overload of civil and criminal cases in courts. In 1983 Judge Posner characterized the backlog of cases in the federal judiciary as a "crisis" (Posner 1983, 761). A decade later, the situation had not improved. As Judge Roger J. Miner of the Second Circuit noted, "the federal courts are confronting a caseload crunch of mammoth proportions" (Miner 1993, 104; cf. Gizzi 1993). The degeneration of the legal profession into a mere "business" and the triumph of avarice, characterized by a rise in frivolous lawsuits and lawyer-stimulated litigation in recent decades, are partly responsible for this condition (Abraham 1986; Kelly 1996, chap. 1). There are real costs associated with such a culture of litigiousness.

An overwhelmed judicial system carries grave democratic implications, not only for the fundamental principle of checks and balances, but for public confidence in government as well. According to Robert Litan (1989), the clogging of judicial dockets causes long queues and considerable delays and expense in the prosecution of civil cases, and that has led to a great deal of public cynicism about the judicial system. This contention is further supported in empirical studies by Sarat (1977) and Tyler (1990, 47–56), which show that citizens who have had direct experience with, and are more knowledgeable about, the legal system hold stronger negative opinions of it. Such perceptions are caused by the below-par performances of judges, which are reflected in their efforts and in the quality of their policy decisions. As Posner (1983, 767) observes, a heavier caseload may induce a judge to "try to limit the growth of his queue by spending less time on each litigated case; or he may delegate more of the judicial function to law clerks and externs." Thus the clogging of judicial dockets may undermine not only the public esteem of the judiciary, but more critically the Constitution's objective to "promote the general welfare" of all members of society.

Here is where specialized courts become invaluable to the expansion of overall judicial capacity, because they can (and do) deflect civil cases of special complexity from generalist courts, thereby allowing the generalist courts to move toward the constitutional objective of promoting the general welfare. Justice Scalia echoed this view during his remarks to the National Conference of Bar Presidents, "If, through specialized courts, a substantial amount of business could be diverted from the regular federal courts, the latter would have a chance of remaining in the future what they have been in the past" (quoted in Revesz 1990, 1120).

In addition to deflecting cases from the generalist courts, judicial specialization and expertise foster the fiscal integrity of the judicial system. The classical insight of Adam Smith regarding the importance of division of labor and its resultant production efficiency in the wealth of nations can provide a useful basis for illustrating this point. One of the real economies of specialization is that it decreases the number of errors and incorrect decisions judges make. In the long run, that can translate into a dramatic reduction in the number of civil and criminal decisions appealed to higher courts, with potentially large savings for U.S. taxpayers. In sum, the presence of specialized courts in the justice system enhances the overall quality of judicial output and efficiency.

Concentration of Judicial Activity
Another important factor that distinguishes specialized courts from generalist courts is that in specialized courts all judicial activity in a given policy area is concentrated in one court. As explained in chapter 2, lawsuits concerning U.S. trade policy are concentrated in the Court of International Trade. Similarly, civil cases involving taxes are adjudged mostly in the U.S. Tax Court. The benefit of such a concentration is, of course, that it eliminates forum-shopping and intercourt conflict; in addition, it enhances harmony, continuity, and predictability in the law. For judges' decisions to be meaningful, judges need to command an excellent understanding of the esoteric legal codes governing international trade or tax matters or

whatever the complex policy area might be. This criterion can be best met by the concentration of judicial activity in one court.

The concentration of judicial business in one court is not without its vices, however. As Richard Posner (1983, 787) has argued, the concentration of judicial activity can stifle the "cross pollination of legal ideas" from one court to another. But it should be emphasized that the growing use of visiting judges designated from other district and circuit courts to sit temporarily on some specialized courts, such as the Federal Circuit, does promote the exchange of legal ideas.

Another vice is that the concentration of judicial activity in one court may lead to intense interest-group influence on judges or even their capture. A popularly accepted idea in institutional analysis and policy formation is that whenever policy definition and decision making are concentrated in the hands of a few political actors, one is likely to find a community of interests or entrepreneurs that will try to shape the process and outcomes of such policy definition (Baumgartner and Jones 1993; Kingdon 1984; Schneider and Teske 1995). Given this idea, organizations that have a stake in the policies that a particular judge will make when appointed may be predisposed to actively support or oppose the nomination of such a judge based on their perception of the judge's stance on the issues relative to their own (see chap.2).

Not surprisingly, some have argued that the concentration of judicial activity in a single court leads to clientelism, that is, the tendency for litigant groups to peddle influence to specialist judges for favors (Baum 1977; Shapiro 1968; Posner 1983, 783; Revesz 1990). This argument is straightforward and convincing. Presumably, such litigant-group influence may occur through several channels, including frequent face-to-face contacts with the same set of judges and in the same judicial forum, and through disproportionate influence of narrow-minded professional bar associations in the judge selection process. It must be noted, though, that the effect of clientelism has not yet been adequately tested beyond its connection to the judicial selection process. We have already seen in chapter 2 that professional bar associations are actively involved in the selection of judges to the courts in their area and that they work hard to influence these judges' decisions. As examined later in chapters 7 and 8, what remains is to determine whether and to what extent industry groups may also affect the decisions of specialized-court judges by using their resources.

Complexity and Salience of Policy Jurisdiction
Another distinguishing feature of specialized courts can be found in the types of policy areas over which such courts preside. The degree of techni-

cal complexity and salience of a given policy area is an important indicator of whether a specialized court will be established to review cases in that area. A casual look at the policy areas in which specialized courts have been established—taxes, trade, intellectual property rights, and the military, to name but four—shows that these courts are most likely to be found not only where the subject matter is complex, but also where the types of cases are relatively routine and the issue is politically salient. William Gormley's insight regarding the typology of regulatory politics in the United States can be useful here in explaining why salience and complexity form important dimensions in the establishment of specialized courts. Gormley (1986) classified regulatory politics by complexity (how difficult the issue is for nonexperts to understand) and salience (how important the issue is to the American public). Issue areas that are high in complexity and high in salience, such as foreign trade and domestic taxes, are the ones most likely to be overseen by a specialized court to augment congressional oversight of bureaucratic implementation in those areas. As John R. Hibbing (1991) concluded in his longitudinal examination of congressional careers in the House of Representatives, there is a remarkable increase these days in the number of conflicting demands placed upon members of Congress by an increasingly insatiable public. Thus, in a general sense, since congressional lawmakers are nonexperts, they may find it advantageous to seek the partnership of a specialized court to help oversee the activities of bureaucratic agencies authorized to implement policy in a highly complex area.

Given the centrality of technical complexity and salience to the establishment of specialized courts, then, one might wonder why such courts have not been created in such complex and salient policy areas as telecommunications and environmental regulation. In the case of environmental regulation, the Supreme Court has attested to the complexity of environmental policy in *Chevron, U.S.A. Inc. v. National Resources Defense Council* (1984, 848). For example, the Clean Air Act and its various amendments, according to the Court, are "a lengthy, detailed, technical, complex, and comprehensive response to a major social issue." And indeed, passionate calls have been made in the past to establish a special environmental court that will review policy decisions of the EPA (Whitney 1973a, 1973b) but these calls have gone unheeded for fear that such a court might exhibit tunnel vision and lead to decadence of environmental law (Dix 1964; Rifkind 1951). Historically, the creation of specialized courts has been the stuff of political maelstrom. Therefore, in order for these types of courts to be established, strong public and political support must converge.

Homogeneous Cases

Finally, specialized courts differ from generalist courts in that they are characterized by a homogeneous set of cases. Homogeneity of cases is defined by two distinct characteristics. First, whether the cases are in international trade policy, tax policy, or military policy, the defendant is almost always the federal government, because most regulatory controversies are sparked by private organizations or persons who are dissatisfied with some ruling of a federal government agency. Second, except in rare instances such as in the Federal Circuit, cases in specialized courts typically concern various aspects of the same substantive policy issue. It is because of the homogeneity of cases that some oppose specialized courts for fear that such courts will not attract top-quality judges. But by uniting all litigation dealing with a single issue area in one court, the logical result is greater efficiency and expertise in judging and disposing of legal controversies in a way that is beneficial to litigants and to the judicial system.

Competing Analytical Models of Decision Making in Specialized Courts

The foregoing discussion on the core features of specialized courts makes clear that these courts deliver a distinctive brand of justice compared to that found in traditional courts, one that can be appropriately termed *specialized justice*. Even though specialized courts have a functional geographic jurisdiction that is nationwide in scope and therefore distinguishes them from most American courts, specialized courts have distinct institutional features that are defined principally by expertise and by a focus on a narrow and well-delineated policy area. The decisional trends of these courts, that is, the factors affecting their decision making and the nature of their decisional output, may be fundamentally different from those found in the generalist courts. From the core characteristics of specialized courts articulated earlier, we can anticipate how judges in these courts reach decisions.

Theoretical Origins of the Two Competing Models

Ever since the influential work of C. Herman Pritchett (1948), in which he explained the importance of values in the behavior of justices of the Roosevelt Court, judicial scholars have probed the ideological character of judges' behavior. They have done so under the assumption that human nature has the power to adapt, albeit in an evolutionary manner, to changing legal, political, and social circumstances rather than simply to adhere to a status quo position. Moreover, scholars perceive "judges and law as human institutions" acting within a larger political context (Peltason 1955, 3). Although this view strikes many as appropriate, some legal practitioners find such assumptions inconsistent with their own understanding of the development of law and of judicial decision making. As a result, two competing models have been developed, which have guided analyses of judicial decision making ever since Pritchett wrote his seminal work. One of these models takes a traditional, static view of law (sometimes called legalism). The other takes a more dynamic view of law in that it emphasizes political, environmental, and behavioral factors as being important in judicial decision making; this is the extralegal view.

The Legal Model

This model postulates that judges make decisions primarily on the basis of legal history; they rely upon the intent of the original framers of the Constitution, legislative history, and legal precedent in light of the facts to arrive at their decisions. Formally, the legal model can be represented as a function of case facts and law:

$$\text{DECISION} = f(\text{CASE FACTS, LAW}) \tag{1}$$

where CASE FACTS and LAW are vectors representing a set of factual and doctrinal variables. A detailed explanation and critique of this model is given by Segal and Spaeth (1993, 32–64), who identified four variants of the legal model: "plain meaning, intent of the framers, precedent, and balancing [of societal interests]" (33). Judges need not employ all four variants to decide a particular regulatory controversy, but they do rely on at least one variant or a combination of them in light of case facts. A careful look at this model shows that its underlying character is quite rigid and mechanical. The model assumes that judges merely discover the law rather than create it and that judges never speak their own minds or inject their own personal policy preferences into their decisions; rather, only the eloquent words of the Constitution or statutes are spoken through judges in an objective and dispassionate manner.

These assumptions have provoked strong reactions from scholars with a more behavioral orientation. Spaeth and Teger (1982, 277) reacted that the assumptions of the legal model constitute nothing more than "weasel words, weasel words all!" On a less feisty note, Jack Peltason observed long ago (1955, 4) that "most political scientists and legal scholars do not believe that 'the law' is an external objective phenomenon that controls the judge and his behavior" and that "traditional [legal] explanations of judicial behavior are no longer in good standing among sophisticates." Realistically, these assumptions are not and cannot be useless. Several research projects have demonstrated their relative utility (Kort 1966; Segal 1984). However, I disagree that the legal model and its assumptions are an adequate representation of judicial behavior, as legal apologists would like us to believe. To see why, we may consult the progenitor of judicial review itself. Chief Justice John Marshall's classic decision in *Marbury v. Madison* (1803) has been extensively analyzed by both legal scholars and social scientists. Much of that analysis attests that Marshall's decision shows, in both its historical context and its meaning, that no serious empirical analysis of judicial review cast in legal terms can be complete without there being a systematic connection to politics. If that were not true, political scientists would have had little or no interest in researching law, leaving only lawyers to conduct such research.

To test all the variants of the legal model simultaneously would prove a daunting, and perhaps an impossible, task. So efforts have been made to validate this model empirically in a piecemeal fashion. Segal (1984), for example, used search-and-seizure cases and developed a probabilistic model of Supreme Court behavior, focusing primarily on the role of precedent and case facts. He reported an "ordered," or incremental, development of standards in the area of search and seizure not previously recognized. Segal's finding suggests that precedent is relied substantially upon by the justices of the Supreme Court in their disposition of legal controversies.

Other scholars such as Gibson (1978, 1981) and Kuklinski and Stanga (1979) have addressed the legal model by examining the role orientation of judges, that is, their perception of how others expect them to behave. They reported that judges' role orientation does matter in their formal, conventional routines. Others such as Nagel (1961) and Ulmer (1973) have taken an indirect tact, believing that there is an indirect linkage between judges' social background and their behavior on the bench, which manifests itself especially when judges decide cases that require them to balance societal interests against the interests of individuals. Such studies, however, have proved unsuccessful because they typically omit an important intervening factor—judges' attitudes (Segal and Spaeth 1993).

While sporadic disagreements have developed about various aspects of the legal model, studies based upon it do commonly show unequivocally that case-specific factors and the legal context of cases are important determinants of decisions at all court levels. There may be yet-untapped variations in the intensity of, or importance attached to, case factors and their legal contexts if we look across different court levels, however. At the Supreme Court, for example, Rohde and Spaeth (1976), Epstein, Walker, and Dixon (1989), Segal and Cover (1989), Tate (1981), and others reported that justices' ideological tendencies, *not* case-specific factors and legal contexts, were the exceptionally powerful correlates of justices' voting behavior. Similarly, using a principal-agent framework to test the compliance of circuit courts to Supreme Court doctrine, Songer, Segal, and Cameron found that while case facts were important in circuit court decisions, judges here exhibited a tendency to shirk and to advance their own policy preferences (1994, 693). And Richard Pacelle and Lawrence Baum (1992) reported that such behavior is most likely when the communication transmitted to circuit court judges is ambiguous.

Focusing at the lower end of the judicial hierarchy, Johnson (1987a) provides some evidence that the legal model accounts for more variation in the responsiveness to Supreme Court decisions by federal district courts than by circuit courts, thus supplying the first systematic, yet preliminary indication that case facts and the legal context of cases may be more salient in district courts than in appellate courts. But there is still much ground to cover. This type of analysis, which compares judges' reliance on the legal model at different court levels, has only recently been applied to specialized courts by my coauthors and me (see Hansen, Johnson, and Unah 1995). There are logical and systemic reasons why judges in lower courts such as the Court of International Trade may pay more attention to case facts and the legal context of cases than they pay to political or ideological factors.

First, district court decisions can be overruled on appeal. About one-third of all district court decisions are appealed to the circuit courts, which is a large number considering that these cases make up most circuit courts' dockets. Roughly 30 percent of the time, these district court decisions are struck down or significantly modified (Howard 1981, chap. 2–3). The court system is organized in a formal, hierarchical fashion to facilitate communication and uniformity in the flow of legal practices. In this system, the line of authority is top-down rather than bottom-up, which makes Supreme Court precedents most authoritative and controlling. The power to correct the errors of federal district courts lies first and foremost with circuit courts and ultimately with the Supreme Court. District court judges who deviate from precedent at time T can be punished by having their decisions reversed or remanded (i.e., softly reversed) on appeal at $T + 1$. In reality, due to the need to protect one's prestige and reputation, no district court–level judge seeks to make a decision that will be overruled by a higher court (Baum 1994b). Thus, strong incentives exist for trial judges to follow precedent and case facts instead of routinely consulting their personal policy preferences.

Also, lower-court judges are typically motivated by the possibility of being recognized with elevation to a higher court, which brings greater remuneration, power, and prestige (Ball 1987; Baum 1994b; Cohen 1992). This possibility of promotion requires judges to establish a strong record that includes as few reversals as possible, since the ABA scrutinizes the totality of a potential judicial nominee's legal record before rating the individual's qualification.

Finally, trial courts are the first courts of record, which implies that judges here have a predisposition to review case facts when they preside over the initial phase of an adversarial process that could eventually wind up being examined by the U.S. Supreme Court.

These three reasons—possibility of reversals, higher-court appointments, and predisposition to case facts—make it logical that lower-court judges consider case facts and the legal context of controversies more seriously than political factors, in contrast to what those justices consider who sit atop the judicial hierarchy and whose decisions cannot be overturned as a matter of routine.[3] Since specialized courts that are situated below the circuit level are functionally equivalent to federal district courts and exhibit the features explained earlier, I hypothesize that judges in these courts consider case-specific factors and the legal context of controversies more strongly in their decisions than they consider political or attitudinal factors.

The Extralegal Model

The extralegal model, whose crux is an orientation toward judges' political preferences, has been advanced as a strong alternative to the legal model. The extralegal model was first ardently proposed by C. Herman Pritchett (1948) when he argued for the inclusion of the "personal element" of jurists in models purporting to explain judicial interpretation and the making of law. In reality, the extralegal model has many dimensions; it focuses on more than just the personal element of judges. Like the legal model, the extralegal model also starts by considering case facts as its base and argues that political and ideological factors (such as interest-group influences and a judge's partisan affiliation) and environmental factors (such as general economic conditions) are more important than the legal context of cases in judicial decision making. The model assumes that judges are interested in maximizing their policy preferences. It is not interpretive coherence that matters most to judges under this model but "good" policy outcomes for society. Thus, according to the extralegal model, judges make decisions by consulting their policy preferences much more readily than by consulting legal precedent. Strong empirical evidence based upon analysis of decisional trends in generalist courts has been furnished in support of this view in specific policy areas such as criminal justice (George and Epstein 1992), labor relations (Spiller and Gely 1992), antitrust regulation (Songer 1987), and civil liberties generally conceived (Richardson and Vines 1967; Segal and Cover 1989; Segal and Spaeth 1993). In the area of international trade, the extralegal model of decision making in the specialized trade courts can be formally represented in reduced form as:

$$\text{DECISION} = f(\text{CASE FACTS, POLITICS, ECONOMICS})\qquad(2)$$

where CASE FACTS, POLITICS, and ECONOMICS are vectors, each representing a set of independent effects, which I enumerate in the next chapter. According to this model, then, precedent and intent are considered by judges as an afterthought. After all, if that were not the case and judges made decisions primarily on the basis of precedent and original intent, law would be static when it must keep pace with changes in society. I define extralegal factors as those political and economic variables that can affect judges' decisions and are unrelated to legal doctrine. These factors include judges' ideological leanings as reflected in their political backgrounds, the direction of lower-court judges' decisions, interest-group influence, and aggregate economic factors that may be relevant to court decisions.

Theoretical Rapprochement

Neither the legal model nor the extralegal model alone is sufficient to explain and predict judicial behavior. Each has its own peculiar weakness. The legal model typically ignores the role of politics; the extralegal model underestimates the importance of legalism. Considered in tandem, the two models have the potential to reinforce each other. Thus, I argue in favor of a theoretical rapprochement whereby the critical features of both models are unified in a single framework so that we can more realistically model judicial behavior, capturing the legal, political, economic, and contextual issues that underlie judicial decisions.

In the Court of International Trade, for example, not only may judges consider the nature of the controversy, precedent, the intent of Congress, and the legal context of the case immediately before them, but they may also consider the potential economic impact their decision will have on workers or the domestic industry as a whole. Moreover, Carp and Rowland (1983) have reported that the political party identification of district court judges is an important correlate of judges' decisions. Similarly, Nagel (1961) reported that the values of judges matter in bipartisan appellate courts and that Democratic judges were more prone to favor regulatory agencies in business regulation and tax cases than were Republican judges, who are usually ideologically predisposed to limit intrusive government regulation. In addition, since money can buy the best lawyer, judges may be swayed by the quality of legal representation. A good model of judicial decision making in specialized courts of international trade should take all these factors into account. Combining equations (1) and (2), we can employ the following unified model to estimate decision making in the specialized trade courts:

DECISION = f(CASE FACTS, LAW, POLITICS, ECONOMICS)   (3)

where CASE FACTS, LAW, POLITICS, and ECONOMICS are vectors as explained earlier.

An integrated model therefore offers the possibility of the most realistic measure of the impact that specialized courts actually have on U.S. trade policy. Perhaps the most comprehensive empirical effort to date in which the two models are conjoined is that of George and Epstein (1992). Using death penalty cases, they reported that individually, the legal and extralegal models behaved "idiopathically"; the legal model underpredicted conservative judicial decisions, while the extralegal model overpredicted them, making it difficult to formulate consistent claims about judges' behavior. They then tested the proposition that the models presented codependent explanations and were able to report better and more consistent findings after integrating critical features of the two models.

Conclusion

In this chapter I have attempted to develop a theory of judicial specialization, focusing on the core features of specialized courts and the virtues of expertise in the U.S. justice system. The federal judicial system continues to experience an increase in case filings of mammoth proportion, as indicated by Judge Miner of the Second Circuit Court of Appeals (Miner 1993). One federal effort to cope with this situation, as Posner (1983) attests, is a growing drift toward specialization of the federal judicial function. Although some view this drift as an unfavorable development, I think that for political scientists it is quite exciting, because it presents us with a historic opportunity to expand our knowledge by testing anew the strength of various theories of judicial behavior and of judicial impact on policy, using institutional contexts that have long been overlooked.

As a matter of course, I have identified four core characteristics or defining features of specialized courts. These courts can be distinguished by (1) development of expertise, which occurs rapidly through repeated access to factually similar cases, (2) the concentration of judicial activity about a given policy area in one court, (3) a focus on fairly complex policy areas, and (4) a homogeneous set of cases. My theoretical argument in this chapter is that as a rule, these features allow judges in specialized courts to develop expertise, which they use to scrutinize legal controversies and to decide them expeditiously and meaningfully. In chapter 6, I provide a refinement of equation (3) by explaining the research design (i.e., independent variables, data, methodology) to test the unified model of specialized-court decision making.

CHAPTER 6

Data, Measures, and Techniques for Analyzing Decision Making in Specialized Courts

In chapter 5, I explained the state of contemporary judicial review, the core characteristics of specialized courts, and the models that may be used to understand specialized court decision making in the area of international trade. This chapter examines how the decisional models will be empirically implemented. I shall discuss here the origin and characteristics of my data, provide a more in-depth explanation of hypotheses discussed in chapter 5, and explain the logic of the methodological techniques that I use in testing the propositions. My data and analysis focus on two specialized courts, the Court of International Trade and the Federal Circuit, and two bureaucratic agencies, the Department of Commerce and the International Trade Commission.

One way to understand the role of expertise in the relationship between specialized courts and administrative agencies is to evaluate how judges in generalist courts settle procedural or substantive questions in cases they have been asked to decide and to use this knowledge as a basis for comparing and analyzing how judges in specialized courts respond to bureaucratic decisions brought to them for review. I argued that judges with expertise in a particular subject area are less likely to defer to bureaucrats than are judges without expertise. Thus, to analyze the role of expertise in judicial review, I start by comparing the level of judicial deference to administrative agencies by generalist and by specialized courts. In doing so, I make an implicit assumption that the issues raised in the cases in the different courts being compared are fixed, just to simplify the analysis and facilitate comparability of court reactions to administrative actions. It is indeed the case that in U.S. trial courts, whether they be specialized or generalist, procedural issues such as pleadings and motions and rules of discovery are similar in character. So while this assumption is imperfect, it is indeed tenable, and quite necessary for the purposes of this analysis. To determine the core factors that condition specialized courts' decision making in the area of trade, I use indicators of judicial behavior derived from the judges' immediate political environment, such as their partisan background, the economic factors relevant to the cases they hear, and the legal and factual information from the cases themselves. These different tasks—comparing decisional trends in various courts and determining factors of decision making—call for the application of different forms of analytical techniques.

In recent years, social scientists have witnessed the development of a number of methodological techniques of inference that do not make stringent assumptions about the distribution of the population from which sampled data originated. For some purposes, that can be an attractive methodological feature. In some aspects of my analysis, I employed these distribution-free or nonparametric statistics to explore the institutional relationship between specialized courts and bureaucracies.

The beauty of using these techniques is that we can quickly and straightforwardly learn the decisional patterns of courts without resorting to using very rigorous and complex methodologies. Specifically, I use these methods to highlight the role of expertise in judicial review by comparing the degree of judicial deference to bureaucratic agencies exhibited by the United States Supreme Court and the Court of International Trade. At first, this type of multilevel comparison may seem odd if we consider the courts involved. Indeed, the Supreme Court and the Court of International Trade are markedly different in several aspects, apart from the similarity they share, which is a geographic jurisdiction of national scope. But it is the magnitude of the difference and what we can learn from it that makes the comparison interesting. Comparing the two courts will increase our understanding of judicial deference by illuminating the fact that these two courts are located at different levels of the judicial hierarchy and at opposite extremes of the expertise dimension. Besides these differences, the two courts also assume quite distinct organizational structures. Generally speaking, the Supreme Court has nine nonexpert justices, who engage in participatory decision making to build the Court's agenda through the so-called rule of four[1] and to issue final decisions on the merits through majority vote. In contrast, the Court of International Trade has no gatekeeping powers; with rare exceptions, each case is heard and decided by only one judge, who has expertise in the subject matter. Are these differences between a quintessential generalist court and a quintessential specialized court manifested in their degree of deference to administrative agencies? As we shall see in chapter 7, the answer is yes.

In addition to this multilevel comparison, I further compare judicial deference at the trial court level, focusing on the (specialized) Court of International Trade and the (generalist) federal district courts. Finally, to determine the core variables that condition specialized-court decision making on the merits, I use probit and logit techniques, which are more theoretically demanding than the nonparametric method and are appropriate for explaining behavior in binary choice situations, that is, where only two alternative outcomes of a process are of concern to the decision maker. Examples include a citizen's decision to vote, a graduate student's decision to visit the corner bar for a beer, or a judge's decision to rule in favor of the plaintiff or the defendant in a case. Indeed, most of the more meaningful and important choices in politics are binary in nature, and that is why maximum likelihood estimation techniques, such as probit and logit, are important techniques with which scholars and aspiring scholars should be familiar.

The probit and logit methods are comparable in terms of the results they produce. In instances where the sample is highly skewed, however, logit is more forgiving than is probit because its **S** shape has "heavier tails" and so is preferred to probit in such a situation (Liao 1994, 24–25). In examining the decision-making behavior of judges of the Court of International Trade, I employ probit. But in modeling the voting behavior of the judges of the Federal Circuit, I employ logit because of a skewed distribution of the data.

The industry data at my disposal extend to only those industries that petitioned the government for relief under the antidumping (AD) and countervailing duty (CVD) trade laws. Resource limitations precluded a more exhaustive data-gathering effort to encompass equally all the trade laws. For example, while sufficient data exist for the AD and CVD cases for the analysis, the data on Section 337 unfair-trade practices are incomplete and so are excluded from the regression models. But where possible, I shall include in the analysis Section 337 cases.[2]

The number of antidumping and countervailing duty appeals decided and published by the Federal Circuit for which I was able to gather data for the full set of independent variables during the period examined was 68. Such a small sample may make the use of an asymptotic (large sample) estimator such as probit or logit problematic because of sensitivity to sample size (Aldrich and Nelson 1984). To check the consistency of my findings about Federal Circuit decision making, I also analyze those data using a linear estimator, weighted least squares (WLS), because of the relatively small sample size and skewness exhibited by the data. I should remind the reader that for both the Court of International Trade and Federal Circuit models, both deferential decisions and policy decisions will be modeled and explained. The main difference between these two types of decisions is that in a deferential decision, a court takes no specific policy stance distinct from that of the agency or lower court, whereas in a policy decision, a court does take a distinct policy stance.

Content Analysis of Judicial Opinions

The data used in this analysis are comprised of primary and secondary data. The primary data describe the legal and factual contexts of cases and were derived by content analysis of published opinions of the Court of International Trade and the Federal Circuit. The data for both courts cover a period of 11 years, from 1980 through 1990. Two reasons motivated the choice of this time frame. First, an incremental and intriguing transformation in the domestic politics of foreign trade occurred during that period. In the 1980s, we witnessed the slow rise of international trade as a controversial partisan issue that both the Republican and Democratic parties relied upon to define themselves. While one can recount a few episodes of trade conflict involving specific industries or regions of the United States, the postwar period up to the late 1960s was one in which trade politics in the United States was largely dormant and uncontroversial. This period was marked by unprecedented growth in the U.S. and Western economies. This boom did not last long, however. The exceptional successes of GATT and its member countries in promoting freer trade[3] finally caught up with U.S. exporters in the 1970s as they faced increasing competition from abroad. Global competition occurred not only in trade but also in financial markets, and it led to strong interest-group and consumer-group activism (Destler and Odell 1987). Intense interest-group pressures stirred Congress into action, leading to passage of amendments that introduced profound changes in existing trade laws and made it easier for industries to acquire regulatory protection.

The second and more immediate reason for focusing on this 1980–90 period is that it trumpeted the growing significance of courts in U.S. trade policy-making. As discussed more extensively in chapter 2, one of the notable changes instituted in trade laws in the 1980s was the expansion of avenues of judicial review of bureaucratic outputs, allowing courts to assume a prominent role in identifying and defining which issues were salient in foreign trade and to make incremental changes to the overall direction of U.S. trade policy.

My content analysis of published judicial opinions followed three steps. First, I developed a coding scheme guided by theoretical considerations and used this scheme as a road map for retrieving information from published opinions. Second, using this scheme, I coded legal and nonlegal information concerning

1. the nature of the case or controversy (i.e., whether the appeal involved a procedural matter, a statutory matter, or a discretionary matter, as defined below)

2. the type of trade law at issue (i.e., whether it was the section of the law that deals with dumping, illegal subsidization, product classification, or presidential power)
3. the type of bureaucratic agency from which the appeal originated (i.e., the ITC, DOC, Customs Service, or USTR)
4. the judge or judges who presided over the matter (also used to determine the political affiliation of the presiding judge or judges), and
5. the decision of the judge or judges to either support (affirm) or reject (reverse) the bureaucracy's decision.

The issue of reliability is key to the data extraction method of content analysis. Reliability is the extent to which coded information from primary sources can be independently reproduced (Krippendorff 1980, 129–33). Substantively, reliability speaks to the amount of confidence we may accord the findings of a study that used this data extraction method. To increase the reliability of the measures, I first clarified and improved my coding scheme as I gained more familiarity with the doctrinal language, opinion writing styles of the judges, and substance of the opinions. Then I tested the consistency of my own coding. Finally, I trained a group of four enthusiastic and meticulous undergraduate seniors to assist in the final data gathering. The students were carefully selected based on their performance in my introductory international trade course and on their expressed interest to attend law school and pursue a legal career after graduating from college. The content analysis was a semester-long project, and participants were each awarded a grade and three academic credits.

Of all the pieces of information sought in the content analysis, the nature of the case was the most elusive and difficult to classify because it required the use of both experience and intuition. It is therefore the item most likely to pose problems of unreliability in the data. This difficulty arises because the entire judicial opinion was used as the recording unit and because each opinion is likely to present several cues about what the nature of the case may be. Coders were instructed to read the entire case to best determine the nature of the case and were instructed to search for and code the enumerated reasons why the case was brought to court. In cases where multiple claims were asserted, coders were instructed to take the claim or issue that the opinion writer deemed dispositive as being the reason for bringing the case to court.

Third, to check the reliability of the nature of the case, I trained a second group of three undergraduate seniors to recode the data after coders in the first group had completed their task. Thus, there was no communication between the first and second groups of coders during the assignment. According to Johnson (1987b, 175) and R. Weber (1990), such communication has the potential to introduce unanticipated errors into the measures because coders may internalize other information outside their specific instructions through group interactions. The task of the second group of coders was to classify only the nature of the case, and the data they produced were used to check for intercoder agreement or reliability. The level of intercoder agreement is 62 percent, which is moderately high when we consider the complexity of the policy area and the fact that coders were instructed to read each opinion in its entirety so as to accurately identify the nature of the controversy.

Unpublished Opinions

For several reasons, data on unpublished opinions are not included in the multivariate analyses reported in this work. Uneven publication rules prevail in federal courts. Some courts publish virtually all their decisions with an opinion, whereas others publish selectively. For example, in the Court of International Trade, by statute, all decided cases must be published in the *U.S. Court of International Trade Reports.*[4] Thus, unpublished opinions pose no concern here. At the circuit level, however, it has been the stated policy of the Judicial Conference of the United States since 1972 to have the courts of appeals publish opinions only selectively, where a case is believed to have precedential value.[5] In the Federal Circuit, according to data I obtained from the Office of the Clerk, there is no systematic evidence to suggest that this policy is being misused. The court issues unpublished opinions quite infrequently.

Moreover, according to rule 47.6 of the Federal Circuit, unpublished opinions are those that the panel has determined unanimously at the time of issuance as not adding significantly to the body of law. Such cases cannot be cited as precedent in court proceedings, suggesting that they have no precedential value, procedural value, or consequence in either promoting or hindering future conflict. In short, these cases do not affect the substance of public policy. Finally, as noted by Donald Songer and Reginald Sheehan (1992, 238), it is extremely difficult and expensive to gather a full set of data on unpublished courts of appeals cases. Considering all these factors, the inevitable conclusion is that the informational value of these cases pales in comparison to the potential costs of researching them. For these reasons, unpublished cases were omitted from my analysis. Similarly, given the limited substantive value of these cases, their exclusion here is not expected to affect the substantive conclusions of the study.

In table 4, I provide brief descriptive information about the outcomes of unpublished international trade cases decided in the Federal Circuit from 1983 through 1990. These data are AD and CVD cases appealed from the Court of International Trade and Section 337 cases appealed from the ITC. During this eight-year period, only 41 trade cases were decided with an unpublished opinion, suggesting that the nonpublication rule is not being abused in the Federal Circuit. The decisions show that the Federal Circuit defers a great deal to the lower court and regulatory agency.

Other Court Data

For my comparative analysis of judicial deference, I rely on Supreme Court decisions in cases involving administrative agencies from 1980 through 1990. Cases were identified via the *Supreme Court Judicial Database.*[6] Case citation was used as the unit of analysis. The data extracted included all cases formally decided by full opinion or per curiam, which yielded a total sample of 340 cases. The direction of agency decisions was obtained by examining *U.S. Reports,* which publishes all opinions formally issued by the Supreme Court. Data on decision-making behavior of federal district courts are the civil decisions of the federal district courts in Houston, Kansas City, and Detroit, from 1981 through 1987.[7] Cases used in the analysis were federal government regulation cases for which a valid federal claim was established and a district court judge had issued a ruling favorable or unfavorable to a federal government agency ($N = 681$).

Independent Variables and Refinement of Hypotheses

In chapter 5, I proposed equation (3) as a general model of decision making in specialized courts that review international trade cases. It was hypothesized that political and economic factors, in addition to case attributes, together condition the behavior of specialized-court judges in the area of foreign trade. In this section, I explain the specific components of this general model and show how these components are important.

TABLE 4. Outcome of Unpublished International Trade Decisions of the Federal Circuit, 1983–90

Federal Circuit Decision	International Trade Commission (Section 337 cases)	Court of International Trade (AD and CVD cases)	Total Unpublished Trade Decisions
Affirm	14 (78%)	16 (70%)	30 (73%)
Reverse	4 (22%)	7 (30%)	11 (27%)
Total	18 (100%)	23 (100%)	41 (100%)

Source: Office of the Clerk, Court of Appeals for the Federal Circuit.

Case Attributes

By case attributes, I mean the specific factual or legal attributes of the case as established by the trial court, including the rules at issue and the manner in which these rules were applied by regulators in the bureaucracy. The following factors satisfy this definition.

The Nature of the Case

In judicial disputes, the nature of the case is critically important in determining how cases are decided. Judicial norms dictate that the clearly articulated facts and rules of practices and procedures are the hallmark of judicial decision making (Kort 1966; Segal 1986); that is especially true at the trial court level, where norm enforcement is the rule rather than the exception. When judges review the decisions of bureaucrats, they typically examine at least one of three crucial aspects of an agency's decision: (1) the choice of procedures that bureaucrats used to arrive at any substantive policy decision (Pierce, Shapiro, and Verkuil 1992, 113); (2) the rationality of the agency's actions in light of the statute; and (3) the agency's use of discretion or interpretation of "facts." There is a difference between questions of fact and questions of law, although this difference is often difficult to discern. For example, the ITC typically investigates domestic industries to determine whether injury has occurred; that is a question of law. What constitutes injury per se as defined by the statute, however, is a question of fact. Because facts are never spelled out completely in statutes, bureaucrats use their discretion. The courts usually review the factually based limits on regulators when judging legal controversies bearing upon issues of statutory interpretation.

A long-standing tradition in the judiciary is that trial courts are responsible for establishing the facts of the case in the litigation process, whereas appellate courts examine how the law was applied by trial court judges and bureaucrats.[8] Thus, the three-pronged strategy of judicial review enumerated earlier is generally more applicable to trial courts, including the Court of International Trade, than to appellate courts. The three-pronged strategy was used as a guide in the content analysis to determine the nature of the case. Cases that claimed that the agency's decision to grant or deny regulatory protection was based on an erroneous procedure were coded 1; those that challenged the agency's interpretation of statutory provisions were coded 2; cases that challenged the agency's discretion to make the decision as it had were coded 3.

Since the Federal Circuit directly reviews the decisions of the Court of International Trade rather than those of the bureaucracy, it is important when examining Federal Circuit review of bureaucratic actions to consider the intervening role of the Court of International Trade.[9] Doing so requires us to consider a three-step process through which cases flow from the federal agencies to the federal courts. First, the bureaucracy decides whether to protect a domestic industry. Second, the Court of International Trade reviews the agency decision and affirms or reverses it based upon the evidentiary record the agency had assembled during its investigation. Finally, the case is appealed to the Federal Circuit, which either affirms or reverses the Court of International Trade decision.

To determine the nature of each case, my assistants and I performed content analysis of each judicial opinion, examining in particular the reasons that triggered the litigation. A priori, I identified three basic reasons (or categories) for litigation, which, as indicated earlier, guided the coding of the nature of the case variable in order of difficulty of reversal. I shall discuss an example of each using actual cases decided in the Court of International Trade. I assume here that cases with clear procedural violations are easier to reverse than those in which bureaucrats relied upon their discretion. This assumption is consistent with the rule announced by the Supreme Court in 1984 in the case of *Chevron, U.S.A. Inc. v. National Resources Defense Council.* In this case, the Court gave substantial power to administrative agencies to interpret ambiguous statements in the law. The Court also stated unequivocally that where Congress is clear, however, agency *interpretation* will be rejected.

The first category identified pertains to litigation that questions the steps (or approach) used by the agency, where litigants charge either that procedural errors have been committed or that the agency failed to consider certain evidence or failed to permit the discovery of business proprietary information to aid in the litigant's defense. Consider, for example, one antidumping case decided in 1989 involving an American importer who sued the U.S. government, challenging the procedure used to impose duties on its foreign supplier, a Swedish company called Extraco, Inc. In the case of *Olympic Adhesives, Inc. v. United States,* the plaintiff, an American importer of animal glue and inedible gelatin from Sweden, sued the DOC, claiming that the agency committed an error in its investigation by neglecting its obligation to reasonably seek all information that is accessible from all relevant sources, so as to conduct a thorough investigation. To determine whether dumping has occurred, the DOC usually compares sales in a foreign producer's home market with sales of similar goods in the U.S. market. In *Olympic Adhesives* case, the agency sought to establish whether fictitious home-market sales had been created by the Swedish exporter (Extraco, Inc.) simply to escape U.S. antidumping duties. After requesting full cooperation but receiving "inadequate" production and sales information from Extraco, the DOC neither sought further informa-

tion from nor notified Olympic Adhesives but instead used the "best information available" (BIA), which was information alleged by U.S. competitors of Extraco. On that basis, the agency found that there was dumping
and imposed duties on animal glue and related products from Sweden. I
present this case as an illustration of an alleged procedural error. In the
coding routine, this and other cases that involved charges of procedural
error by bureaucrats were coded 1. These types of cases make up 18 percent of all the cases ($N = 114$) in the Court of International Trade model
and 19 percent ($N = 12$) of the appeals of administered protection cases
used in the multivariate model of Federal Circuit decision making.

The second major reason for litigation concerns cases that challenge
the agency's interpretation of statutory provisions or charge that the
agency's actions will have a significant detrimental impact upon the
administration of U.S. trade laws. These cases pose a higher level of
difficulty of reversal for judges than those cases concerned merely with
procedural issues. The example I present for this category is *Fundicao
Tupy S.A. v. United States* (1987). In this case the plaintiff, a Brazilian
exporter, challenged the interpretation of section 612 of the trade act,
which authorizes the ITC to cumulatively assess the volume and effects of
imports from two or more countries to determine whether injury to an
American industry has occurred. The exporter charged that the ITC's
interpretation of the cumulation provision was meaningless and that under
this interpretation, the statute interfered directly with the president's
authority to conduct foreign affairs. Cases in this category were coded 2
and make up 28 percent of the Court of International Trade cases ($N = 179$) and 18 percent of the Federal Circuit cases ($N = 11$).

The final category concerns litigation that charges that, on the basis of
its broad discretion, the agency acted capriciously in the manner that it
made its decision. These are cases for which the governing statute provides
little or no guidance, requiring bureaucrats to fill in the gaps. I should note
that although bureaucrats have broad discretion, courts have repeatedly
stated that this grant of discretion is not unlimited and "cannot bind a
court" (for example, *Bureau of Alcohol v. Federal Labor Relations Authority* 1983, 98). Thus, in *Canadian Meat Council v. United States* (1987), the
plaintiff charged that the DOC abused its discretion when it concluded in
its CVD investigation that a subsidy to swine producers bestowed competitive benefits on pork packers who export frozen pork to the United States.
The agency relied on its broad discretion to *assume* that a direct economic
benefit existed because, in its judgment, swine is "the primary input" for
pork and that it was unnecessary to formally investigate whether benefits
passed from an upstream (swine growers) to a downstream (pork packers)
firm. In court, the DOC complained that the statute "gives little guidance"

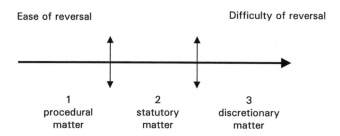

Fig. 3. Nature of the case in unidimensional space showing ease of reversal

and the DOC therefore used its discretion. The court was unpersuaded and remanded the case. These types of cases that question agents' use of discretion and interpretation, and which I consider the most difficult to reverse, are coded 3. Fifty-four percent of the Court of International Trade cases ($N = 349$) and 63 percent ($N = 36$) of the Federal Circuit cases fell in this category.

This coding is assumed to be interval in scale and is depicted in a unidimensional space in figure 3. (See the data appendix for the description and sources of other data.) No claim is made, however, that the distances are equal. In other words, I do not claim that the distance from 1 to 2 is the same as the distance from 2 to 3. I do claim that the direction translates into a progressively higher level of difficulty for judges to reverse trade cases.

The nature of the case is expected to condition the decisions of Court of International Trade and Federal Circuit judges, and as one moves from procedural issues to discretionary issues, the decision to reverse an agency action is expected to get relatively more difficult for the judge to make. Because procedures generally have a limiting effect on bureaucratic behavior, specialized-court judges are more likely to agree with the policy decisions of bureaucrats based on the application of procedures and less likely to concede on issues of agency discretion. Clearly, bureaucrats do have broad discretion to implement public policy and courts are expected to defer to them within reason, but judges recognize that bureaucratic discretion is not unlimited and is not binding on courts.

Import Duty
As required by law, antidumping and countervailing duty cases appealed to the Court of International Trade generally have received at least a preliminary duty determination, signifying the severity of the alleged unfair practice. In this respect, the policy actions of bureaucrats are important in

predicting what Court of International Trade judges will do as well as what judges in the Federal Circuit will do. One of the most important roles of the courts is to correct the "errors" that may have been committed by bureaucrats in implementing trade policy. If the decision of the regulators is reasonable (i.e., it falls within acceptable boundaries of the law) and the duty they imposed is reasonably high, and if both of these actions were based on accurate factual foundation, the courts will be expected to support the regulatory action taken by bureaucrats. When the outcome of a bureaucratic investigation is negative, meaning that no violation was found, there is no duty imposed; these cases are coded 0. In instances where there is a violation, the duty variable is coded as the actual rate of duty imposed by the regulators. Of all the cases considered, the highest duty assessed on goods from a single country between 1980 and 1990 was 241 percent on in-shell pistachio nuts from Iran in 1985. A higher duty rate signifies greater certainty on the part of regulators about the seriousness of the violation and about the veracity of their findings. In such instances, the court is expected to uphold bureaucratic decisions to protect U.S. firms.

Agency Structure

Also potentially important to the decision-making process of the courts is the nature of the agency from which a case was appealed. Agency structure here refers to those conditions that form the signature of an agency. They include an agency's internal "culture," the path that potential decisions must traverse to become official policy choices (typically defined by agency practices and procedures), the number of individuals in charge of making final command decisions in an agency, or the agency's ability to resist outside political influences. All these conditions influence the criteria for decision making used by an agency to accomplish its stated goals.

The tasks of the regulatory agencies examined here are different, as explained in chapter 3. In addition, the agencies operate under different institutional rules, which may affect their vulnerability and responsiveness to judicial control.[10] For example, the Commission holds trial-style hearings with an adversarial process quite similar to that typically found in real courts, and thus its decisions should be more likely to be upheld by real courts. Furthermore, given that the six commissioners serve staggered nine-year terms and thus are appointed by different presidents with certain partisan constraints, they are less likely to be controlled by the president than would be his politically appointed head of the DOC. Thus, a president may be able to influence or change the policy orientation of the DOC much more easily and quickly than he would be able to change that of the Commission, leading to frustration and frequent violations of legal precedent by the DOC. Therefore, we should expect the courts to show more support for an independent regulatory commission such as the ITC than an executive-level agency such as the DOC. I represent agency structure with a dichotomous variable. Cases appealed from the ITC were coded 0; those from the DOC were coded 1.

Policy Direction

A final case-specific attribute that may condition the decisions of specialized-court judges in foreign trade is the direction of the bureaucratic policy decision. This attribute is an important indicator of whether the trade courts have a direct impact in moving trade policy in either a protectionist or a free-trade direction. The decisions of the ITC and DOC result either in a movement toward greater protection for U.S. industries through the imposition of higher tariff rates or in the maintenance of freer trade through the denial of such protection. Policy direction is measured as a dichotomous variable based on the agency decision. It is coded 1 if agency decision is protectionist and 0 if the status quo (free trade) is maintained. Using this variable, the policy direction of court decisions can be determined easily by looking at whether the courts affirm or reverse the agency's decision.

Economic Factors

The economic data used in this study include data on industry and U.S. government activity on import, export, and production.[11] At the heart of regulatory petitions in international trade are economic considerations whose importance extends well beyond the bureaucracy to influence court decisions to award or reject protection sought by U.S. industries. To control for economic circumstances surrounding each case appealed to the courts, I use a number of case-specific economic factors. The outcome of a given legal controversy may be predicated upon economic considerations such as the balance of trade between the United States and the foreign country involved in the legal controversy with a U.S. firm. I use the U.S. trade balance with the country named as the unfair trader in each case as a control variable in explaining court decisions. I expect the courts to rule in favor of granting protection for the domestic industry if the United States has a high trade deficit with the country named as an unfair trader in a particular legal action. Also important is the extent to which the volume of imports of a particular product penetrating U.S. markets poses a threat of high competition for domestically produced goods of similar characteristics. When such a threat exists, we should expect the courts to rule in favor of protection for the domestic industry. Foreign penetration is measured here (as in Hansen 1990) as the ratio of imports to domestic consumption (see appendix C1).

Other economic factors considered are those measuring industry performance. Industry performance is a good predictor of whether a firm will seek regulatory protection against foreign competitors in the first place. Presumably an economically healthy firm has no incentive to incur the expense necessary to fight for regulatory protection. Profits are typically a good indicator of industry performance, with high profits signifying good industry performance. However, there are strong incentives for petitioning firms to deny the general public access to sensitive information such as profit, which could be used as a weapon by market competitors or opponents in the regulatory process. Moreover, proprietary information that agencies have concerning petitioning firms' profits are usually not open to public review. Thus, as an alternative measure of industry performance, I use yearly capital expenditures of the U.S. industry involved in a case as a surrogate for industry profit and as an indicator of economic injury resulting from unfairly traded imports. Capital expenditures show whether a firm is making the necessary investment to innovate and stay competitive in global markets; it also shows the extent of the general health of an industry and is expected to have an influence on the decisions of judges to sustain or reverse the ruling of trade regulators.

Political Factors

Political Affiliation of Judges
The political affiliation of judges is used as a surrogate for ideology for three specific purposes. These are to measure: (1) the potential microlevel or judge-specific ideological influences in decision making, (2) the relative impact of the ideological composition of the courts in their decisions, and (3) Democratic and Republican judges' support for administrative agencies. Partisan affiliation of the presiding judge in a case in the Court of International Trade was measured as a dichotomous variable (coded 0 if a judge identifies as a Republican and 1 if Democrat). A slightly different measure of political ideology was adopted for judges of the Federal Circuit. Since circuit courts typically use three-judge panels, the party affiliation of the majority of each panel was used to account for the political influence of the judges. A dummy variable was used to represent the panel majority (coded 1 if Democratic and 0 if Republican).

Partisanship has historically played a crucial role in American trade politics. From the years after the Great Depression up until the late 1960s, Republicans were generally in favor of protectionist trade policy while

Democrats were in favor of freer trade. These roles have since been reversed, starting from the late 1960s, as a result of structural developments in world trade competition such as capital mobility and the reaction to these developments from domestic interests and labor unions (Ray 1989). As international trade has become an area that both parties are increasingly relying upon to define themselves, Republicans now are perceived as the champions of freer trade and Democrats are viewed as the ones increasingly taking a more protectionist stance in foreign trade matters (Keech and Pak 1995, 1136). The recent debates over the ratification of the North American Free Trade Agreement (NAFTA) and the Uruguay Round of GATT underscore this difference. In the House of Representatives, for example, NAFTA passed by a narrow margin on a vote of 234 to 200, with a stronger Republican backing (75 percent) than Democratic (40 percent) (Dutt 1993). In recent decades, trade has simply not elicited a distinctively strong ideological fervor among American elites, including judges. Therefore, the direction of impact of judges' ideology on judicial decisions cannot be determined with absolute certainty. But it is noteworthy that in the period here examined, the courts were populated by judges appointed by Republican presidents.

Concentration Ratio
Concentration ratio represents the percentage of total output by the four largest firms in an industry. Concentration ratios are commonly used by economists as an indicator of industry market structure and are recorded here at the four-digit standard industrial classification (SIC) level. The SIC is a comprehensive statistical classification standard, which defines industries in terms of all goods and services manufactured in the United States. Classifications range from the two-digit level (broad category) to the seven-digit level (extremely specific category). For instance, a classification of 48 represents the communications industry, 481 represents radiotelephone communications, and 4812 represents paging systems and beepers.

   In this study, I use the four-digit SIC for concentration ratio (the best and most disaggregated measure available) as a proxy for industry political power or organizational ability (Baldwin 1985; Hansen 1990; Grier, Munger, and Roberts 1994). A high concentration ratio means that an industry is able to control the free-rider problem and lower the cost of organization, because a small number of similar-sized firms facilitates the formation and enforcement of agreements. A high concentration ratio also implies access to greater financial resources, which are necessary to hire superior legal counsel and to finance the high costs associated with legal research in an international trade case.[12] A concentrated industry therefore has the ability to exert influence on court decisions. As Galanter

(1974) noted, the "haves" do indeed come out ahead of the "have nots" when it comes to fighting legal conflicts out in court.[13]

Although federal judges have life tenure, are independent of any political entity, and operate outside the normal flow of politics, research indicates that judges may respond to political pressure in their decision making (Carp and Rowland 1983; Epstein and Rowland 1991; Howard 1981). If Baum's (1977) and Shapiro's (1968) claims that specialized-court judges are highly susceptible to clientelism hold, then industries with greater concentration ratios and therefore greater political power may be able to exert sufficient pressure on judges to have bureaucratic decisions reversed or affirmed in their favor.

Reputation

Reputation is conceptualized as a summary of the ideological commitment of a nation to the standing rules of GATT. Ever since GATT was created, the organization has maintained regulations designed to promote free trade and to deter the practices of dumping and illegal subsidization by national governments. Nations that are signatories of GATT's antidumping or subsidy codes in principle agree to and in practice are expected to abide by this legal framework. Nevertheless, in times of economic difficulty nations that are not GATT members, as well as those that are, may abandon their commitment to the ideal of free trade in order to accommodate domestic interests (Milner 1993). The opportunity for such behavior is great because of imperfect information and enforcement. However, one would expect highly committed nations to be more dedicated to avoiding the temptation to violate the rules of GATT and therefore have fewer antidumping and countervailing duty cases filed against them, ceteris paribus. A member or nonmember nation that is accused of frequently violating GATT rules may develop a reputation as an unfair trader. In court, we should expect judges to be more lenient toward countries that are perceived to have a good reputation. Reputation is operationalized as the total yearly number of antidumping and countervailing duty cases initiated worldwide against each country, whether or not the case went to court.

By this definition, table 5 reveals Japan to be the worst offender of unfair trading practices, with 84 cases filed against it in the period here examined. Moreover, in terms of U.S. administrative agency decisions appealed to the Court of International Trade, 14.7 percent of all cases appealed between 1980 and 1990 involved Japan, as indicated in table 6. Indeed, Japan is not only the most frequent participant in the court, it is also one of the most active in filing suits against U.S. firms and the U.S. government. As indicated in table 6, India, Japan, and Taiwan have the distinction of being the most frequent plaintiffs in the Court of International Trade, with each country initiating legal actions in at least 53 percent of the suits in which it is a direct party. But France, Canada, and Italy are not far behind as frequent plaintiffs.

The Probit and Logit Models

Judicial decisions have discrete rather than continuous outcomes. Judges can either affirm a bureaucratic policy decision (coded 1) or reverse it (coded 0). And, still within the confines of their opinion, they can issue a protectionist ruling or a free-trade one. Due to this categorical nature of the outcome, ordinary least squares (OLS) methodology is inappropriate and cannot be trusted to yield efficient estimates; the assumption of normality is violated (Gujarati 1988, chap. 15).

Let the probability that the court affirms an agency decision equal 1 and the probability that the court reverses an agency decision equal 0. At any given period, we can expect the court to base its decision Y on knowledge of certain pertinent information, $x_{1i}, x_{2i}, \ldots, x_{ki}$, about the case as well as the political and economic environments. Given the binary nature of this choice, we can write the outcome equations:

$$\text{Prob } (Y = 1|x_{1i}, x_{2i}, \ldots, x_{ki}) = F\beta'$$
$$\text{Prob } (Y = 0|x_{1i}, x_{2i}, \ldots, x_{ki}) = 1 - F\beta'$$

TABLE 5. Reputational Ranking of Countries Most Frequently Targeted in Antidumping and Countervailing Duty Cases Worldwide, 1980–90

Country	Reputational Rank	Number of Cases	Ratio
Japan	1	84	15.8
Italy	2	57	10.8
Mexico	3	39	7.4
France	3	39	7.4
Canada	4	35	6.6
Brazil	5	34	6.4
Taiwan	6	31	5.8
South Korea	7	29	5.5
China	8	21	4.0
United Kingdom	9	19	3.6
(West) Germany	10	13	2.5
Sweden	11	12	2.3

Source: Operations of the Trade Agreements Program published by the U.S. International Trade Commission.

where F is a cumulative distribution function and the vector β' reflects the effects of changes in x (a vector of independent variables) on the probability of Y. This formulation suggests a linear probability model,

$$y = E(y) + (y - E[y]).$$
Since $E[y] = \beta'x$, then
$$y = \beta'x + \varepsilon.$$

This linear probability model has one important problem. This problem lies with the random component, ε, which represents all unobserved influences and randomness in the dependent variable. We cannot assume that ε is normally distributed with mean of 0 and standard deviation of 1. Indeed, the variance is nonconstant; therefore ε is heteroschedastic (Gujarati 1988, chap. 15). Consequently, predicted court decisions will fall outside the 0 and 1 interval, making it impossible to derive meaningful inferences about the behavior of judges in the CIT and the Federal Circuit. To correct this anomaly, we need to constrain the distribution of the random term, ε, in the (0,1) range so as to construct a model that will be consistent with the theory that judges' decisions generally either affirm or

TABLE 6. Top-Ranking Litigators of Antidumping and Countervailing Duty Cases in the Court of International Trade, 1980–90

Rank	Country	Number of Cases	Percent	Ratio as Plaintiff
1	Japan	90	14.7	.53
2	Italy	58	9.5	.45
3	Mexico	51	9.3	.36
4	Canada	46	8.5	.49
5	France	40	6.5	.51
6	Taiwan	35	5.7	.53
7	Brazil	31	5.1	.37
8	S. Korea	29	4.7	.31
9	China	22	3.6	.20
9	India	22	3.6	.55
11	United Kingdom	21	3.4	.38
12	(West) Germany	16	2.6	.25
13	Sweden	14	2.3	.23
14	Colombia	12	2.0	.36
15	Belgium	11	1.8	.09
15	Spain	11	1.8	.36
17	Romania	8	1.3	.25

Note: These 17 foreign nations account for 86.4 percent of all the international trade disputes reviewed by the Court of International Trade between 1980 and 1990. Plaintiff ratio represents the proportion of cases in which the corresponding country initiated legal action at the court.

reverse an agency action and that trade court judges' decisions generally either favor or oppose protectionism.

Assuming that the random component, ε, follows a cumulative normal distribution, we can write the probit model

$$Prob\ (Y = 1) = \int_{-\infty}^{\beta'x} \varphi(t)dt = \Phi\ (\beta'x)$$

where $\beta'x$ can assume any value ≥ 0, and $\Phi(.)$ is the standard normal distribution function. It can be shown that the probit model restrains the random component, ε, to values that fall only in the $(0,1)$ range (Greene 1993, chap. 21). Given that, we can now write the general outcome equation for the Court of International Trade:

Prob $(Y = 1) = F(\beta'\mathbf{x})$

= f(Import Duty, Nature of the Case, Agency Structure,

Party Affiliation of Judge(s), Concentration Ratio,

Reputation, Country Trade Deficit, Capital Expenditures,

Judge-Specific Influence)

Furthermore, assuming that the random component, ε, follows a logistic distribution, we can write the logistic function as:

$$Prob\ (Y = 1) = \frac{e^{z_i}}{1 + e^{z_i}}$$

where $Z_i = \Sigma b_k X_{ik}$, the systematic component.

Given that, we can write the decision model for the Federal Circuit:

Prob $(Y = 1)$ = f(Import Duty, Nature of the Case, Agency

Structure, Party Affiliation of Panel Majority,

Concentration Ratio, Country Trade Deficit,

Capital Foreign Penetration)

Conclusion

In this chapter, I have examined the data and explained the proposed analytical techniques to test the hypotheses as explained in this chapter and in chapter 5. Given that one of the main objectives of this study is to determine the core independent variables that condition the decision-making behavior of judges who operate with considerable expertise, I have proposed to use probit and logit techniques, which are appropriate for modeling court decisions because of their discrete outcome. But due to limitations in the Federal Circuit data, I shall also employ weighted least squares to estimate the Federal Circuit model as a way of checking the consistency of the findings. A brief discussion is given in appendix C2. I seek also to explore the role of expertise in the relationship between courts and administrative agencies more generally. I shall examine this relationship by comparing judicial responses to administrative decisions between courts at different levels of the judicial hierarchy and across courts located at the trial and appellate levels.

Although legal scholars have produced a large number of articles that seek to explain the behavior of judges in the area of international trade, those works have focused almost exclusively on addressing the rightness or wrongness of judicial decisions. My purpose here is not to take a moral stance on legal theory but to examine *why* specialized-court judges issue the kinds of decisions that they do. The result of the analyses and their implications are explained in the final three chapters.

Part 3
Findings and Implications of Specialized Trade Courts

CHAPTER 7

The Court of International Trade and the Politics of U.S. Trade Policy-Making

It is as much the duty of government to render prompt justice against itself in favor of citizens as it is to administer the same between private individuals.

Abraham Lincoln, First Message to Congress

The rest of this work is devoted to explaining the results and implications of the empirical analyses of the relationship between specialized courts and administrative agencies. This chapter reports the findings of the analysis of specialized-court decision making at the trial level, focusing on the Court of International Trade and its potential impact on public policy. Chapter 8 focuses on specialized courts of appeals. Two issues form the analytical focus of this chapter: judicial deference and judicial protectionism. I begin by examining here judicial deference to administrative agencies in light of the stated policy of the Supreme Court that courts should defer to regulatory agency interpretation of statutes when such interpretation is deemed reasonable. Later, in the section "To Protect or Not to Protect . . . ," I examine the policy decisions and substantive impact of the Court of International Trade. But first, I shall give a brief summary of some of the key findings of the analysis.

How much deference is there at the Court of International Trade, and does the court exert significant substantive influence on trade policy? The results of this analysis debunk the popular wisdom that courts as a whole give unprecedented deference to agency construction of statutes and that judges are ineffective in influencing public policy because of excessive deference. The Court of International Trade is indeed heeding Abraham Lincoln's sage admonition that one condition for a strong democracy obtains in an environment where judges are willing to render prompt justice against their employer, the federal government, in favor of private individ-

131

uals. The court *is* ruling against the federal government in a substantial number of legal controversies.

A further examination of the deference hypothesis, taking into account different types of regulatory agencies, reveals some interesting dynamics. For instance, when agencies have their day in court, judges accord them varying degrees of trust, corresponding to the agencies' institutional structures. For reasons having to do with autonomy and the decisional strategies of bureaucracies, courts tend to agree with independent regulatory agencies more frequently than they agree with executive-level agencies.

The analysis in this chapter ends with an examination of specialized courts to determine their protectionist tendencies and the core variables that condition their decision making in circumscribed policy areas such as international trade. I examine the factual characteristics of the cases as well as their political and economic circumstances to develop an understanding of how judges arrive at their policy judgments. The results consistently indicate that contextual case facts are critical in specialized-court decision making at the trial court level. The effect of political factors is generally small. Of the political variables employed in the analysis, only industry political power evinces decisional impact on the judges, though not consistently across all models. In a similar vein, the cumulative effect of the judges' political affiliation is important only in appeals from the ITC, not in appeals from the DOC. With regard to the claim that specialized courts serve only policy-neutral objectives, the data reveal *strong protectionist tendencies* in the Court of International Trade.

Judicial Deference in Generalist vs. Specialized Trial Courts

I argued in chapter 5 that because the business of specialized courts is concentrated in a limited policy area, judges who sit on these courts have expertise and are at least as knowledgeable as bureaucrats who implement policy in the area. Hence, specialized courts are able to play a significant role, beyond their policy-neutral virtues, in shaping public policy. The traditional focus of judicial research on generalist courts has led to the all-too-familiar conclusion that courts as a whole defer significantly to administrators charged with implementing legislative enactments (Shapiro 1968; Sheehan 1992; Jackson 1991, 67; cf. Spaeth and Teger 1982, 278). Although this conclusion is valid and convincing, it is indeed limited to generalist courts. I therefore question its generalizability to specialty courts such as the U.S. Court of International Trade, the U.S. Tax Court, and several others in the U.S. justice system, and I test here its applicability to specialized courts. My hypothesis is that by virtue of their expertise, specialized courts do defer significantly *less* to the bureaucrats charged with implementing public policy than do generalist courts.

To validate this claim, I conducted two different tests in which I analyzed how federal agencies have fared in courts at different levels of the judicial pyramid throughout the 1980s. First, I compared the rate of judicial deference in the federal district courts to that of the Court of International Trade. Second, I compared deference between the U.S. Supreme Court and the Court of International Trade. I limit my focus to formally decided cases, including those decided per curiam.

My definition of judicial deference mirrors that of Spaeth and Teger (1982, 278). Deference occurs when a judge votes to uphold an agency's actions; conversely, deference is absent when a judge votes to overturn, modify, or remand an agency's actions. So conceived, the concept of judicial deference makes no definitive claims about the quality, objectivity, or moral correctness of the agency decision or court decision itself. Furthermore, deference in and of itself tells us little about the resultant policy decision of a court except when critically analyzed in conjunction with an agency's policy direction. Only the level of decisional agreement, as opposed to the policy direction, matters in this definition. Later on I shall incorporate the policy direction of the agency into the analysis to determine court impact on policy. Table 7 reports the outcome of the analysis, which compares the dynamics of the interaction between courts and administrative agencies.

The analysis shows that the Supreme Court defers to agency interpretation of statutes 72 percent of the time and reverses 28 percent of the time. This finding is consistent with the findings of Sheehan (1992) on the Supreme Court and Willison (1986) on the D.C. Court of Appeals. But what is most striking here is that, as predicted, the Court of International Trade, which is a specialized court, defers to agencies at a significantly lower rate (59 percent) and reverses at a correspondingly higher rate (41 percent) compared to the Supreme Court. The Supreme Court and the Court of International Trade are located at opposite extremes of the expertise dimension, and they both cover a geographic jurisdiction of national scope. For these reasons, comparing how the two courts respond to bureaucratic agencies is logical. But some may argue that comparing deference between the highest court of the land and the Court of International Trade is inappropriate or unilluminating.

To attempt to dispel such skepticism, I compare judicial deference of two types of courts that both operate at the trial level. The result is still impressive. As indicated also in table 7, the federal district courts defer to agency regulators 73 percent of the time and reverse regulators only 27 percent of the time, compared to the 41 percent reversal rate for the Court of International Trade. As with the Supreme Court, the behavior of the federal district courts is statistically different from that of the Court of International Trade ($p \leq .05$).

One of the factors driving these differences in the rates of deference is the level of expertise of judges in their interaction with bureaucratic agencies. Specialized-court judges use their expertise in a complex policy area to critically examine agency practices. Consequently, those bureaucratic agencies appearing before the specialized court generally fared worse than those appearing before the generalist courts, that is, the Supreme Court and the federal district courts, which may be limited because of the complexity of the regulatory issues being reviewed.

Bureaucrats are typically distinguished from other government officials on the basis of expertise and ability to solve complex policy problems (Rourke 1984). Specialized-court judges also possess a high level of expertise that in many cases is comparable to, or even exceeds, that of bureaucrats, unlike judges in generalist courts. The findings here suggest that because of their substantive expertise and familiarity with bureau-

TABLE 7. A Comparative Look at Judicial Deference in Generalist vs. Specialized Courts

Court Decision	Generalist		Specialized
	United States Supreme Court (1980–90)[a]	Federal District Courts (1981–87)	Court of International Trade (1980–90)[b]
Reverse agency	95 (28%)	181 (27%)	510 (41%)
Affirm agency	245 (72%)	500 (73%)	786 (59%)
Total	340 (100%)	681 (100%)	1296 (100%)

Note: Data for the U.S. Supreme Court were extracted from the U.S. Supreme Court Judicial Database, 1991, ICPSR no. 9422, compiled by Harold J. Spaeth. Data for the federal district courts were extracted from the Federal District Court Civil Decisions in Detroit, Houston, and Kanas City, ICPSR no. 9367, compiled by C. K. Rowland. Data for the Court of International Trade (CIT) here refer to all cases appealed from the International Trade Commission, Department of Commerce, U.S. Customs Service, and U.S. Trade Representative and were published in the U.S. Court of International Trade Reports. Cases appealed from the Department of Labor, which typically involved adjustment assistance for U.S. industries and workers, were excluded. These CIT data were compiled by the author.

[a]The number of cases before the Supreme Court that are reversed or affirmed varies by agency (Sheehan 1992).

[b]The difference in the affirm and reverse rates between the Supreme Court and the Court of International Trade is 13 percent. Using a difference-in-proportion test, this difference is significant at the .05 level. Similarly, the difference in the affirm and reverse rates between the Court of International Trade and the federal district courts is 14 percent and is significant at the .05 level.

cratic practices, specialized-court judges display greater confidence than their generalist colleagues when evaluating bureaucratic actions. More important, specialized judges use their expertise and knowledge to overturn a significantly larger number of bureaucratic decisions.

Implications and the Dynamics of Judicial Review

Thus far in this chapter we have seen that because of its relative expertise, the Court of International Trade is reluctant simply to defer to the statutory interpretation reached by bureaucratic agencies charged with implementing U.S. trade laws. The court's reluctance to defer to agency actions would surely suggest that it is imposing discipline on trade administrators and would lead some to suspect that the court does indeed have a substantial impact one way or the other on trade policy-making. We cannot conclude from table 7 that this suspicion proves true, however. First, do Court of International Trade decisions lead to more protectionism? I will address this important question throughout this chapter by examining those cases in which the court defers to the bureaucracy and those in which it rejects the arguments of the bureaucracy and legitimizes an alternative policy argument instead. Second, does court impact vary between different types of agencies? In table 8, I investigate the court's substantive impact on the behavior of different types of bureaucratic agencies. Then, in table 9, I address the question of substantive impact of the court on public policy.

Table 8 shows the litigation success rates of the ITC and the DOC. The results suggest that the structure of an agency, defined in chapter 6 as

TABLE 8. Court of International Trade Decisions with Respect to Administrative Agency, 1980–90

Court Decision[a]	Administrative Agency		Total
	International Trade Commission	International Trade Administration	
Affirm	149 (64%)	220 (54%)	369 (58%)
Reverse	83 (36%)	184 (46%)	267 (42%)
Total	232 (100%)	404 (100%)	636 (100%)

Note: Data include antidumping (section 731) and countervailing duty (section 701) cases appealed to the Court of International Trade from the International Trade Commission and the Department of Commerce.

[a]A chi-square test of agency success rate at the court with 1 degree of freedom shows that the court is significantly more likely to affirm cases from the International Trade Commission than cases from the Department of Commerce: $\chi^2_{(1\ \text{d.f.})} = 5.77$ ($p \leq .02$).

a composite of those conditions that form the signature of an agency, matters significantly in the nature of court decisions. The Court of International Trade agrees with (affirms) the ITC 64 percent of the time but agrees with the DOC only 54 percent of the time. Stated somewhat differently, the rate of agreement between the court and agencies is 10 points higher for the ITC than for the DOC. A chi-square test indicates that the difference in success rates between the two agencies is significant at the .02 level.

This finding has several political implications. The task of modern international trade regulation is bifurcated as a safeguard mechanism for the entire American foreign trade system; and the actions of both administering agencies have either a foreign target or a domestic target. The DOC investigates and rules on the behavior of foreign firms or governments, whereas the ITC investigates and rules on the economic health of the American industry seeking regulatory protection. The first implication, therefore, is that the differences in responsibility and target of the agency investigations may account for some of the observed variance in the court's treatment of these agencies. Second, the decisional processes of the two agencies are different. The process of investigation is more adversarial and more courtlike at the six-member ITC than at the DOC, which has a single political appointee as the chief trade administrator, the undersecretary of commerce for international trade. The adversarial decision style of the ITC is more likely to expose the "truth," thereby leading to fewer reversals in court than the decisional style of the DOC, which is characterized more by rule making than by adversarial procedure.

Third, although evidence suggests that both agencies are indeed susceptible to external political pressures (see Baldwin 1985; Hansen 1990; Hansen and Park 1995; Moore 1992), the ITC may be more politically insulated and less responsive to external political pressures than the DOC. For example, in a 1993 *New York Times* article, South Carolina Democratic Senator Ernest Hollings, then chair of the Senate Commerce Committee, was said to be so influential at the international trade administration branch of the DOC that his staffer actually characterized him as "an 800-pound tiger" that enforces dumping curbs (Passell 1993, D1). Moreover, the fact that the DOC is headed by one political appointee who may be easily controlled makes the agency more susceptible to direct political influence. For example, the president can change the policy orientation of the DOC more sharply and more quickly than he can change the policy orientation of the Commission. This controllability is likely to create tension in the DOC; hence legal precedents may be violated more frequently by this agency than by the ITC, resulting in more frequent reversals by the Court of International Trade.

Substantive Impact of Court of International Trade Deference

Looking now at the potential substantive impact of the Court of International Trade deference on trade policy implementation, in table 9 I consider the likelihood that the court will affirm or reverse protectionist and nonprotectionist trade decisions in antidumping and countervailing duty cases. Impact is a nebulous concept that means different things to different people; therefore, I shall first explain my conception of impact as used in this study.

Political scientists typically view *impact* as "postdecisional events" (Canon 1991, 435). This definition refers to events undertaken by those who must enforce court decisions and those who must abide by them. For example, there was a sharp increase in the number of legal abortions in the United States between 1974 and 1980 after the 1973 Supreme Court decision in *Roe v. Wade* legalizing abortion (Rosenberg 1995, 394). In international trade policy, there was a significant rise in the number of antidumping petitions filed with the ITC following the 1987 decision of the Federal Circuit in *Bingham and Taylor Division, Virginia Industries, Inc. v. United States* that the ITC must use "cross-cumulation" when conducting economic analysis to support a preliminary injury determination.[1]

Defined this way, that is, as postdecisional events, impact would be difficult to assess across a range of international trade cases because to do so would require expensive and in-depth case studies of numerous court decisions. But even if one were to conduct such case studies, the selection of cases for examination would likely be biased in favor of newsworthy cases and against the majority of ordinary cases that never make it to the *Wall Street Journal*, for example.

Thus I adopt here the more lenient and therefore more generalizable conceptualization of *impact* as the extent to which the courts are able to shift trade policy implementation in either a protectionist or nonprotectionist direction through their decision to reverse or affirm a bureaucratic action. This definition is consistent with the meaning of *impact* discussed by Songer (1987, 831), Wasby (1970, chap. 2), and Segal and Spaeth (1993, chap. 9), which is that a court's policy leadership may be exercised through decisional trends that signal its inclination toward a particular policy direction.

I follow this definition of *impact* in my discussion of the role of specialized courts in public policy-making. I analyze policy impact in two ways, first nonparametrically, using a bivariate method, and then parametrically, using a multivariate method. Table 9 shows that although the

Court of International Trade has an impact in that it reverses a remarkably high total percentage of protectionist and nonprotectionist decisions (42 percent), there is no disparate treatment of the two kinds of regulatory decisions. From the perspective of interagreement between court and agency choices, we can conclude that the court is not treating protectionist and nonprotectionist decisions of the agencies differently. The data show only a 1 percent difference in the rate of affirmance between protectionist and nonprotectionist cases, and this difference is clearly not statistically significant. In the aggregate, the Court of International Trade seems to be shunning prescriptive policy-making, striving instead to uphold the status quo in antidumping and countervailing duty cases.

Multivariate Analysis of Decision Making in the Court of International Trade

In chapter 5 I posed the hypothesis that because international trade is a policy area defined by both economic and political considerations, the courts deciding cases in this area consider not only the factual context of the controversies but also the political and economic circumstances surrounding the cases in deciding whether to uphold or deny agency grant of protection to domestic firms or industries. In the remainder of this chapter, I shall explain the result of this general hypothesis. In doing so, I will reexamine my findings concerning the role of the structure of an agency in court decisions.

Table 10 reports the findings of two separate econometric models pertaining to the interaction between the Court of International Trade and administrative agencies in antidumping and countervailing duty cases. The dependent variable is the court's decision to reverse (coded 0) or

TABLE 9. Court of International Trade Deference to Agencies with Respect to Policy, 1980–90

| Court Decision[a] | Agency Decision | | Total |
	Protectionist	Non-protectionist	
Affirm	237 (58%)	134 (59%)	371 (58%)
Reverse	174 (42%)	94 (41%)	268 (42%)
Total	411 (100%)	228 (100%)	639 (100%)

Note: Data include antidumping (section 731) and countervailing duty (section 701) cases appealed to the Court of International Trade from the International Trade Commission and the Department of Commerce.

[a]A chi-square test of court deference to agency shows no statistically significant impact on policy: $\chi^2_{(1\,d.f.)} = .074$ (n.s.)

affirm (coded 1) a bureaucratic action. Thus, this section of the analysis pertains only to the potential deferential behavior of the court. In both models I used a single dichotomous variable to control for the policy direction of the regulatory decision as a way of examining whether the Court of International Trade is shifting policy implementation in a protectionist or free-trade direction. In addition, in both models I controlled for the political affiliation of the judges to capture the impact of ideological characteristics on court decisions.

In the literature on the behavior of courts, scholars have furnished extensive documentation that judges base their decisions largely on values or attitudes (Carp and Rowland 1983; Tate 1981; Segal and Spaeth 1993; Murphy 1964). Given that the evidence has come from the activities of generalist courts, I propose to test whether this basis for decision making obtains for specialized court judges. The impact of values on court decisions may be introduced through the judges' backgrounds and routine interactions among themselves during formal conferences or informal conversations. Moreover, given that most cases appealed to the Court of International Trade are decided by a single judge, I also developed an unrestricted model that includes a dummy variable for each of the judges so as to test for judge-specific differences.

Both models in table 10 fit the data reasonably well, although the inclusion of individual partisan characteristics in the unrestricted model shows no remarkable improvement over the restricted model. Each model predicts about 63 percent of the cases correctly, with an 11 percent reduction in error for the unrestricted model and a 6 percent reduction in error for the restricted model. The lack of improvement in the unrestricted model is corroborated by a nested chi-square (or log-likelihood ratio) test with 13 degrees of freedom, which indicates that individual judge characteristics are not important predictors of judicial deference to administrative agencies. We failed, then, to reject the null hypothesis that individual judge characteristics are unimportant, even at the 10 percent level.[2] Since the interpretation of raw probit estimates is not straightforward, I included a measure of the relative impact of each variable determined through sensitivity analysis (see Greene 1993, 635–46).

Looking at contextual case factors, for example, we can see that consistent with prior expectation, when all other variables are held at their mean, cases in which a high import duty has been levied are 11.1 percent more likely to be affirmed by the Court of International Trade than are those with a low duty rate. Furthermore, the findings reaffirm the earlier reported role of agency structure and bureaucratic policy output. Holding other potential influences at their mean, the court is 11.4 percent less likely to affirm a decision of the DOC than a decision of the ITC. And as before,

TABLE 10. Determinants of Court of International Trade Deference to Agencies in Antidumping and Countervailing Duty Cases, 1980–90

Variables	Restricted Model (1)			Unrestricted Model (2)		
	MLE	MLE/SE	Impact	MLE	MLE/SE	Impact
Case Factors						
Import Duty	.005**	2.396	.112**	.005**	2.003	.111**
Agency	−.291**	−2.278	−.108**	−.307**	−2.316	−.114**
Nature of the Case	−.158**	−2.117	−.095**	−.205***	−2.561	−.122***
Policy Direction	−.103	−.687	−.034	−.127	−.821	−.042
U.S. Plaintiff	−.028	−.231	−.010	−.015	−.117	−.006
Foreign Plaintiff	−.364	−1.073	−.047	−.309	−.875	−.004
Political Factors						
Political Affiliation	−.133	−1.011	−.045	−.113	−.277	−.038
Judge						
DiCarlo (R)				.196	.817	.056
Restani (I)				−.102	−.416	−.026
Aquilino (I)				−.504*	−1.725	−.095†
Tsoucalas (R)				.020	.074	.004
Musgrave (R)				−.129	−.371	−.018
Watson (D)				−.256	−.700	−.075
Newman (R)				−.252	−.956	−.056
Maletz (D)				−.093	−.207	−.015
Re (D)				.919	1.413	.092
Boe (R)				−.451	−1.312	−.065
Ford (R)				.342	.676	.032
Landis (R)				−.619	−1.252	−.059
Richardson (R)				−.422	−.660	−.028
Constant	1.142***	3.731	—	1.396***	3.661	—
Number of cases	526			526		
−2xlog likelihood	691.56‡			673.5‡		
Correctly predicted	62%			63%		
Reduction in error	6%			11%		

Note: Probability of deference when all variables are held at their mean is .6 for both models. Data for both models include all antidumping and countervailing duty cases appealed from the International Trade Commission and the Department of Commerce. The dependent variable is Court of International Trade decision to affirm agency action (coded 1) or reverse it (coded 0). The Court affirmed bureaucratic action 311 times and reversed (or remanded) 215 times. In both models, Judge Carman was used as the control judge because he is closest to the median in terms of the number of cases presided over. A nested chi-square test shows that the individual judge characteristics are statistically insignificant even at the 10 percent level. Entries are unstandardized probit estimates.

**p ≤ .05 one-tailed test; ***p ≤ .01 one-tailed test; †p ≤ .10 two-tailed test; ‡p ≤ .01 two-tailed test the court does not appear to be treating protectionist cases differently from nonprotectionist ones, as indicated by the insignificance of the policy direction variable. Thus far, examining the interaction between the Court of International Trade and the regulatory agencies in terms of deference, there is no strong evidence that the court is moving trade policy implementation in either a protectionist or nonprotectionist direction. This conclusion is only preliminary. The substantive impact of the court is further examined in the section that considers the interaction in terms of the policy decisions of the court.

Meanwhile, the analysis confirms the argument raised in chapter 6 that the Court of International Trade is less likely to affirm cases that are difficult to reverse than cases for which regulatory decision was predicated upon statutory guidelines or procedures. In other words, cases that challenge regulatory decisions claiming abuse of discretion are less likely to be affirmed than those claiming that regulatory decisions were based upon improper procedure. Presumably, procedures promote fairness and have a salutary effect upon administrative behavior, especially where the decision-making process is deliberative in nature. Even though the Supreme Court has ruled in *Chevron* that courts should accord agencies considerable deference, the Court of International Trade is not extending administrators as much deference as they might expect.

Finally, I use two dummy variables to control for the type of plaintiff.[3] The purpose here is to test whether judges have a proclivity to rule in favor of the administrative agency's decision when the case is brought by a domestic industry. I find that in this particular instance, the type of plaintiff does not matter.

As was stated earlier, the reason for estimating two models in table 10 is to determine whether the cumulative effect of political affiliation of the judges counts in their decision making. My data indicate that when both protectionist and nonprotectionist cases are considered together, political party affiliation of the judges has no significant effect, even when variables for individual judges' characteristics are excluded from consideration. Although numerous studies of judicial decision making have found a causal link between partisanship and judicial decisions, this trend is by no means universal. Party affiliation of Court of International Trade judges is largely orthogonal to judicial deference to administrative agencies' interpretation of the law. The general inference to be drawn from table 10 is that case characteristics—such as the amount of import duty imposed, the structure of the administrative agency from which a case originated, and the nature of the controversy—are more important in explaining Court of International Trade decisions than are political factors such as party affiliation of the judges.[4]

To Protect or Not to Protect at the United States Court of International Trade

I next examine the role of (1) case factors such as import duty, regulatory policy direction, and nature of the case; (2) political factors such as partisanship, concentration ratio (proxy for industry political power), and the international reputation of the country named as the unfair trader in a case; and (3) economic factors such as country-specific trade deficit and industry capital expenditures in judicial protectionism. I do so by consolidating the protectionist and nonprotectionist decisions as the dependent variable and analyzing them jointly to determine the core independent factors conditioning whether the court would award protection or refuse to award protection to American industries allegedly injured or threatened with injury by reason of dumped or subsidized imports.[5] The result, reported in table 11, shows that the data do fit the model well, predicting 63 percent of the cases correctly, with a 21 percent reduction in error for the full model and 13 percent for the restricted model. The full model is more representative of the court, especially in light of the assignment of cases to individual judges as opposed to a panel of judges. So throughout, I shall base my explanation of the determinants of the court's protectionist decisions on the full model.

I tested for the importance of individual judge characteristics in protectionist or free-trade decisions of the Court of International Trade to determine how deeply politics permeates the character of the court. As before, I undertake this test in two ways, first with a dummy variable for political affiliation of all the judges, then with a variable for each judge so as to capture the role of individual characteristics.

Generally speaking, the analysis indicates that political factors are of little predictive value in judicial protectionism. First, among the judges of the court, only one Republican and one Democrat—Newman and Maletz, respectively—differ significantly from the excluded judge, Judge Gregory Carman. Moreover, using a nested chi-square test, we fail to reject the null hypothesis that judge characteristics are unimportant, even at the 40 percent level. Second, the political affiliation of the judges, represented by a dummy variable, fails to reach statistical significance in the full model. So despite much theorizing in the political landscape that Democrats are more protectionist and Republicans more status quo (free-trade) oriented, this widespread belief does not seem to hold when it comes to Court of International Trade judges.[6] Thus, the partisan characteristics of specialized-court judges are not only unimportant in defining the interaction between the judges and administrative agencies, as illustrated in table 10, but they are also largely orthogonal to protectionism, as illustrated in table 11.

TABLE 11. Determinants of Court of International Trade Protectionism in Antidumping and Countervailing Duty Cases, 1980–90

Independent Variables	Restricted Model		Full Model		
	MLE	MLE/SE	MLE	MLE/SE	Impact
Case Factors					
Import Duty	.005**	2.360	.005**	2.172	.114**
Nature of the Case	−.096	−1.281	−.115*	−1.426	−.071*
Policy Direction	.630***	4.051	.624***	3.893	.210***
Agency Structure	−.359***	−2.755	−.352***	−2.613	−.134***
U.S. Plaintiff	−.040	−.310	−.040	−.309	−.015
Foreign Plaintiff	−.055	−.156	−.055	−.156	−.007
Political Factors					
Political Affiliation of Judges	−.269^b	−1.976	.214	.438	.075
Concentrated Ratio	.006**	1.936	.007**	2.095	.098**
Reputation	−.005	−.799	−.004	−.607	−.033
Economic Factors					
Country Trade Deficit	.004	.740	.006	.962	.061
Foreign Penetration	.214	.461	.029	.060	.003
Capital Expenditures	−.00008	−1.291	−.00008	−1.134	−.056
Judge					
DiCarlo (R)			.066	.274	.019
Restani (I)			−.018	−.074	−.005
Aquilino (I)			−.188	−.636	−.037
Tsoucalas (R)			−.057	−.215	−.013
Musgrave (R)			−.148	−.426	−.022
Watson (D)			−.539	−1.130	−.162
Newman (R)			−.437†	−1.660	−.100†
Maletz (D)			−.963†	−1.804	−.162†
Ford (R)			.973	1.605	.085
Landis (R)			−.217	−.443	−.021
Boe (R)			−.315	−.898	−.047
Rao (D)			−.502	−.878	−.065
Constant	.285	.836	.387	.911	—
All Variables at Mean	—	—	—	—	.53
Number of cases	526		526		
−2log likelihood	682.96‡		669.18‡		
Correctly predicted	69%		63%		
Reduction in error	13%		21%		

Note: Dependent variable is Court of International Trade decision favoring regulatory protection (coded 1) or reversing regulatory protection (coded 0). The data include all antidumping and countervailing duty cases appealed to the court from the International Trade Commission and Department of Commerce. In both models, the court affirmed protectionist decisions 53 percent of the time ($N = 278$) and reversed or remanded protectionist decisions 47 percent of the time ($N = 248$). Entries are unstandardized probit estimates.

*$p \leq .10$ one-tailed test; **$p \leq .05$ one-tailed; ***$p \leq .01$ one-tailed; †$p \leq .10$ two-tailed; ‡$p \leq .05$ two-tailed.

On the basis of the discussion of clientelism given by Lawrence Baum (1977) and Martin Shapiro (1968), I hypothesized that because of their expertise, specialized judges may be influenced by external political pressures through legal advocacy or case selection in their decision to grant or deny protection to industries. This hypothesis is supported here. Concentrated industries, which are assumed to command formidable political resources, are more likely to be successful in pressuring the court to rule in their favor than smaller, less-concentrated ones.

Concentrated industries are those that possess organizational advantages. They have the capacity to control the free-rider problem (Grier, Munger, and Roberts 1994), possess the resources necessary to hire superior legal representation and to undertake the huge expense of $150,000 to $550,000 necessary to successfully pursue an antidumping remedy, for example, plus the $50,000 to $85,000 it costs on average to pursue litigation at the Court of International Trade.[7] The impact of concentration ratio is moderately strong and significant. Highly concentrated industries, as defined at the four-digit Standard Industrial Classification (SIC) level, have a 9.8 percent higher probability than less-concentrated industries of being able to convince the court to rule in their favor. The implication of this finding is that while smaller U.S. firms that ordinarily have smaller financial and organizational resources may be provided limited technical and legal assistance with their agency petition through the Trade Remedy Assistance Center (TRAC) of the ITC, they are still at a great disadvantage in terms of their ability to successfully appeal their cases to court and win.

Given that international trade is first and foremost an economic issue, I controlled for the role of case-specific economic circumstances on trade court decisions, using as indicators the U.S. trade deficit with the foreign country named in a given case, the penetration of foreign imports into the United States, and the petitioning U.S. industry's capital expenditures. Yet none of these variables was significant in explaining whether the court is more likely to make a protectionist decision. This finding, however, does provide strong support for the theoretical argument that lower federal courts, such as the Court of International Trade, base their decisions less on extralegal factors and more on case-specific factors and the law.

Judges' reliance on case-specific factors and the law forms the hallmark of judicial decision making at the trial court level. On this basis, I examined the importance of case-specific factors such as the amount of import duty, the nature of the controversy, the structure of the administrative agency, the direction of administrative agency policy decision, and the type of plaintiff in the case. In comparative terms, case factors perform better than political or economic factors. But more specifically, a most notable finding here is the performance of the policy direction variable, which shows strong evidence that the Court of International Trade has a protectionist rather than a free-trade bent in deciding antidumping and countervailing duty cases.

In general, when all other variables are held constant at their mean, the Court of International Trade is more likely to rule in favor of protection if the import duty imposed by the bureaucracy is high rather than low and if the bureaucracy rules in favor of protection for the domestic industry. The court is less likely to protect domestic industries if the controversy originated from the DOC rather than from the ITC, however. This finding confirms my previously reported finding that the court treats the two administrative agencies differently, presumably because of differences in their institutional structure.

Finally, when all the variables in the model are held constant at their mean, there is a 53 percent cumulative probability that the court will rule in favor of protectionism over free trade. While this finding is not suggestive of a zealous court imposing its own will to force dramatic shifts in American trade policy, it does suggest a propensity toward protectionism rather than toward free trade. This conclusion is further supported by the bivariate analysis of court-agency decisional congruence in table 12, showing a higher percentage of protectionist decisions than nonprotectionist ones, and by the analysis of policy outcomes of individual judges' decisions in table 13, showing that more often than not, a majority of the judges render protectionist rather than nonprotectionist decisions.

Agency-Specific Analysis in the Dynamics of Judicial Protectionism

One of the consistent findings throughout the probit results discussed thus far is that the Court of International Trade accords different administrative agencies distinct treatment. But more needs to be said about the decisional patterns of the Court of International Trade with regard to these agencies. For example, given that the two agencies follow distinct decisional processes and make different types of economic analyses, are there detectable patterns concerning which factual, political, or economic conditions the court considers important when reviewing cases from these agencies? To address this question, I separated all the cases according to the agency from which the controversy originated and analyzed these cases separately to see if there are any factors that are particularly important when the court reviews cases from each agency. Once again, the dependent variable is coded 1 if the Court of International Trade rules in a protectionist direction and 0 if the court rules in a nonprotectionist direction. Given that the two agencies have different decision-making strategies and

TABLE 12. International Trade Policy Congruence between Court of International Trade and Administrative Agencies, 1980–90

Court Policy Direction[a]	Agency Policy Direction		
	Protectionist	Nonprotectionist	Total
Protectionist	237 (58%)	94 (41%)	331 (52%)
Nonprotectionist	174 (42%)	134 (59%)	308 (48%)
Total	411 (100%)	228 (100%)	639 (100%)

Note: Data include administered protection cases, for example, antidumping (section 731) and countervailing duty (section 701) cases, appealed to the Court of International Trade from the International Trade Commission and the Department of Commerce.

[a]A chi-square test of the relationshihp between court and agency policy decisions shows that the court is significantly more likely to agree than disagree with agency policy decision; $\chi^2_{(1\,d.f.)} = 15.87$ ($p \leq .001$).

TABLE 13. Trade Policy Outcomes of Court of International Trade Judges' Decisions in Antidumping and Countervailing Duty Cases

Judge	Cases	Protectionist Outcome	Non-protectionist Outcome	Majority of Decisions[a]
DiCarlo (R)	93	55 (59%)	38 (41%)	P**
Carman (R)	56	30 (53%)	26 (47%)	P**
Restani (I)	113	62 (55%)	51 (45%)	P**
Aquilino (I)	37	18 (48%)	19 (52%)	NP**
Tsoucalas (R)	53	31 (58%)	22 (42%)	P**
Musgrave (R)	23	14 (61%)	9 (39%)	P**
Watson (D)	101	46 (45%)	55 (55%)	NP**
Newman (R)	49	20 (41%)	29 (59%)	NP**
Maletz (D)	32	9 (28%)	23 (62%)	NP**
Re (D)	11	6 (55%)	5 (45%)	P**
Boe (R)	20	9 (45%)	11 (55%)	NP**
Ford (R)	10	8 (80%)	2 (20%)	P**
Landis (R)	11	5 (45%)	6 (55%)	NP**
Rao (D)	20	11 (55%)	9 (45%)	P**
Richardson (R)	5	4 (80%)	1 (20%)	P**
3-judge panel	4	2 (50%)	2 (50%)	NP[ns]
Court	638	330 (52%)	308 (48%)	P**

Note: Entries are based on antidumping and countervailing duty cases only. A decision is considered protectionist if a judge affirms a protectionist agency decision or reverses a nonprotectionist agency decision.

[a]P = majority protectionist outcome; NP = majority nonprotectionist outcome

**$p \leq .01$ (confidence interval test for proportions)

functions, it would be interesting to see if these differences manifest themselves in the court's decisional trends and whether my previous conclusion, that contextual case factors are most important, continues to hold up. To accomplish this examination, I use the same independent measures listed in table 11 to examine ITC cases separately from DOC cases.

The outcome of the analysis performed on cases from the ITC is reported in table 14. Here the model does very well in predicting protectionist decisions of the court, showing that 76 percent of the cases are predicted correctly, with a full 46 percent reduction in error.

This model showcases the importance of economic factors in ITC decisions as well as in decisions of the Court of International Trade. As pointed out in chapter 3, trade statutes contain elaborate economic standards to which the Commission must adhere when conducting its investigations. As a tangential matter, the data provide evidence that the ITC does rely on the economic guidelines mandated in the statutes for its decisions. Independent support for this inference is offered by Anderson (1993), who found that statutory guidelines are more important than bureaucratic discretion in ITC decisions, although he agrees that discretion does play a large role.

The analysis here clearly shows that economic conditions also play a crucial role in Court of International Trade decisions to protect U.S. industries against unfair foreign trade practices. The court is more likely to rule in favor of protection for U.S. industries in cases where there is a high foreign import penetration but less likely to do so for firms or industries with higher capital expenditures, presumably because such expenditures are a sign of sound economic health in the industry. The U.S. trade deficit with the country named as the unfair trader evinces no statistically significant impact. Here political variables also show a small-to-moderate impact on court decisions. For example, industry concentration ratio is significant, suggesting that specialized-court judges do respond to good legal advocacy, case preparation, and case selection. Plaintiffs from highly concentrated industries—those that possess strong political power and organizational advantages—are better able to persuade judges to rule in their favor, holding other factors constant at their mean. This finding is consistent with much of the empirical literature on the effectiveness of interest-group activity in the political process. In a slightly different vein, the dummy variable representing political affiliation of the judges is not significant, although a nested chi-square test of the model with and without individual judges does show that the effect of the individual judges combined is significant at the .01 level.

Finally, among the case factors for which I controlled was the type of plaintiff involved in the case, whether foreign or domestic. For cases orig-

TABLE 14. Court of International Trade Review of International Trade Commission Decisions, 1980–90

Independent Variables	Restricted Model		Full Model		
	MLE	MLE/SE	MLE	MLE/SE	Impact
Case Factors					
Import Duty	.021**	2.423	.032***	2.915	.614***
Nature of the Case	−.168	−1.236	−.046	−.276	−.027
Policy Direction	.871***	3.346	1.146***	3.459	.393***
U.S. Plaintiff	.244	.961	.750**	2.260	.245**
Foreign Plaintiff	−.478	−.722	.022	.029	.003
Political Factors					
Political Affiliations of Judges	−.370	−1.589	−.241	−.256	−.083
Concentration Ratio	.014**	2.425	.019***	2.550	.249***
Reputation	−.016	−1.148	−.004	−.027	−.003
Economic Factors					
Country Trade Deficits	−.005	−.406	.006	.454	.057
Foreign Penetration	1.019	1.080	2.324**	2.042	.195**
Capital Expenditures	−.0003***	−2.597	−.0004***	−2.498	−.252***
Judge					
DiCarlo (R)			.238	.517	.058
Restani (I)			.515	.853	.086
Aquilino (I)			5.212	.214	.623
Tsoucalas (R)			−.969†	−1.711	−.211†
Musgrave (R)			.603	.731	.069
Watson (D)			−.114	−.129	−.036
Newman (R)			−.419	−.844	−.096
Maletz (D)			−3.816	−.107	−.418
Ford (R)			5.001	.125	.426
Landis (R)			.904	1.138	.092
Boe (R)			1.137	1.620	.142
Rao (D)			.593	.904	.080
Constant	−.546	−1.043	−1.988**	2.459	—
All variables at their mean	—	—	—	—	.77
Number of cases	191		191		
−2xlog likelihood	208.82‡		181.29‡		
Correctly predicted	69%		76%		
Reduction in error	29%		46%		

Note: Dependent variable is Court of International Trade decision favoring regulatory protection (coded 1) or reversing regulatory protection (coded 0). The data include all antidumping and countervailing duty cases appealed to the court from the International Trade Commission. In both models, the court affirmed protectionist decisions 55 percent of the time ($N = 106$) and reversed or remanded protectionist decisions 45 percent of the time ($N = 85$). Entries are unstandardized probit estimates.

**p ≤ .05 one-tailed test; ***p ≤ .01 one-tailed test; †p ≤ .10 two-tailed test; ‡p ≤ .01 two-tailed test inating from the ITC, it matters significantly whether the plaintiff is a U.S. firm or a foreign firm. The court is more likely to provide protection if the plaintiff is strictly an American firm rather than a domestic firm and a foreign firm combined. The appeals in which an import-competing domestic firm is the sole plaintiff are those in which regulators have found insufficient evidence to warrant regulatory protection for the domestic industry. Note that by law, a firm is representing its entire industry when it petitions for regulatory protection with federal agencies. It appears that in court such import-competing U.S. plaintiffs are able, more often than not, to gain the sympathies of judges regarding the difficulties facing their industry, such as layoffs, unemployment, and declining performance ratios, and the likelihood that such difficulties will be exacerbated because of failure to win regulatory protection from the government. When all the variables are held at their mean, the cumulative odds are considerably high (77 percent) that the court will rule in favor of protection for the domestic industry.

I now turn to appeals from the DOC. In table 15, I model Court of International Trade decisions in cases originating from the DOC. The results are less impressive than those reported for the ITC model. Although the model is plausible, predicting 62 percent of the cases correctly with a 29 percent reduction in error, only two case factors—the nature of the controversy and the policy decision of the bureaucracy—are important in the court's decisions. The fact that the policy direction of the agency is positive and significant suggests that the court has a protectionist inclination toward cases appealed from the DOC.

Conclusion

The results of the analysis reported in this chapter suggest a number of conclusions. Specialized courts are thought historically to serve only policy-neutral objectives. But this analysis suggests that the Court of International Trade, which is a specialized court, does have nonneutral substantive impact on U.S. foreign trade policy. As government becomes increasingly specialized, the reality we face is that modern bureaucratic experts are clearly exerting increasing influence on public policy. Oftentimes political leaders are passive in controlling bureaucratic behavior and in enforcing the bureaucratic contract. As Landes and Posner (1975) pointed out in discussing the usefulness of an independent judiciary in the legislative realm, it is up to the courts to ensure that the power and discretion of bureaucrats is exercised in accordance with guidelines mandated in the statute. Because of the complexity of certain public policies and because of the intractability of administrative discretion, the usefulness of

TABLE 15. **Court of International Trade Review of Department of Commerce Decisions, 1980–90**

Independent Variables	Restricted Model		Full Model		
	MLE	MLE/SE	MLE	MLE/SE	Impact
Case Factors					
Import Duty	.002	.327	.0009	.327	.020
Nature of the Case	−.147*	−1.432	−.175**	−1.715	−.104**
Policy Direction	.418*	1.902	.544**	2.283	.142**
U.S. Plaintiff	−.158	−1.085	−.147	−.957	−.058
Foreign Plaintiff	−.079	−.191	.069	.159	.009
Political Factors					
Political Affiliations of Judges	−.286	1.611	.253	.406	−.083
Concentration Ratio	.003	.800	.001	.310	.013
Reputation	−.002	−.280	−.003	−.419	−.025
Economic Factors					
Country Trade Deficits	.008	1.192	.008	1.086	.077
Foreign Penetration	−.028	−.049	−.238	−.400	−.025
Capital Expenditures	.00003	.403	.00008	.912	.055
Judge					
DiCarlo (R)			.081	.256	.025
Restani (I)			−.201	−.630	−.058
Aquilino (I)			−.739‡	−2.015	−.156‡
Tsoucalas (R)			−.043	−.122	−.010
Musgrave (R)			−.426	−1.020	−.067
Watson (D)			−.764	−1.258	−.193
Newman (R)			−.600	−1.617	−.127
Maletz (D)			−.986	−1.517	−.183
Ford (R)			.540	.781	.051
Landis (R)			−.532	−.782	−.046
Boe (R)			−.786†	−1.775	−.120†
Rao (D)			−.921	−1.227	−.104
Constant	.024	.064	.325	.633	—
All variables on average	—	—	—	—	.46
Number of cases	335		335		
−2xlog likelihood	449.8‡		443.16‡		
Correctly predicted	58%		62%		
Reduction in error	17%		29%		

Note: Dependent variable is Court of International Trade decision in favor of regulatory protection (coded 1) or in opposition to regulatory protection (coded 0). The data include all antidumping and countervailing duty cases appealed to the court from the Department of Commerce. The court affirmed protectionist decisions 51 percent of the time ($N = 172$) and reversed or remanded protectionist decisions 49 percent of the time ($N = 163$). Entries are unstandardized probit estimates.

*$p \leq .10$ one-tailed test; **$p \leq .05$ one-tailed test; ***$p \leq .01$ one-tailed test; †$p \leq .10$ two-tailed test; ‡$p \leq .05$ or better two-tailed test

having judges who are themselves experts in complex policies is increasingly being recognized as a means to "tame" bureaucratic behavior. This expertise is exemplified by the judges of the Court of International Trade in New York City in their ability to review and consequently reverse a high proportion of complex implementation decisions of the DOC and ITC.

The Court of International Trade shows a propensity toward protectionism. The court seems to be more restrained than activist, however, in that between 1980 and 1990, the court has avoided prescriptive policy-making. A most exciting and indeed most consistent finding is that even though there are no dramatic shifts in substantive trade policy brought on by the court, there is unmistakable evidence in the court's decisional trends that it does have an impact on the behavior of the regulatory agencies, especially the DOC, whose decisions the court reverses more frequently than decisions of the more politically insulated ITC. This finding underscores the importance of politics and institutional structure in defining the outlook of a bureaucracy and its interaction with external actors.

In almost all the models estimated, I consistently find that case-specific legal or factual attributes constitute the core determinants of specialized trial court decisions. This conclusion supports the findings of others, such as Johnson (1987a) and Carp and Rowland (1983), who examined trial courts that have a more generalist orientation. Overall, political factors do not significantly and consistently explain Court of International Trade decisions. Only by isolating the cases according to agency type do we find the cumulative effect of individual judge characteristics making an important imprint on court decisions. Although industry political power does make a strong showing in several of the models, it does not exert a consistent and overpowering impact throughout the analysis. The conclusion as far as the impact of politics is concerned is that, generally speaking, judges do respond, albeit modestly, to litigant pressure when making protectionist or free-trade judgments.

Mine is one of the first systematic analyses of judicial behavior in which the political characteristics of judges do not play a decisive role in explaining how judges reach their decisions. This outcome can be attributed to the *expertise* of the judges of the specialty court here analyzed. These judges base their decisions more on their commanding knowledge of the case facts and of agency practices than on extralegal or political concerns. Although economic factors do play an important role in court decisions, this role is limited to legal controversies emanating from the ITC, largely because the Commission relies heavily on economic analysis for its decisions.

CHAPTER 8

The Specialized Courts of Appeals and the Politics of Protectionism

This chapter presents the second set of empirical results of the hypotheses posed in chapter 5 and refined in chapter 6. The analysis reported here is similar in many ways to the discussion given in chapter 7 concerning the analysis of trial court review of ITC and DOC actions; however, the focus is on the interaction between the Court of Appeals for the Federal Circuit and these agencies. In this introductory section, I want to highlight some of the key findings of the analysis. The work reported here shows unmistakably that appeals courts draw a distinction between different types of federal regulatory agencies and respond to grievances from these agencies accordingly. For example, the specialized Federal Circuit court affirms a significantly greater proportion of cases challenging ITC actions than those challenging DOC actions, perhaps due to institutional differences between the two agencies.

Furthermore, the Federal Circuit defers a great deal to agency interpretation of statutes. This result goes against the theoretical expectation for a specialized appellate court, suggesting that the Federal Circuit is best characterized as a semispecialized appellate court. The highly deferential behavior of the Federal Circuit may suggest, on the surface, that the court is not exerting noteworthy policy impact on American trade policy. But upon controlling for agency policy direction, I find that the Federal Circuit *does* in fact have far more than policy-neutral effects on American public policy.

Finally, I model the voting behavior of the judges of the court to determine the core factors conditioning judicial protectionism, the situation whereby Federal Circuit decisions lead to the imposition of numerical tariffs or quotas meant to assist American industries or firms that are suffering due to unfair foreign trade practices. Here, I find that political factors such as the political power or organizational ability of industries and case-specific factors such as the direction of the bureaucratic policy decision are more important than economic factors such as foreign import penetration and country-specific trade deficit in determining whether the Federal Circuit will uphold protection for an American industry or firm.

Judicial Deference in Generalist vs. Specialized Appellate Courts

The starting point of analysis for the specialized courts of appeals is an examination of the extent of judicial deference demonstrated by the Federal Circuit to the administrative agencies that implement trade policy. Generally speaking, judicial deference serves as a barometer of the extent to which courts are independently exercising an active check on bureaucratic power or discretion. Given that, it is imperative that any serious analysis of courts of appeals' review of agency actions include an examination of the deferential trends that exist in these courts. As pointed out in chapter 7, judicial deference implies interagreement between two or more decision-making systems, for example, between a specialized court and a bureaucratic agency. And, throughout this work, a deferential situation has been viewed as one in which a court agrees with the decisional choice of an agency. To conduct a fully meaningful analysis of deference, however, it is not sufficient simply to analyze specialized court deference to agencies without providing a reasonable basis for comparison.

I provided such a comparison by analyzing deference in a number of judicial settings. First, I compared the level of judicial deference between the U.S. Supreme Court (the quintessential generalist court) and the Federal Circuit (a specialized appellate court). Then I compared deference across the Federal Circuit and the District of Columbia Circuit, a generalist court recognized as the dominant litigation venue for federal regulatory agencies (Howard 1981; Melnick 1983). These comparisons allow us to observe any broad decisional trend that may exist in generalist and specialized appellate courts. Table 16 reports the rates of judicial deference among appellate courts. It is shown that the Supreme Court defers to bureaucratic agencies 72 percent of the time and disagrees 28 percent of the time. The Federal Circuit has a similar, though slightly higher, rate of deference to administrative agencies (76 percent). Statistically speaking, there is no difference in the rates of deference between the Supreme Court and the Federal Circuit. Thus we see here that the Federal Circuit is not disciplining the ITC and DOC through high rates of reversal, as might be expected of a specialized appellate court.

Let us consider now the rates of deference across the circuit courts of appeals. My analysis shows that the specialized Federal Circuit court is considerably more deferential to regulators (76 percent) than is the D.C. Circuit (66 percent). Of course there are some noteworthy differences in the data, which may help place this finding in perspective. In David Willison's 1986 study from which I extracted the D.C. Circuit data, a wide variety of regulatory agencies and policy areas were involved, including the Federal Communications Commission (FCC), Federal Energy Regulatory Commission (FERC), Interstate Commerce Commission (ICC), National Labor Relations Board (NLRB), and Environmental Protection Agency (EPA), whereas my Federal Circuit data involved only the ITC and DOC and only the area of trade policy. Although the D.C. and Federal Circuit courts are situated on the same judicial level, these differences in jurisdiction between the courts may help explain their decisional trends about deference.

I argued in chapter 5 that specialized court judges are repositories of knowledge about the law and about the substantive policy area(s) in which their court has jurisdiction. Based upon this argument, I hypothesized that specialized-court judges are likely to delve more deeply into the substance of bureaucratic choices and therefore less likely to defer to bureaucrats than are generalist judges. This hypothesis and its predicate sound logical enough. In the previous chapter, the hypothesis was confirmed for the U.S. Court of International Trade. It is not confirmed here, however. In fact, the opposite prediction is supported ($p < .05$). Before discussing the possible reasons for this antithetic outcome, it should be noted first that the high rate of deference found for the Federal

TABLE 16.   Judicial Deference in Generalist vs. Specialized Appellate Courts

	Generalist		Specialized
Court Decision[a]	United States Supreme Court (1980–90)[b]	Court of Appeals for the D.C. Circuit (1981–84)[c]	Court of Appeals for the Federal Circuit (1980–90)
Reverse Agency	95 (28%)	174 (34%)	26 (24%)
Affirm Agency	245 (72%)	337 (66%)	83 (76%)
Total	340 (100%)	511 (100%)	109 (100%)

Note: Data for the U.S. Supreme Court were extracted from the U.S. Supreme Court Judicial Database, 1991, ICPSR no. 9422, compiled by Harold J. Spaeth. Data for the District of Columbia Circuit were extracted from Willison 1986, table 2. Data for the Federal Circuit refer to all cases appealed from the International Trade Commission and Department of Commerce and are published in the U.S. Court of Appeals for the Federal Circuit Reports. These data were compiled by the author. Data for both circuit courts include published unanimous and nonunanimous decisions.

[a]The number of cases that are reversed or affirmed by the different courts varies by agency.

[b]The difference in the reverse and affirm rates between the Supreme Court and the Federal Circuit is only 4 percent. Using a difference-in-proportions test, this difference is not statistically significant.

[c]The difference in the reverse and affirm rates between the D.C. Circuit and the Federal Circuit is 10 percent. Using a difference-in-proportions test, this difference is significant at the .05 level.

Circuit does hold informational value. It lends empirical support to the conclusion reached by some practitioners, such as Charlene Barshefsky and Michael J. Firth (1988, 1206), who analyzed the 1988 trade decisions of the Federal Circuit, and Perla M. Kuhn (1986, 1096), who analyzed the 1985 trade decisions of the court. In both studies, these practitioners found that the Federal Circuit showed a proclivity toward deference to the regulators charged with administering the trade laws, but especially to the Court of International Trade.

There are several plausible explanations for why the Federal Circuit is so deferential to regulatory agencies. The most plausible explanation is that judges of this court recognize trade as an area that requires expertise; they further recognize that they are simply not as specialized as are bureaucrats in the ITC and DOC who implement U.S. trade policy. Recall that Congress did not intend the Federal Circuit to be a highly specialized court, as evidenced by the court's multiple subject matter jurisdiction. Because the Federal Circuit is not highly specialized, judges think it logical to defer to the expertise of the trade administrators.

A second explanation is that the Federal Circuit's tendency to defer to regulators may be due to organizational life-cycle effects (Porter 1985; Unah 1995). The court is, after all, quite young, having been elevated to the circuit level and assigned an expanded jurisdiction only in 1982. Partly for this reason, the Federal Circuit lacks a strong body of legal precedent from the Supreme Court in international trade matters from which to draw. This reality makes it difficult for judges of the court to overcome the uncertainty usually associated with any newly created and evolving organization trying to define itself in a complex and indeed unfriendly political environment.

Unlike social policy areas, such as individual civil liberties and civil rights, or economic policy areas, such as antitrust and securities regulation, where the Supreme Court has maintained a forceful and an active national voice, the Court has been reluctant to review international trade, even cases under the popular antidumping and countervailing duty laws. For example, I requested and obtained from the clerk of the Federal Circuit data on the court's trade decisions that were appealed to the Supreme Court. From 1983 to January 1995, there were 37 international trade cases involving antidumping, countervailing duty, and unfair practices in import trade that were appealed to the Supreme Court. All were denied certiorari by the High Court.[1] Thus, it seems that partly because of the dearth of legal guidance and authority from the nation's highest tribunal, there may be a certain level of reluctance on the part of Federal Circuit judges as a group to be activist. And the Supreme Court is giving silent approbation to the Federal Circuit's practice, which is to approve a high proportion of agency actions instead of imposing greater discipline on the agencies by reversing their decisions.

There is another aspect to this explanation, and it deals with institutional integrity of the Federal Circuit. Because the Federal Circuit was created during a period of much controversy over the virtues and vices of judicial specialization, the judges are mindful of safeguarding the institutional integrity of their court. The high rate of deference to agencies is a sign that Federal Circuit judges are proceeding cautiously (some would say too much so) in exercising their responsibility, perhaps because they are leery of rejuvenating the long-standing political criticisms of specialized courts that such courts are afflicted with tunnel vision, clientelism, capture by advocacy coalitions, and juristic decadence (see Bruff 1991; Shapiro 1968; Posner 1983).

Another possible explanation of the deferential tendencies of the Federal Circuit is that the court is responding positively to the interest of the federal government, which, generally speaking, is to protect American firms and industries from unfair trading practices of foreign firms. Under this interpretation, federal agencies are actively complying with the court's rulings, which in turn obviates the need to discipline agencies through frequent reversal of their decisions.

Bureaucratic Politics and Judicial Review: ITC vs. DOC in the Specialized Court of Appeals

To what extent does the Federal Circuit respond differently to the two administrative agencies charged with implementing American trade laws? Just because the court exhibits a deferential tendency toward the administrative agencies does not mean that there is no variation in how well the court is checking the practices of each agency. To address this possibility, I probe how the agencies have fared when they had their day in court. Table 17 reports bivariate analysis of Federal Circuit support for the regulatory agencies (panel A), controlling for policy direction (panels B and C).

Several notable findings emerge. First, the controls for policy direction provide preliminary evidence that the Federal Circuit does exhibit a strong favorable tendency toward protectionism as opposed to free trade. As we shall see in the subsequent discussion of the determinants of judicial protectionism, this finding is later corroborated through multivariate analysis, using antidumping and countervailing duty cases. Second, and perhaps most important from the perspective of institutional analysis, there is a striking difference in the manner that the Federal Circuit responds to cases appealed from the ITC compared to those appealed from the DOC. In other words, the type of agency from which court cases

TABLE 17. Bivariate Analysis of Specialized Court of Appeals Support for Administrative Agencies, Controlling for Policy Direction

Court Decision	(A) Administrative Agency[a]			(B) Protectionist Policy[b]			(C) Nonprotectionist Policy[c]		
	International Trade Commission	Dept. of Commerce	Total	International Trade Commission	Dept. of Commerce	Total	International Trade Commission	Dept. of Commerce	Total
Favorable	49 (84%)	34 (67%)	83 (76%)	26 (90%)	22 (65%)	48 (76%)	18 (78%)	9 (69%)	27 (78%)
Unfavorable	9 (16%)	17 (33%)	26 (24%)	3 (10%)	12 (35%)	15 (24%)	5 (22%)	4 (31%)	9 (22%)
Total	58 (100%)	51 (100%)	109 (100%)	29 (100%)	34 (100%)	63 (100%)	23 (100%)	13 (100%)	36 (100%)

Note: Data are administered protection cases, including antidumping (section 731), countervailing duty (section 701), and unfair practices in import trade (section 337), decided by published opinion by the Court of Appeals for the Federal Circuit, 1980–90.

[a] A chi-square test with 1 degree of freedom was conducted to assess agency success rate at the Federal Circuit. The court is significantly more likely to support decisions of the International Trade Commission than those of the Department of Commerce: $\chi^2_{(1\,d.f.)} = 4.74$ ($p \leq .05$).

[b] A chi-square test with 1 degree of freedom was conducted to determine Federal Circuit support for administrative agencies when their regulatory decision is protectionist. The Federal Circuit gives significantly strong support to these agencies when their decision is protectionist: $\chi^2_{(1\,d.f.)} = 5.37$ ($p \leq .02$).

[c] A chi-square test with 1 degree of freedom was conducted to determine Federal Circuit support for administrative agencies when the policy is nonprotectionist. However, the Federal Circuit support for agencies is weak when the policy these agencies announce is nonprotectionist: $\chi^2_{(1\,d.f.)} = 3.61$ (n.s.).

originate matters. The ITC performs considerably better in court, winning 84 percent of its cases, while the DOC claims victory in only 67 percent of its cases. The 17 percent difference in the rates of success is statistically significant ($p \leq .05$). Although past research has suggested that the ITC does respond to external political pressure (Hansen 1990; Moore 1992), as does the DOC (Hansen and Park 1995), it appears that the Commission is generally more resistant to outside political pressures, more likely to make decisions on the basis of statutory directives (Anderson 1993), and therefore relatively less likely to be overruled on appeal than is the DOC.

Structural differences between the ITC and DOC may be partly responsible for their relatively skewed success rates in the Federal Circuit. As a bipartisan, quasi-judicial body of experts, the ITC makes decisions on a majority-rule basis through collegial deliberation, and its decisions need not be consensual. Indeed, it is not unusual for the commissioners to express strong disagreements with each other over investigative standards and over the meaning of the statutory scheme (Kaplan 1991, 143). Although the ITC is bipartisan, it is not necessarily the case that the commissioners are apolitical. Indeed, the policy disagreements observed in the ITC often reflect ideological differences among the commissioners in terms of their individual views toward trade, for example, promoting industries and safeguarding good jobs by awarding industries the protection they seek or encouraging competition and safeguarding the interest of consumers by refusing to award industries the protection they seek. Ben Wildavsky, who examined recent policy and interpersonal disagreements among ITC commissioners, characterizes these disagreements as "a microcosm of the fierce passions and political maneuvering that the nation's often arcane unfair-trading laws stir up (1995, 2637).

The benefit of such disagreements, though, is that the agency's deliberative decisional strategy lends itself to statutory interpretation that is less arbitrary and less political than may be found in an executive-level agency such as the DOC, which has only one agency head. Consequently, the ITC is more likely to make policy choices that are consistent with legal precedents set by the Federal Circuit than is the DOC, whose single agency head can be easily controlled and manipulated by the president and Congress.

In addition, the adversarial procedure used by the ITC allows the agency to develop a more comprehensive administrative record, which holds functional as well as symbolic value. Not only does a more complete record reduce the informational costs associated with judicial review, it also lessens the Federal Circuit's reliance upon its relative expertise. As Hansen, Johnson, and Unah (1995) have shown, specialized-court judges who rely on their expertise for their decisions tend to take a more discriminating look at agency performance than do generalist judges and to show little deference to these agencies. This finding suggests that because the DOC's administrative record is less detailed, the Federal Circuit, more often than not, is relying upon its relative expertise to examine and conse- quently to reverse the DOC's decisions.

Determinants of Specialized Court of Appeals Deference to Administrative Agencies in International Trade

Table 18 reports the outcome of three econometric models estimated to determine the core variables that condition specialized courts of appeals support for administrative agencies in antidumping and countervailing duty cases. These cases were chosen because (1) the laws governing them are extremely popular with domestic petitioners seeking relief from the federal government; (2) these laws are of a highly politicized nature from the standpoint of petitioners (Hansen and Prusa 1993a; cf. Goldstein 1993, 197); and (3) these laws give greater power to the bureaucracy than to the president, which makes judicial review all the more important and neces- sary.

I estimated three separate models in table 18 to allow us to reexamine the independent impact of regulatory policy outcome and of the structure (i.e., type) of the administrative agency on appeals courts' decisions. Doing so also permits us to compare the relative importance of case fac- tors—such as the nature of the controversy, import duty, and the structure of the agency—against economic and political factors—such as partisan- ship, country trade deficit, and foreign import penetration. The dependent variable is the Federal Circuit decision to affirm (coded 1) or reverse (coded 0) a regulatory agency's action. The models were estimated via logit. However, because of a small sample size and a skewed dependent variable, the models were also estimated using weighted least squares (WLS) to check the consistency of the findings (see table D1 in appendix D).[2]

As hypothesized in chapter 6, the full model performs better than either the contextual fact model alone or the politics-and-economics model alone (see table 18). The full model predicted 85 percent of the cases correctly, with an impressive 50 percent reduction in error. The Akaike's Information Criterion (AIC) for comparing regression models also indi- cates that the full model best explains court decisions. Note that a smaller AIC is better (see Amemiya 1980).[3]

The nature of the case, which Judge Bennett (1991, 330) suggests is typically the focus of review at the Federal Circuit, has an intercoder agreement ratio of 61 percent. This ratio is moderately strong and signals that the analysis can be successfully replicated. I find that, holding other potential influences constant at their mean, if a case challenges regulators' discretion-based interpretation of the statute, there is a 36.3 percent higher probability that the Federal Circuit will affirm rather than reverse the agency interpretation.

The results reaffirm the earlier reported finding of the importance of agency structure and regulatory policy outcome in the decision making of specialized appeals courts. Agency structure, viewed as those conditions that define an agency—such as its decisional style and the extent of its

TABLE 18. Determinants of Specialized Court of Appeals Deference to Administrative Agencies in Antidumping and Countervailing Duty Cases, 1980–90

Independent Variable	Contextual Fact Model (1)		Politics and Economics Model (2)		General Model (3)		
	MLE	MLE/SE	MLE	MLE/SE	MLE	MLE/SE	Impact
Case Factors							
Nature of the Case[a]	.739	1.781*			1.772	2.523**	.363**
Import Duty	.023	1.095			.099	2.208**	.512**
Agency Structure	−2.270	−2.441**			−3.991	−2.806**	−.486**
Policy Direction	.581	.729			.274	.266	.031
Political Factors							
Political Affiliation of Panel Majority[b]			−1.239	−1.746*	−1.993	−1.744*	−.249*
Concentration Ratio			−.003	−.227	.010	.404	.049
Economic Factors							
Country Trade Deficit			.059	1.150	.151	2.415**	.406
Foreign penetration			.736	.221	4.644	.972	.150
Constant	2.395	1.42	1.841	1.707*	3.664	1.017	—
−2xlog likelihood	56***	61***	43***				
Correctly predicted	77%	71%	85%				
AIC	60.45	65	50.56				
Reduction in error	18.74%	—	50%				

Note: Entries are unstandardized logit estimates. The number of cases for the models is 57, 56, and 55, respectively. The dependent variable is Court of Appeals for the Federal Circuit decision to affirm a bureaucratic agency decision (coded 1) or reverse it (coded 0). Data include antidumping and countervailing duty cases appealed to the court from the International Trade Commission and the Department of Commerce. The court affirmed 71 percent of the cases and reverse 29 percent.

[a]Intercoder agreement = .61.
[b]Odd number of circuit judges in a panel is typically three or higher.
*$p \leq .10$ one-tailed test; **$p \leq .05$ one-tailed test; ***$p \leq .01$ two-tailed test

political independence—is a powerful indicator of court support for agencies. Judges of the Federal Circuit are significantly less likely to agree with regulatory decisions of the DOC than those of the ITC for reasons that I believe stem from differences in institutional arrangements (e.g., differences in the level of autonomy and in decision-making styles) between the agencies and from differences in their responsiveness to external political influence.

I tested whether judicial deference is related to regulatory policy, but regulatory policy fails to reach statistical significance here. The analysis also shows that, controlling for other decisional factors, a high import duty significantly improves the chances that the Federal Circuit will agree with the final decision reached by regulators in the bureaucracy, controlling for other decisional trends. These findings are consistent with the findings of others who conclude that case characteristics play a strong role in the decision making of circuit courts of appeals (Johnson 1987a; Songer, Segal, and Cameron 1994; Songer and Haire 1992). Despite the norm that appellate judges take case characteristics as given to apply the law, appeals court judges do base their rulings on the characteristics of the cases themselves.

Because of the economic nature of trade cases, I tested for the effects of industry economic performance on appellate court deference, using annual capital expenditures as an indicator of industry health. The variable was consistently insignificant and so was excluded from the reported analysis after I determined that expenditures were uncorrelated with other determinants of court decisions. As evidence that the specialized court of appeals does respond to case-specific economic circumstances, however, I find that when the United States holds a high trade deficit with a country named as an unfair trader in a lawsuit, judges of the Federal Circuit are 40.6 percent more likely to agree with the decision reached by trade regulators about the condition of the U.S. industries than when the deficit is low, controlling for other independent effects.

Political scientists have long recognized the importance of extralegal factors in judicial decision making. So I controlled for political influences on appeals court decision making with two variables that measure (1) industry political power (concentration ratio) and (2) political affiliation of the judicial panel majority deciding each case. A concentrated industry is typically assumed to possess sufficient political power and resources to hire superior legal representation, develop winning strategies (e.g., in case selection), and pressure appeals judges to affirm or reverse regulatory decisions in the industry's favor. While political scientists (e.g., Baum 1977; Shapiro 1968) and legal practitioners (e.g., Posner 1983; Rifkind 1951) have predicted that specialized courts, such as the Federal Circuit, will fall prey to clientelism and influence peddling by advocacy groups, my preliminary findings here do not support this claim. This finding is only preliminary because the dependent variable here is not the direction of the court's *policy* decision, whose variability may be dependent upon political pressure. Later on in this chapter, I shall incorporate the policy direction of the Federal Circuit's decisions as the dependent variable to reexamine the potential influence of industry political power and organizational ability.

It has long been reported that the background of judges, such as their political party affiliation, correlates strongly with their decisional propensities. Furthermore, it is traditionally believed that Democratic judges tend to favor regulatory agencies significantly more than Republican judges do, based upon political preferences over government regulation (Nagel 1961, 847). My findings here support only the first part of this view, not the second. In the Federal Circuit, for example, political party affiliation of the judges in any given panel does appear clearly to have a strong effect on the decisions judges reach in international trade controversies. However, controlling for agency policy direction and other economic and political determinants, a panel with a Democratic majority (coded 1) is significantly *less* likely to affirm bureaucratic decisions than one comprised of a majority of Republican judges (coded 0). Stated differently, panels with Republican majorities are more proagency than panels with Democratic majorities, or Democrats are more activist.

Independent accounts lend credence to this finding. For example, Willison (1986, 322–24) reported that in the D.C. Circuit, where most federal agencies take their cases for review, a majority of the judges "displayed fairly high levels of support for all agencies combined . . . . [but] agency support tends to increase as one moves from Democratic to Republican judges."

That the partisan background of judges is important in their interaction with bureaucrats is further supported in table 19, which reports marginals for specialized appeals court support for bureaucratic agencies by party of the panel majority. It is unmistakable that panel composition is significantly related to decisional trends. The court of appeals rules in favor of regulatory agencies in 82 percent of the cases in which Republican judges constitute a panel majority, compared to 69 percent of the cases in which Democratic judges make up a majority.

Although majority-Republican panels prove to be more proagency than their majority-Democratic counterparts, that does not necessarily mean that majority-Republican panels are more protectionist than majority-Democratic ones. In table 20, I further explore the policy implications of partisanship in the Federal Circuit, controlling for policy direction of agency decisions. Since the 1970s, Democrats in the United States have been viewed as the party of Main Street, organized labor, and protection-ism, while Republicans have been viewed as the champions of Wall Street, big business, and free trade. But my data indicate that Federal Circuit pan-els with a Republican majority are considerably more likely to support protectionist regulatory decisions than are panels with a Democratic majority (table 20, part A). In terms of support for nonprotectionist regu-latory decisions, the data show no statistically significant difference between the two types of panels (table 20, part B). Overall, these results raise the possibility that the decisional trends in the Federal Circuit might be due to the ideological congruence in partisan composition between the bureaucratic agencies and the Federal Circuit during the 1980s. Recall that during this period, Reagan-Bush Republican appointees dominated both the Federal Circuit and the regulatory agencies here analyzed. As the Republican-dominated regulatory agencies found cause to protect Ameri-can industries from unfair-trade practices, the Republican-dominated Federal Circuit found legal bases for approbation.

Determinants of Judicial Protectionism in the Federal Circuit

Judges in the United States think it iconoclastic to argue that judges make public policy. After all, the legal model, which judges view as the guiding principle for their decisions, repudiates active policy-making. American judges perceive themselves to be dispassionate arbiters of the law; and in that capacity as arbiters, they view themselves as individuals who hold no

TABLE 19. Partisan Support for Agency in Administered Protection Cases Decided in the Federal Circuit

Court Decision	Court Panel Majority[a]		Total
	Democratic	Republican	
Favorable	35 (69%)	49 (82%)	84 (76%)
Unfavorable	16 (31%)	11 (18%)	27 (24%)
Total	51 (100%)	60 (100%)	111 (100%)

Note: Data are administered protection cases, including antidumping (section 731), countervailing duty (section 701), and unfair practices in import trade cases (section 337), fully decided by the Court of Appeals for the Federal Circuit, 1980–90. These cases originate from either the International Trade Com-mission or the Department of Commerce.

[a]A chi-square test with 1 degree of freedom was conducted to determine the differences in partisan sup-port for the administrative agencies. Panels with a majority of Republican judges are significantly more likely to support the bureaucratic agency than panels in which the majority is Democratic: $\chi^2_{(1\ d.f.)} = 2.55$ ($p \le .10$).

concrete policy views, preferences, ability, or interest to make public policy. One passage in the letter sent to me by the longest-serving active-duty federal judge, Judge Giles S. Rich of the Federal Circuit, underscores this view:

> I suggest to you that where "policy formation" is concerned, the attitude of the [Federal Circuit] as I know it is that policy is none of our business and we leave it to the policy makers, Congress and the Administration. We are not in a position to acquire the knowledge necessary to make policy, such as holding public hearings, compiling data and the like, as Congress does.[4]

This perception has served judges well throughout American history in perpetuating the myth that legalism always rules. But many outside the legal profession, for example, social scientists who study law and courts, are unpersuaded that judges do not make policy through their rulings and are equally unpersuaded that judges' personal values and preferences do not impinge upon their rulings. Is the Federal Circuit making decisions that move trade policy incrementally toward a protectionist or free-trade direction? I examine here judicial protectionism in the nation's newest

TABLE 20.   Partisan Support in Administered Protection Cases by Panel Majority

Court Decision	Court Panel Majority[a]		Total
	Democratic	Republican	
A. Support for Protectionist Policy			
Favorable	13 (57%)	28 (85%)	41 (73%)
Unfavorable	10 (43%)	5 (15%)	15 (27%)
Total	23 (100%)	33 (100%)	56 (100%)
B. Support for Nonprotectionist Policy			
Favorable	19 (76%)	16 (80%)	35 (78%)
Unfavorable	6 (24%)	4 (20%)	10 (22%)
Total	25 (100%)	20 (100%)	45 (100%)

Note: Data are administered protection cases, including antidumping (section 731), countervailing duty (section 701), and unfair practices in import trade (section 337), fully decided by the Federal Circuit, 1980–90.

[a]A chi-square test with 1 degree of freedom was conducted to determine court panel majority support for protectionist trade policy. Result shows panels with a Republican majority being significantly more protectionist than panels with a Democratic majority: $\chi^2_{(1\ d.f.)} = 5.55$ ($p \le .02$). A chi-square with 1 degree of freedom was conducted to test court panel majority support for nonprotectionist policy. Result shows no significant difference between panels with a Democratic majority and those with a Republican majority: $\chi^2_{(1\ d.f.)} = .103$ (n.s.).

intermediate court of special jurisdiction in order to determine its policy and juristic propensities through a determination of the specific factors conditioning the protectionist (coded 1) or nonprotectionist (coded 0) outcomes of the court.

Thus far in this chapter, I have focused mostly on judicial deference or support for agencies, and I have controlled for agency policy direction as a way of detecting the court's policy imprint. Little policy imprint was discovered, although at a more micro level, judicial panels where Republicans comprise a majority *were* found to be more likely to rule in favor of protectionism than panels populated by Democratic judges. In the multivariate analysis reported in this section, however, I incorporate the policy decisions of the Federal Circuit itself as the dependent variable. As did other judicial scholars before me, I assume that judges are political actors who hold policy preference and oftentimes render policy decisions according to those preferences (Peltason 1955; Howard 1981; Carp and Rowland 1983).

Table 21 reports the outcome of three separate models of the determinants of protectionism by specialized courts of appeals in administered protection cases. Consistent with theoretical expectation, the full model does better than either the fact model or the politics-and-economics model alone. This finding is indicated by the smaller index of Akaike's Information Criterion (AIC). The findings indicate that the null model (that the variables have a 0 impact on Federal Circuit protectionism) is unequivocally rejected ($p < .01$). Overall, the model categorized 79 percent of the cases correctly, with a full 54 percent reduction in error. If all the variables are held constant at their mean, the cumulative odds of a court decision favoring protection are 55 percent; but if all the variables are set at one standard deviation above or below the mean to simulate an increased chance of a protectionist decision, the Federal Circuit is almost 100 percent likely to protect the domestic industry; this figure compares with a .2 percent probability that the court would protect the domestic industry if the signs for the variables are reversed to simulate a situation where it is harder for the court to rule in favor of protection.

In this model of protectionism, political and case-specific attributes seem to be most important. Economic attributes such as country trade deficit and foreign import penetration have no remarkable impact. We should recognize, however, that this outcome is limited to antidumping and countervailing duty cases, which are only two important subsets of the Federal Circuit's international trade docket. The outcome of the case factors confirms the earlier reported finding that the international trade courts do favor protectionism.

For example, when all variables are held constant at their mean, the

TABLE 21. Determinants of Specialized Court of Appeals Protectionism in Administered Protection Cases

Variables	Contextual Fact Model		Politics and Economics Model		General Model		
	MLE	MLE/SE	MLE	MLE/SE	MLE	MLE/SE	Impact
Case Factors							
Import Duty	.010	.605			.027	1.041	.240
Policy Direction	2.018**	2.988			3.517***	3.221	.676***
Lower Court							
Decision	−.068	−.111			2.284*	1.796	.508*
Political Factors							
Political							
Affiliation of							
Panel Majority			−.787	−.897	1.927	1.225	.446
Lower Court							
Decision x							
Political							
Affiliation of							
Panel Majority			−1.118	−1.195	−5.323**	2.514	−.841**
Concentration							
Ratio			.003	.225	.005**	2.052	.508**
Economic Factors							
Country Trade							
Deficit			.040	1.094	.093*	1.444	.393*
Foreign							
Penetration			−1.182	.424	−2.264	−.562	−.123
Constant	−1.307	−1.960	1.021	1.043	−4.734**	−2.057	—
All Variables at:							
Mean							.55
Protectionist$_{(\pm1 \text{ S.D.})}$							.998
Nonprot.$_{(\pm1 \text{ S.D.})}$							.002
Sample	58		56		56		
−2xlog likelihood	67.57†		69†		48†		
Correctly predicted	72%		64%		79%		
AIC	71.57		74.05		55.67		
Reduction in error	40%		23%		54%		

Note: Entries are unstandardized logit estimates. The dependent variable is Court of Appeals for the Federal Circuit decision in favor of protectionism (coded 1) or free trade (coded 0). Data include antidumping and countervailing duty cases appealed to the court from the International Trade Commission and the Department of Commerce.

*p ≤ .10 one-tailed; **p ≤ .05 one-tailed; ***p ≤ .01 one-tailed; †p ≤ .01 two-tailed

Federal Circuit is 67.6 percent more likely to grant protection to a domestic petitioner if the agency policy decision is protectionist than if it is non-protectionist. Also, the court is about 51 percent more likely to grant protection when the Court of International Trade affirms rather than reverses the decision of the agency based on the administrative record. In judicial parlance, these two outcomes strongly suggest that the Federal Circuit is not practicing an "error correction" strategy, which political scientists typically associate with an activist court. Instead, the Federal Circuit is playing a strong legitimizing role in promoting U.S. protectionism, as suggested by its high rate of deference to the Court of International Trade and the trade bureaucracies. Thus, as Charlene Barshefsky and Michael J. Firth (1988) noted, the Federal Circuit is missing opportunities to impose greater discipline on agency practices and failing to seriously consider the wider political implications of its behavior.

I have already reported that Republican judges show a greater tendency than Democratic judges to support regulatory agencies and that majority Republican panels are more inclined than Democratic panels to protect American industries and firms. This multivariate analysis supports these conclusions but also introduces an interesting dynamic concerning the intervening role of the Court of International Trade in Federal Circuit decision making. Analyzing the policy responses of the Federal Circuit, I find that differences between Democratic and Republican panel majorities are mediated by the ruling of the Court of International Trade, as indicated by the interaction of Court of International Trade decision and partisanship of the panel majority. As indicated by the interaction variable, a panel that has a Democratic majority is significantly less likely to grant protection to U.S industries than one populated by Republican judges if and only if the lower court agreed with the interpretation reached by regulators. This finding is not too surprising given the Federal Circuit's apparent tendency to defer to regulators at the ITC and DOC and to judges at the Court of International Trade (Kuhn 1986).

Finally, I find support for the contention of some political scientists (e.g., Baum [1977] and Shapiro [1968]) and legal scholars (e.g., Rifkind [1951] and Posner [1985]) that specialized courts may respond to political pressure of industry interests, leading to biased policy decisions. Following the lead of Hansen (1990), Baldwin (1985), Grier, Munger, and Roberts (1994), and others, I used industry concentration ratio as a surrogate for political power and organizational ability. The analysis shows that a highly concentrated industry is better able to convince the Federal Circuit to rule in favor of protection than an industry that is less concentrated and therefore politically weak. This finding is consistent with the pluralist theory of interest-group contestation discussed in chapter 4. It confirms an indubitable political reality: On average, an industry or firm that possesses organizational advantages in both resource accumulation and ability to hire superior legal counsel to advocate the industry or firm's causes before a panel of judges enjoys more successes in court.

Conclusion

The purposes of this chapter were to analyze the relationship between the specialized courts of appeals and the bureaucracies charged with implementing American trade policy and to determine the core correlates of judicial protectionism. Based upon the hypotheses explained in chapter 5 and refined in chapter 6, I set out to accomplish several objectives. First, I was interested in examining the level of appellate judicial deference to administrative agencies. To do so I first compared judicial deference between the Supreme Court and the Federal Circuit, two courts located at different levels of the federal appellate system, and found that both courts deferred to bureaucratic agencies at a fairly high rate. Then I examined judicial deference across two circuit courts, the Federal Circuit and the D.C. Circuit, and found that the former seemed considerably more deferential than the latter, which was contrary to expectation. I offered a number of plausible explanations for the deferential behavior of the Federal Circuit, the most notable one being that the Federal Circuit is not specialized in the real sense of the word because of its multiple subject matter jurisdiction.

My second objective was to examine the role of institutional design in the impact of specialized appellate courts on bureaucracy. Using the ITC and the DOC, my data indicate that the institutional structures of the agencies do make a substantial difference in appellate review. Because of its relative independence from external political influence and manipulation and because of its extremely courtlike decision-making strategies, the ITC wins more of its legal challenges than does the DOC.

The Supreme Court decided the landmark international trade case of *Zenith Radio Corp. v. United States* in 1978. In *Zenith Radio,* the Court deferred the interpretation of ambiguous statutory concepts to the administrators charged with implementing trade policy. Since then, there have been virtually no other administered protection cases that have been granted certiorari and fully reviewed by the High Court, even though several petitions for review have been filed. Although Chief Justice William H. Rehnquist announced in the inaugural session of the Federal Circuit in 1982 that the Federal Circuit would be placed under the judicial microscope, that has not happened, especially in the area of international trade. This unwillingness to review Federal Circuit decisions makes the Federal

Circuit tantamount to a miniature supreme court, capable of issuing peremptory decisions and exerting sustained impact on the direction of public policy.

Therefore, my third objective was to examine the extent to which the Federal Circuit was influencing the direction of trade policy implementation in the United States. The data reveal that in the 1980s when American industries and their employees cried out for governmental assistance against unfair-trade competition from abroad, the Federal Circuit did respond positively to a majority of these requests. The court shows a proclivity toward protection for American industries.

In recent years, Congress has enacted significant procedural amendments to U.S. trade laws to make it easier for businesses to obtain protection. They include expanding executive authority over trade and expanding opportunities for judicial review as a way of checking that executive authority. The findings reported in this book suggest that the federal courts, particularly the Court of International Trade and the Federal Circuit, have become yet another avenue for the congressional abdication of responsibility over foreign commerce. Through incremental amendments, Congress has required industries to fight their trade battles in court, and the courts are responding favorably to these industries, therefore legitimizing American protectionism.

Fourth, I was interested in examining the factors that condition appellate courts' decisions to protect American industries from unfair trading practices of foreign companies. I called this the *policy model* of protectionism (as opposed to a *deference model,* referring to interagreement between courts and agencies). In this policy model, I find that the Federal Circuit is more likely to rule in favor of protection if the bureaucracy rules in favor of protection and the Court of International Trade agrees; if the plaintiff in the case is a highly concentrated U.S. industry, meaning that it has the power to apply pressure on judges and to convince them to award protection, or if the United States holds a high trade deficit with the trading partner named as the unfair trader. Conversely, the Federal Circuit is less likely to support protection for the domestic industry if the panel deciding the case has a Democratic rather than a Republican majority and the challenged agency action was upheld in the lower court.

As public policy issues become more and more complex, specialized courts increasingly are being called upon to settle disputes to minimize conflict between generalist courts. It is my hope that the findings reported here will serve as an important springboard for the development of greater understanding of the behavior and contributions of specialized courts in the dissemination of civil justice in the United States.

CHAPTER 9

Conclusions and Implications: Expertise, Bureaucratic Context, and Judicial Review of U.S. Trade Policy-Making

The United States is the leading prosecutor of unfair-trade practices cases in the world.[1] This fact is not surprising if we consider our strong belief in due process and individual liberty and the growth of litigiousness in American society since the 1960s. The United States achieved this status as the leading prosecutor of unfair-trade practices cases partly because of the nation's historical approach to trade. This approach has been one of openness rather than closure, starting from the end of the Second World War up to the late 1970s, when policymakers began the process of instituting profound changes that openly diverged from the official policy of openness in international trade. Many supporters of the policy of openness, however, including this author, argue that in an imperfect international environment, where compliance with both bilateral and multilateral trade rules is difficult to monitor and enforce, making it possible for aggrieved parties to seek redress of their grievances in court is an acceptable way of moving closer to a level playing field.

The demand and supply of trade regulation in the United States used to be, for all practical purposes, a matter of economics and politics. But even though the investigation of unfair-trade practices in the United States is carried out by experts operating within a competitive political environment and using economic guidelines, the whole process is "more like a judicial contest rather than a political event" (Boltuck and Litan 1991, 2). For scholars interested in American foreign trade policy and its history, the growth of judicial review of international trade remedies is an important phenomenon that will help shape the future of trade policy in American society and relations with trading partners. Yet, we find virtually no systematic empirical studies of the interaction between courts and the administrative agencies responsible for implementing U.S. foreign trade policy.

This study began with a straightforward objective, which was to explain the interconnections between judicial review and bureaucratic implementation in the unique context of mutual expertise of courts and bureaucratic agencies. To accomplish this objective, I have used international trade as a policy venue and have developed and presented several arguments in the preceding chapters in this regard. Two of the principal arguments are (1) that the level of expertise of judges and bureaucrats undergirds the variation in the stream of policy outputs emanating from the interaction between courts and bureaucratic agencies—that is, expertise matters in the relationship between courts and agencies, and (2) that specialized courts *do* have substantive impact on public policy.

To address the main objective of the study and develop the arguments presented, I pursued several intermediate inquiries: Do specialized-court judges hold inferior qualifications relative to generalist-court judges? What are the core characteristics and virtues of specialized courts in the U.S. system of justice and the administrative state? How critical is the bureaucratic context in judicial response to administrative task decisions? What impact do courts with narrow jurisdiction and expertise have on the substantive direction of public policy? Finally, what are the core independent conditions that best explain the behavior of judges who review and evaluate bureaucratic task decisions in complex policy areas that are both economic and political in nature? In this concluding chapter, I give a summary of the principal findings and implications of the study.

Distinctiveness

This study makes several contributions to political science and to the study of political institutions, particularly in regard to the idea of judicial oversight. For social scientists, this study provides, from a political science perspective, the first systematic empirical analysis of the interaction between the bureaucratic agencies in charge of implementing U.S. international trade laws and the specialized courts designated to review their decisions. Political scientists and economists who study administered protection do show their awareness of the existence of judicial review of trade decisions, but this awareness rarely progressed beyond passing observations into actual empirical study of the issue. Indeed, their observations are all too often perfunctory, limited to statements like "appeals from [agency] decisions are handled by the Court of International Trade and the Court of Appeals for the Federal Circuit" (Baldwin 1985, 89). It is my hope that this study will increase the knowledge base available to scholars and help spur further research into the characteristics of specialized courts, their contributions to civil justice, and their relationships with government agencies.

Indeed, the prime motivation for this project was my own lack of understanding of judicial oversight conducted by specialized courts. I have no illusion that these courts are in the mainstream of the American judicial system. Specialized courts are little known, even though they play important roles in the civil justice system. In fact, some who are familiar with specialized courts have taken the position that specialized courts are not really courts because they lack a generalist orientation and that specialized courts are unnecessary because their functional similarity with bureaucratic agencies leads to duplication and inefficiency in government (Shapiro 1968). I disagree. I argue instead that specialized courts are necessary to improve overall judicial capacity and public policy in their areas of jurisdiction. When the Founding Fathers framed the Constitution, they erred on the side of safety and inefficiency, not convenience and efficiency, when, in order to build an enduring system of government, they erected an institutional framework of checks and balances: three independent branches of government, a bicameral legislature, and veto power for the president. We can think of specialized courts similarly; they provide more room for needed deliberation and safety in the entire system of policy implementation in the United States.

In his 1988 essay on judicial incursions into the bureaucratic ambit and bureaucratic responses to such incursions, professor Martin Shapiro complained about the dearth of studies on judicial review of agency action and offered the explanation that political scientists are reluctant to conduct research on this subject because they perceive it as ruled by "an impenetrable body of legal-doctrinal esoterica" (ix). Another contribution of this study, then, is its demystification of some of the daunting images of research that this perception invokes. The study proves that while judicial evaluation of bureaucratic performance can be complex, especially in highly stylized and technical areas such as trade policy, it need not be an impenetrable area of study.

Because this is the first empirical study of its kind, it is difficult to place all the findings and contributions in a comparative context and to assess fully their implications. Although I make no claim that my answers to the questions posed earlier represent the last word on the subject, I do hope that my analysis will lead us to a better understanding of court-bureaucracy relationships, particularly within the context of an institutional symmetry defined by expertise. While many more quite specific findings of the interaction between bureaucratic agencies and specialized courts were discussed in the preceding individual chapters, I shall use the remainder of this chapter to highlight the principal substantive findings and implications of this research.

Bureaucratic Context and Institutional Form

A major substantive finding concerns bureaucratic context. With regard to federal bureaucratic agencies, this study shows that judicial response to administrative agencies varies between independent regulatory commissions and executive-level regulatory agencies and between generalist and specialized courts. Administrative agencies come in various forms and have different levels of resilience in the face of external political pressure. Agencies must adapt to the competing demands of external political actors while protecting their turf, autonomy, and programs. Agencies serve more or less as policy advocates for domestic interests and networks that have a stake in the agencies' policy outputs (Moe 1982; Wood and Waterman 1991). They must adapt themselves to the vague mandates and conflicting demands of politicians who are guided by quite different incentives and motivations (Weingast 1984, Weingast and Moran 1983; McCubbins and Schwartz 1984).

We must bear in mind that bureaucratic adaptation must accommodate not only the conflicting demands of the president and Congress, but also those of courts. American courts are the designated invigilators of the policy process, to the extent that the process interferes with constitutional rights. Today courts are more vigilant than ever and agencies must be mindful of this fact. The active presence of courts in the venue of implementation, the finality of their decisions, and their power to restrain agency behavior pose a potential threat to bureaucratic autonomy and to the flexibility that bureaucrats may need to define appropriate strategies for optimal policy delivery. In light of the many potential constraints and the conflicting and oftentimes nebulous messages with which bureaucratic agencies are presented on a continuing basis, they must do no less than respond pragmatically to the extent that the political system allows. That implies that agencies must continually perform a balancing act to meet the conflicting demands of key external actors. Unfortunately, because of differences in institutional form, some agencies are better equipped than others are to undertake such a balancing act, and herein lies a key determinant of the extent to which external forces are able to shape the behavior of bureaucratic agencies.

My analysis of the data on court-bureaucracy interaction shows consistently that executive-level agencies, such as the Department of Commerce, are significantly more susceptible to conflicting political pressures. When a bureaucracy succumbs to political pressures, its policy choices typically become inconsistent, arbitrary, and oftentimes overzealous. According to Boltuck and Litan (1991), these are all afflictions of the DOC. My data show that executive-level agencies, such as the DOC, fare considerably worse than independent regulatory commissions, such as the International Trade Commission, when called upon to defend their policy choices before judges. Independent regulatory commissions, such as the ITC, being bipartisan, quasi-judicial, and extremely courtlike in their decision-making strategies, are significantly less susceptible to external political influence and tend to give a more textual interpretation of statutory schemes than do executive-level agencies. Executive-level agencies face greater uncertainty, are more likely to show the symptom of "bureaucratic drift," and make decisions that are more likely to be overturned by the courts than those of independent regulatory commissions.

Judicial Expertise and the Deference Hypothesis

Another principal substantive contribution of this work deals with judicial expertise and deference. There is a functional dissimilarity among courts that partially explains the variation in judicial responses to administrative agencies. This functional dissimilarity is defined by the level of expertise and specialization that a given court commands. As discussed extensively in chapter 5, there are sharp differences between specialized courts and generalist courts, with the former commanding far greater expertise in their area(s) of concentration than the latter in theirs. Interestingly, this difference in expertise exists not only between generalist and specialized courts but also between different specialized courts. For instance, the Court of International Trade appears to be the quintessential specialized court because its decisional tasks are concentrated only in foreign trade matters, which allows judges to amass a wealth of experience in the area.

The analysis suggests that during the 1980s, Federal Circuit judges generally exhibited a lower level of expertise in trade matters than judges of the Court of International Trade. This difference is partly because the Federal Circuit has jurisdiction over a larger number of specific policy areas than the Court of International Trade does, and so its decisional focus is more diverse, tending to reduce the intensity of specialization. These differences in the expertise of the courts are manifested in the nature of their responsiveness to arguments challenging bureaucratic choices. To the extent that the difference in the number of jurisdictional concentration areas between the two courts remains, there is no reason to expect the Federal Circuit to be able to match the substantive expertise of the Court of International Trade in international trade matters.

Contrary to the popular claim that courts as a whole give extraordinary deference to administrative agencies because of agency expertise and closeness to the policies as well as to citizens served, my analysis suggests that, at the trial court level, specialized courts embrace uncertainty far more courageously than do generalist courts in their dealings with the bureaucracy. It is possible that the level of uncertainty differs between the two judicial environments. But assuming that all things are equal, specialized courts at the trial level defer to administrative agencies at a significantly lower rate than their generalist counterparts do. In comparison, specialized courts at the appellate level, for example, the Federal Circuit, show a higher level of deference to administrative agencies than do some of their generalist counterparts. These inferences are of course most germane to the courts and policy area here analyzed. It is left to future analyses of specialized courts to refute or authenticate these inferences using other courts and policy areas. In summary, not all courts are predisposed to deference. Rather, the type of court (as defined by its institutional structure) and the location of a court within the judicial pyramid—whether at the trial or appellate level—determine the level of deference a court shows.

Policy Impact of Judicial Review

Another major substantive contribution concerns the policy impact of judicial review. Political scientists have long embraced the idea that judges make public policy through the judgments they render in legal controversies. It is commonplace, however, for judicial scholars to discuss judicial review by merely pointing to the number of lower-court or administrative agency decisions that a higher court has reversed or affirmed (see, e.g., Crowley 1987; Handberg 1979; Spaeth and Teger 1982). This type of analysis is important in informing us of the deferential propensities of courts but tells us little about the potential impact of courts on public policy-making (for a rare exception, see Sheehan 1992). My study of specialized courts incorporates the policy direction of the bureaucratic decision in order to determine potential policy impact. Note that the impact of courts need not be limited to policy; courts can also have an impact on the bureaucracy itself.

The most profound medium through which courts have an impact on bureaucratic behavior is the tangible costs they routinely impose on agencies through adverse decisions, which strain agency operating budgets and personnel resources during compliance efforts. Impact can also be detected through the policy disruption that courts provoke when they reverse or remand even a small number of agency decisions and define new procedures for use by agencies to meet statutory and constitutional requirements. My findings indicate that judicial reversals and remands of agency action are quite common. Indeed, in specialized trial courts, such as the Court of International Trade, reversals and remands occur in 41 percent of the cases, and in 24 percent of the cases in specialized appellate courts.

In the 1980s, American industries and workers sounded an alarm against unfair foreign trade practices, doing so at a level that prompted one presidential candidate, Walter Mondale, in 1984 to vow vigorous retaliation in order to protect American businesses and workers. As Mondale learned, even in such a context, it can be bad politics for a would-be president to carry a protectionist banner. Most interestingly, however, we witnessed during the 1980s a phenomenon whereby the international trade courts reached out and helped American industries and workers against the perils of foreign dumping and subsidization. The *significance* of this development is that it represents the culmination of a strategic effort by Congress to protect itself from industry pressures and safeguard American trade policy by devolving more and more of its trade responsibility to others. Given that the courts of international trade are willing to legitimize the protectionism of the legislative and executive branches, one would expect Congress to continue to devolve its constitutional responsibilities over trade to the executive branch, and to enact even wider authority for the courts to oversee executive implementation of those responsibilities.

Integrating Legal and Extralegal Theories

The final major substantive contribution concerns the theories of judicial decision making. Recognizing that extant theories of judicial decision making that focus on either legalism or extralegal factors alone are incomplete and thus have explanatory and predictive weaknesses (e.g., George and Epstein 1992; Songer and Haire 1992; Johnson 1987a), I developed and tested an integrated model that combines economic, political, and case-specific legal circumstances in a way that more realistically reflects judicial decision making in the courts here examined. I find that this full model best explains the decisions of courts having jurisdiction over policy areas that are inherently political and economic.

Given the inclusive character of this model, it is possible to examine the long-standing claim that has been made by some political scientists and legal practitioners about the weaknesses of specialized courts. The most popular criticism of specialized courts is that their unidimensional focus makes them highly susceptible to clientelism and capture by interest groups that have a direct stake in what the courts do (Posner 1985; Shapiro 1968; Baum 1977). My analysis shows that the Court of International Trade does respond to interest-group pressure, but only when we model the policy decisions of the court, not when we concern ourselves with judicial deference to agency actions. This finding suggests that further empirical studies need to be conducted so that we may fully understand how and why specialized courts respond to interest-group pressure.

In addition, this study underscores the importance of case characteristics in the decisions of lower-court judges, controlling for behavioral and environmental conditions. The importance of behavioral indices in judicial decision making has recently been stated most forcefully by Segal and Spaeth (1993) in their explication of the attitudinal model of judicial behavior. The basic premise of their argument is that justices atop the judicial hierarchy face neither the threat of reversal by a higher court, which is faced by lower-court judges, nor the opportunity of appointment to a higher court, which is available to lower-court judges. Because these incentives do not play a role in the set of decision strategies open to Supreme Court justices, Segal and Spaeth conclude that justices make judgments largely on the basis of their own ideological or attitudinal predilections in light of case facts. My analysis of lower courts complements this conclusion chiefly because it arrives at a different conclusion. Generally speaking, for reasons that may verge on career and professional goals, lower-court judges rely less on behavioral predicates and more on case characteristics when settling legal controversies.

Appendix A: Supplement to Chapter 2

TABLE A1. Background Characteristics and Qualification of Federal Circuit Judges

Judge	Stated Party Affiliation	Year Appointed (Age)	Appointing President	Area(s) of Legal Expertise Prior to Appointment	Prior Federal Government Prosecutorial and Other Experiences	American Bar Association Rating[a]
Rich, Giles S.	Ind.	1956 (52)	Eisenhower	Patent and trademark	Legislative aid, helped draft Patent Act of 1952	—
Davis, Oscar H.	Dem.	1962 (48)	Kennedy	Benefits and claims	Justice Dept. Civil Division; deputy solicitor general	—
Cowen, Wilson	Dem.	1964 (59)	Johnson	Government contract	Assistant to secretary of agriculture	Well Qualified
Nichols, Philip	Dem.	1964 (57)	Johnson	Taxation and customs	Justice Dept. Lands Division; Treasury Dept.; commissioner of customs	Qualified
Skelton, Byron G.	Dem.	1966 (61)	Johnson	Government contract		Well Qualified
Baldwin, Phillip B.	Dem.	1968 (44)	Johnson	Criminal		Qualified
Kashiwa, Shiro	Rep.	1971 (59)	Nixon	Corporate and realty	Justice Dept. Lands Division	Qualified
Bennett, Marion T.	Rep.	1972 (58)	Nixon	Government contract	Member of Congress, served in House Commerce Committee	Exceptionally Well Qualified
Markey, Howard T.	Rep.	1972 (52)	Nixon	Patent and trademark		Well Qualified
Miller, Jack R.	Rep.	1973 (57)	Nixon	Patent and taxation	Counsel, Internal Revenue Service; senator	Qualified
Friedman, Daniel M.	Ind.	1978 (62)	Carter	Securities and exchange; antitrust; administrative	Counsel, Securities and Exchange Commission; counsel, Justice Dept. Antitrust Division	Well Qualified
Smith, Edward S.	Dem.	1978 (59)	Carter	Taxation	Assistant to attorney general, Justice Dept. Tax Division	Well Qualified
Nies, Helen W.	Ind.	1980 (55)	Carter	Patent and trademark	Justice Dept. Alien Property Office; Price Stabilization Office	Well Qualified

Name	Party	Year (age)	President	Field of expertise	Prior position	ABA rating[a]
Bissell, Jean G.	Rep.	1984 (48)	Reagan	Commercial; banking and business		Qualified
Newman, Pauline	Rep.	1984 (57)	Reagan	Patent and trademark		Qualified
Archer, Glenn L.	Rep.	1985 (56)	Reagan	Taxation and corporate	Justice Dept. Tax Division	Qualified
Mayer, Haldane R.	Rep.	1987 (46)	Reagan	Benefits and claims	Assistant to Chief Justice Burger; Merit Systems Protection Board	Well Qualified
Michel, Paul R.	Rep.	1988 (47)	Reagan	Patent and antitrust; criminal; general trial expert	Justice Dept. Office of Public Integrity; administrative aide and counsel to Sen. Arlen Spector (R-PA.)	Qualified
Clevenger, Raymond	Rep.	1990 (53)	Bush	Federal administrative	General counsel, Department of Transportation	Qualified
Lourie, Alan D.	Rep.	1990 (55)	Bush	Patent and trademark	From private sector worked closely with Commerce Dept. and U.S. trade representative	Well Qualified
Plager, S. Jay	Rep.	1990 (59)	Bush	Government contract	Counselor, Health and Human Services; administrator, Office of Management and Budget	Qualified
Rader, Randall R.	Rep.	1990 (41)	Bush	Patent and trademark	Counsel, Senate Judiciary Committee; Claims Court judge	Qualified
Schall, Alvin A.	Rep.	1992 (48)	Bush	Government contract; civilian personnel	Assistant to the attorney general	Well Qualified
Bryson, William C.	Dem.	1994 (49)	Clinton	Criminal; general trial expert	Special counsel, justice Dept. Criminal Division; deputy solicitor general	Well Qualified

Source: Court of Appeals for the Federal Circuit—A History, 1982–1990, edited by Marion T. Bennett; "Report Concerning the Nomination of Judges of the Court of Appeals for the Federal Circuit," Journal of Patent and Trademark Office Society (September 1988): 599–607; Almanac of the Federal Judiciary, vols. 1 and 2 (1996); Who's Who in American Law; Judicial Yellow Book, 1996; author's mail survey of Federal Circuit judges; American Bar Association (ABA).

[a] ABA ratings are based upon a nominee's integrity, legal competence, and judicial temperament to sit on the federal bench. Ratings were unavailable for all judges.

TABLE A2. Background Characteristics and Qualification of Court of International Trade Judges

Judge (Party Affiliation)	Home State	Year Appointed (Age)	Appointing President	Area(s) of Legal Expertise Prior to Appointment	Prior Federal Government Prosecutorial and Other Experience	American Bar Association Rating
Rao, Paul P. (D)	Unknown	1948 (49)	Truman	None known	None known	Unavailable
Ford, Morgan (D)	North Dakota	1948 (38)	Truman	General practice	None known	Unavailable
Richardson, Scovel (R)	Tennessee	1957 (45)	Eisenhower	None known	None known	Unavailable
Landis, Frederick (D)	Indiana	1965 (53)	Johnson	None known	None known	Unavailable
Maletz, Herbert (D)	Massachusetts	1967 (54)	Johnson	None known	None known	Qualified
Newman, Bernard (R)	New York	1968 (61)	Johnson	None known	None known	Well Qualified
Re, Edward (D)	New York	1969 (49)	Johnson	None known	Justice Dept. special hearing officer; Federal Judicial Center; Foreign Claims Settlement Commission; assistant secretary of state for educational and cultural affairs	Qualified
Rosenstein, Samuel (D)	Kentucky	1967 (58)	Johnson	None known	None known	Well Qualified
Watson, James (D)	New York	1966 (44)	Johnson	None known	None known	Unavailable
Boe, Nils (R)	South Dakota	1971 (58)	Nixon	None known	Director, Office of Intergovernmental Relations; director, Office of Emergency Preparedness	Well Qualified
Restani, Jane (I)	California	1983 (35)	Reagan	Civil and commercial law	Director, commercial litigation branch, civil division of Justice Department	Unavailable

Name	State	Year (age)	President	Expertise	Prior experience	ABA Rating
Carman, Gregory (R)	New York	1984 (47)	Reagan	Military and international law	Member of Congress, served in House Banking, Finance and Urban Affairs Committee	Unavailable
DiCarlo, Dominick (R)	New York	1984 (56)	Reagan	None known	Assistant secretary of state of international narcotic matters	Unavailable
Aquilino, Thomas (I)	New York	1985 (47)	Reagan	International trade	None known	Unavailable
Tsoucalas, Nicholas (R)	New York	1986 (59)	Reagan	Criminal	U.S. attorney, federal district of New York	Unavailable
Musgrave, R. Kenton (R)	California	1987 (60)	Reagan	Corporate; international trade	None known	Qualified
Goldberg, Richard (R)	North Dakota	1991 (64)	Bush	None known	Undersecretary for international affairs and commodity programs, Dept. of Agriculture	Qualified
Pogue, Donald C. (D)	Connecticut	1995 (48)	Clinton	Labor and employment	None known	Well Qualified
Wallach, Evan J. (D)	Nevada	1995 (46)	Clinton	Constitutional	General counsel and public policy adviser to Sen. Harry Reid	Qualified

Source: Who's Who in American Law; Almanac of the Federal Judiciary, vols. 1 and 2; author's mail survey of Court of International Trade judges; obituary notes published in Court of International Trade Reports; Congressional Directory of the 103d Congress (1992–93); Judicial Yellow Book; American Bar Association (ABA) ratings obtained from the ABA. Ratings for many of the judges were unavailable from the ABA.

A3. Sample Questionnaire Sent to Judges of the Court of International Trade and the Federal Circuit

January 11, 1994

Helen W. Nies, Chief Judge
U.S. Court of Appeals for the Federal Circuit
717 Madison Place, N.W.
Washington, D.C. 20439

Dear Judge Nies:

I am conducting a study on the impact of the Court of Appeals for the Federal Circuit on U.S. trade policy implementation. In my study, I argue that the judiciary has been given less than deserved attention by political scientists who study U.S. public policy formation. However, to proceed with my work, I need to know the party identification of the Judges of the Court of Appeals for the Federal Circuit. This information is very important for my analysis.

I have examined several published sources including the *Congressional Directory, Who is Who in American Law* and other places that list the biographical information of the judges of this court. However, I have been able to identify only a few of the judges' party identification (PID). Your PID is one of those I have not been able to identify and I seek to enlist your assistance in this regard. I realize that some judges may be unwilling to give out this information. But let me assure you that the information you provide is strictly for academic research purpose and I will not publish it in a journal if you so indicate.

My party identification is: Democrat _____; Independent_____;
Republican_____
I want this information to remain confidential_____
This information may be published in a journal_____

Please return this letter to me in the enclosed self-addressed stamped envelope. Thank you very much for helping me to study the role of the Court of Appeals for the Federal Circuit in U.S. trade policy-making.

Sincerely,

A4. Response from Judge Giles Sutherland Rich

21 Jan. '94

Dear Mr. Unah,

The probable reason you don't find my party affiliation published anywhere is that I have never regarded it as important -- never having been in politics. I was a Newyorker until I came to Washington in 1956. I was generally inclined toward FDR until he tried to run for his last term on the theory he was indispensable but could never bring myself to register democratic because New York was being run by Tammany Hall. Fortuitously, I registered republican when Eisenhower ran and thus made it possible for him to nominate me to be a Federal judge.

You can determine the party affiliation of a judge with about 98% accuracy by looking at the party of the President who appoints him/her. Presidents just don't nominate judges of the party out of power, except for a couple of elevations to appear nonpartisan. Just watch what is done in filling the over 100 existing vacancies.

From my 38 years as a Federal judge, I will tell you that "party identification" has next to nothing to do with whatever effect the Court of Appeals of the Federal Circuit (CAFC) has on U.S.trade <u>policy</u>. As to its implementation, of course, its role is to see that the laws made by the initial policy makers, the Congress, are correctly applied. The Judiciary or "Third Branch", as you well know, is not a policy making branch of government. Congress in enacting laws, approved by the president in office at the time, is the policy maker. The remaining branch, the Administration through one or more Agencies such as I.T.C. or Congress may have something to say policywise. Unless the Agencies get too far out of line with the law as Congress has written it, I think you will find the judiciary will leave them alone on policy matters. When they do get too far out of line, the courts are going to see that Congress's policy prevails. These are, of course, personal views.

Otherwise than as above stated,I have never observed during the 12-year life of the CAFC that party affiliation has played any role whatsoever in how the judges go about deciding trade policy cases. It is not a factor that is ever mentioned, discussed,or observed. Once a judge is appointed for life, whatever his affiliation was tends to be forgotten.

I suggest to you that where "policy formation" is concerned, the attitude in the CAFC as I know it is that policy is none of our business and we leave it to the policy makers, Congress and the Administration. We are not in a position to acquire the knowledge necessary to make policy, such as holding public hearings, compiling data and the like, as Congress does.

Good luck

Sincerely,

Giles S. Rich

Appendix B: Supplement to Chapter 3

B1. The Distributive Effects of a Tariff on Various Sectors of the Domestic Economy

In April 1995, the Clinton administration, led by then U.S. Trade Representative Mickey Kantor, threatened to impose 100 percent tariff on Japanese luxury cars imported to the United States if, by the end of June 1995, Japan did not open its market to U.S. cars and car parts. While a tariff rate of 100 percent is extreme and may perilously lead to autarky, lower tariff rates are nonetheless imposed on foreign goods on a continuing basis. In this appendix, I use the following demand-and-supply graph to perform a partial equilibrium analysis of the distributive impact of tariffs on various sectors of the domestic economy, namely, the U.S. government, producers, and consumers.

Assume that U.S. producers currently produce and supply q_1 cars to the market at a price of p. This quantity supplied is insufficient to meet consumer demand for cars, which is at q_2. To make up for this shortage, it is necessary to import $q_2 - q_1$, leading to the equilibrium point (p,q_2). This excess demand creates downward pressures on prices, but the initial equilibrium at (p,q_2) remains unchanged unless there is some outside "shock" to the market, such as a government action that actually imposes tariff on imports. Suppose government officials respond to the pressures of producers by imposing tariff (t) on the foreign good. This raises the import price to $p + t$. Consequently, domestic producers increase their production to q_3, with a producer surplus gain corresponding to area A. Imports fall to $q_4 - q_3$, creating a new equilibrium $(p + t, q_4)$. Area B is the deadweight (social) loss resulting from inefficient domestic production due to the tariff. Area C represents a revenue gain for the government in the form of tariff. Area D represents another deadweight loss to consumers from the tariff. In the absence of any compensation mechanism (see Becker 1985), consumers are therefore the biggest losers when a tariff is imposed on imports. Consumers lose what domestic producers and the government gain; in addi-

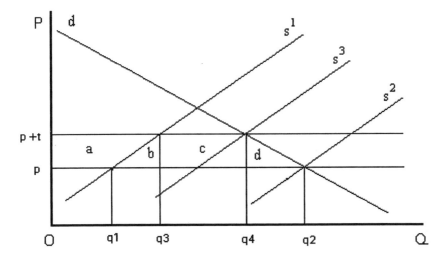

Fig. B1.   Distributive effects of a tariff on sectors of the domestic economy

tion, they suffer a loss in consumer surplus corresponding to areas *B* and *D* (for a more extensive treatment, see B. Yarbrough and R. Yarbrough 1991, chap. 7).

Appendix C: Supplement to Chapter 6

C1. Measures and Data Sources

Court Decisions. Data on decisions at the Court of International Trade and other case-specific information were obtained from the *United States Court of International Trade,* 1980–90 Annual Reports. When the Court of International Trade affirms a challenged agency action, the decision is coded 1, while reversed actions are coded 0. Data for the Federal Circuit were obtained from the U.S. Court of Appeals for the Federal Circuit reports, 1980–90. Decisions favorable to the agency were coded 1; those otherwise were coded 0. For both courts, remand decisions were interpreted as "soft reversals" and so were coded 0.

Agency, Policy Direction, and Duty. Data on all ITC (coded 0) and DOC (coded 1) cases from 1980 through 1990 were obtained from the ITC annual reports for 1979–91 and the U.S. Federal Register for the same years. The policy direction variable was coded 1 (for a positive agency decision) if the agency ruled in favor of granting protection to the U.S. industry; it was coded 0 otherwise. The size of the duty for each case is reported in the U.S. Federal Register. The data include all countervailing duty and antidumping cases appealed to the Court of International Trade in this period. To incorporate economic factors in the models, products involved in each case were categorized at the four-digit Standard Industrial Classification (SIC) level using the *U.S. Bureau of the Census Numerical List of Manufactured Products* for various years.

Concentration Ratios. Concentration ratios measure the percentage of output by the four largest firms in an industry. Concentrated ratios are recorded here at the four-digit SIC level and are available in *U.S. Bureau of the Census, Subject Statistics,* various years.

$$\text{Foreign Penetration} = \frac{Imports}{domestic\ consumption}$$

where domestic consumption = shipments - exports + imports. Foreign penetration was computed at the four-digit SIC level from data on imports, exports, and shipments from the *U.S. Bureau of the Census Annual Survey of Manufacturers* (shipments), *U.S. Exports of Domestic Merchandise, SIC-Based Products by World Areas,* and *U.S. Imports for Consumption, SIC-Based Products by World Areas.*

Capital Expenditures.   Capital expenditures are available at the four-digit SIC level from the *U.S. Bureau of the Census, Annual Survey of Manufacturers.*

Reputation.   Reputation is measured by the yearly number of antidumping and countervailing duty actions initiated against each country accused in a court case as an unfair trader. These data are available in *Operations of the Trade Agreements Program* published by the United States Trade Representative.

Country Trade Deficit.   Country trade deficit is the trade balance (foreign imports - U.S. exports) between the United States and each country involved in a case, obtained from the *Direction of Trade Statistics Yearbook,* various years, published by the International Monetary Fund.

C2.   The Weighted Least Squares Model

The small number of antidumping and countervailing duty cases decided by the Federal Circuit suggest the reanalysis of the data through an alternative technique. An estimator that is less sensitive to sample size is weighted least squares (WLS). I rely on this method, proposed by Goldberger (1964, 249–50), to check the substantive results of the logit model. This is a technique calling for the estimation of a binary choice model through ordinary least squares (OLS) and then performing a correction for heteroschedasticity, using predicted values derived from the OLS model. Two steps are involved.

First, estimate the decision-making model for the Federal Circuit,

$$\text{Prob }(Y = 1|x_{1i}, x_{2i}, \ldots, x_{ki}) = F(\beta'x)$$

where $\beta'x = E(Y|X_i) = \hat{Y}$. Set all values in which $\hat{Y} \geq 1$ equal to .99 and all values in which $\hat{Y} \leq 0$ equal to .01. Using these restricted values, create a weight variable, ω.

$$\omega = \sqrt{E\left(y_i|x_i\right) * 1 - E\left(y_i|x_i\right)}$$
$$= \sqrt{\hat{y}_i * \left(1 - \hat{y}_i\right)}$$

Second, using ω, estimate a general model such as the following, which corrects for heteroschedasticity.

$$\frac{Y_i}{\omega} = \frac{\beta_0}{\omega} + \frac{\beta_1 x_1}{\omega} + \dots\dots + \frac{\beta_k x_j}{\omega} + \frac{\varepsilon_i}{\omega} \quad\Bigg|$$ *intercept suppressed*

The decision-making model for the Court of Appeals for the Federal Circuit is stated as follows:

Prob $(Y = 1)$ = f(Import Duty, Nature of the Case, Agency Structure,

Party Affiliation of Panel Majority, Concentration

Ratio, Country Trade Deficit, Capital Foreign

Penetration)

Appendix D: Supplement to Chapter 8

TABLE D1. Determinants of Specialized Court of Appeals Deference in AD and CVD Cases, 1980–90 (WLS Estimates)

Independent Variable	Contextual Fact Model		Politics and Economics Model		General Model	
	MLE	SE	MLE	SE	MLE	SE
Case Factors						
Nature of the Case[a]	.144	.069**			.169	.070**
Import Duty	.005	.003*			.007	.004*
Agency	−.351	.128**			−.443	.131***
Policy Direction	−.127	.125			−.173	.126
Political Factors						
Political Affiliation of Panel Majority[b]			−.237	.132*	−.254	.126**
Concentration Ratio			−.0006	.003	−.001	.003
Economic Factors						
Country Trade Deficit			.012	.007*	.015	.006**
Foreign Penetrations			.139	.589	.527	.569
Constant	.969	.272**	.874	.200***	1.206	.384***
Adjusted R^2	.75		.72		.77	
Durbin-Watson	1.95		1.98		1.98	
Number of cases	57		56		55	
F-statistic	35.95		29.79		21.66	
Significance	$p < .001$		$p < .001$		$p < .001$	

Note: Entries are unstandardized weighted least squares (WLS) estimates. The data include antidumping and countervailing duty cases appealed to the Court of Appeals for the Federal Circuit from the International Trade Commission and the Department of Commerce.

[a]Inter-coder agreement = .61.

[b]Odd number of circuit judges in a panel is typically three or higher.

*$p \leq .10$ one-tailed; **$p \leq .05$ one-tailed; ***$p \leq .01$ one-tailed

Notes

Chapter 1

1. Chief Justice Burger made this remark in 1982 during a time of national debate to create more specialized courts, quoted in Middleton 1983, 23.

2. Apart from the power to act pursuant to such congressional delegation, the executive claims its own power to act in international trade matters pursuant to its foreign relations powers. The legal precedent for this power was stated by Justice George Sutherland in his opinion in *United States v. Curtiss-Wright Corp.* that the executive is the "sole organ of the federal government in the field of international relations" (1936, 320).

3. See *Marubeni America Corp. v. United States,* 17 CIT 360–65 (1993).

4. For further confirmation of Shapiro's contention, see the statement of Chief Justice Warren Burger quoted in Middleton 1983, 23.

5. Quoted in Middleton 1983, 23.

6. Among all federal administrative agencies, the Social Security Administration (SSA) has the greatest number of ALJs. In 1986, for example, despite personnel cutbacks by the Reagan administration, there were 750 ALJs in the SSA alone (Cofer 1986, 229).

Chapter 2

1. This bill was the Tariff Act of July 4, 1789. It was the second statute passed by the First Congress and was meant to legislate duties on enumerated imports.

2. Senate, *New Title for Board of General Appraisers,* 69th Cong., 1st sess., 1926, S. Rept. 781, 1–2.

3. For a more complete history of the Court of Customs, see Reed 1996, chap. 4; Re 1981.

4. House, *Customs Court Act of 1980,* 96th Cong., 2d sess., 1980, H. Rept. 1235, 18.

5. Senate Subcommittee on Improvements in Judicial Machinery of the Committee on the Judiciary, *Customs Court Act of 1979, Hearings on S.R. 1654,* 96th Cong., 1st sess., 10 September 1979.

6. The only significant opposition to creating the Court of International Trade came from the AFL-CIO on the grounds that "[b]usinesses, consumers, workers and communities throughout the nation are affected by trade. [Therefore] the dis-

trict courts, which are in the communities [across the nation], are the best equipped to handle issues related to these effects, because they are not solely trade problems, but domestic problems created by trade" (statement of Dr. Rudolph Oswald testifying on behalf of the AFL-CIO before the Subcommittee on Improvements in Judicial Machinery [Ibid., 71–72]). The union's chief concern was the administration of adjustment assistance to workers displaced from their jobs due to foreign trade competition. The union failed in its attempt to leave this issue in the hands of the federal district courts.

7. *Congressional Record,* 96th Cong., 2d sess., 1980, 26, pt. 20: 27063–64.

8. The Commerce Court is the "black sheep" of specialized courts. It existed from 1910 to 1913, during the administration of William H. Taft. The court's creation was fervently pushed by railroad interests, and after it was established to review Interstate Commerce Commission decisions, significant evidence emerged that the court was catering to the interests of the railroad trusts and tycoons. That sparked a political maelstrom, prompting Congress to quickly abolish the court just three years after it was created (Lorch 1967, 67–69; Bruff 1991).

9. It should be noted that the extent to which a president makes a patronage appointment may also depend upon how sensitive such a president is to charges of nepotism, especially in the context of modern media scrutiny of judicial appointments.

10. The ABA started rating judicial nominees for the Justice Department and the Senate Judiciary Committee in 1952. Until the Bush administration, the ABA rated nominees under a four-point scale as "Exceptionally Well Qualified," "Well Qualified," "Qualified," and "Not Qualified." In April 1989, at the urging of the Department of Justice, five Republican members of the Senate Judiciary Committee called for hearings to scrutinize the ABA's role in the appointment process, charging that the ABA has a liberal ideological bias, which it claimed was manifested in low rating of conservative nominees (Biskupic 1989). The most pointed example that right-wingers use to criticize the ABA is the "Not Qualified" rating of judge Robert Bork of the D.C. Circuit when he was nominated in 1987 to replace retiring Supreme Court justice Lewis Powell. In June 1989, the ABA agreed to remove the "Exceptionally Well Qualified" category from its rating scale, leaving the other three. For all tables using ABA rating in this book, the "Exceptionally Well Qualified" rating is merged with the "Well Qualified" rating for all presidents before George Bush to facilitate comparison of the judges.

11. Many presidents have expressed painful disappointment with some of their appointments. For example, at the Supreme Court level, Republican president Dwight Eisenhower is said to have quibbled that his appointment of Chief Justice Earl Warren was "the biggest damn-fooled mistake" he had ever made (quoted in O'Brien 1993, 106).

12. This practice applies to the Democratic party as well. Numerous instances exist where the appointment efforts of Republican presidents have been thwarted by a Democratic Senate (Biskupic 1989). In spite of that, there are factors that may temper the effect of partisanship in the Senate. Senators from the president's party do share some common institutional interests with senators from the other party.

For example, institutional integrity is damaged when the Senate goes along with the president on a nominee of questionable merit. So even for specialized courts, especially a specialized court located in Washington, D.C., and having jurisdiction over certain grievances involving the Senate itself, it is unlikely that senators from the president's party would place overwhelming emphasis on partisanship over qualification.

13. This quotation is from a letter to the author written on January 21, 1994, by Federal Circuit judge Giles Sutherland Rich and is used here by permission of Judge Rich. The full text of the letter appears in appendix A4.

14. See *Almanac of the Federal Judiciary* 1996, vol. 2, *Lawyers' Comments 'about the Federal Circuit,* 1–3. New York: Aspen Law and Business Publishers.

15. These unions include the United Auto Workers, the United Steelworkers of America, the Amalgamated Clothing and Textile Workers, the International Union of Electronic and Electrical Workers, the International Ladies Garment Workers, and the United Mine Workers (Cohodas 1988).

Chapter 3

1. The Office of the USTR is not formally an agency, although it is organized as one. The office was created by Congress in 1962 to serve as liaison between the legislative and executive branches in trade matters. The USTR also negotiates executive agreements such as the North American Free Trade Agreement (NAFTA) and other agreements sponsored by the General Agreement on Tariff and Trade (GATT), such as the recently completed Uruguay Round. Since the creation of this office, U.S. trade representatives have seen the job of managing international trade grow increasingly complex. Because of the salience of trade, the rise in global competitiveness, and the need to maintain adequate response to these developments, the number of employees in this office has grown remarkably since 1962. In addition, the USTR has become one of the most visible and most prestigious positions in the executive branch.

2. There are other agencies that are also concerned with some aspects of international trade. For example, the Department of Labor is concerned with international trade to the extent that it affects American workers. This agency administers the adjustment assistance program, which is designed to assist workers who have been negatively affected by trade competition. The Department of Agriculture is also intimately involved in some aspects of U.S. international trade. But these two agencies are not analyzed in this book.

3. Except for sections that are specifically designated as referring to the International Trade Administration, the terms *DOC* and *ITA* are used interchangeably throughout this book.

4. Domestic firms that depend on imports and are party to the proceedings at the administrative level may also appeal an affirmative agency decision to the courts, but such firms usually ally themselves with the foreign firm and participate as intervenors.

5. See McCraw 1984 for an exposition of regulatory history in the United

States, including the critical roles played by four prophets of regulation: Charles Francis Adams, Louis D. Brandeis, James M. Landis, and Alfred E. Kahn.

6. Note that the budget of the foreign and commercial services section of the ITA is included with the budget of the trade development section and reported jointly (see *Budget of the United States Government,* 1980–87).

7. See *Trade and Tariff Act of 1984,* Public Law 98–573, U.S. Code 1994 Edition, vol. 9, title 19, sec. 1677(b).

8. See Murray 1991, 39.

9. See U.S. International Trade Commission 1992, 5.

10. *Trade and Tariff Act of 1984,* Public Law 98–573, U.S. Code 1994 Edition, vol. 9, title 19, sec. 1677(10).

11. Recently in the case of *Calabrian Corp. v. United States* (1992), the Court of International Trade ruled that the International Trade Commission may use price as a determinant of the "like" product. See also U.S. International Trade Commission 1992, and *Granges Metallverken A.B. v. United States* (1989).

12. See the discussion in Knoll 1989, 80; see also U.S. International Trade Commission 1986, 13–17.

13. *House, Trade Remedies Reform Act of 1984,* 98th Cong., 2d Sess., 1984, H. Rept 725, 37.

14. Some of these cases include *Copperweld Corp. v. United States* (1988); *Hyundai Pipe Co., Ltd. v. U.S. International Trade Commission* (1988); *Alberta Pork Producers' Marketing Board v. United States* (1987); and *Fundicao Tupy S.A. v. United States* (1988).

Chapter 4

1. See Anthony Lewis, "A Profound Contempt," *New York Times,* 21 May 1984, A17. The agency's practice eventually led the Court of Appeals for the Ninth Circuit to issue a circuitwide injunction against continued nonacquiescence in the case of *Lopez v. Heckler* (1984). A more detailed discussion of nonacquiescence in the SSA is given by Derthick (1990, chap. 7).

2. Note that Lowi did not declare faith in such a process because in his view, "it impairs legitimacy by converting government from a moralistic to a mechanistic institution" (1984, 65).

3. For a recent discussion of the life-cycle thesis and its application to public policy, see Baumgartner and Jones 1993.

4. In his original usage of this concept, Stigler failed to make any distinction between bureaucrats and legislators. He simply referred to them both as "regulator," perhaps because he thought the distinction unimportant at the time.

5. The legal precedent goes back to the FDR administration when in October 1933 the president decided, for policy reasons, to fire William E. Humphrey, a conservative member of the Federal Trade Commission (FTC), who had been appointed by President Hoover. The agency had authority over many economic policies key to the New Deal. In a unanimous opinion by Justice Sutherland, the Supreme Court decided in *Humphrey's Executor v. United States* (1935) that since the FTC was created by Congress to carry into effect legislative policies, commis-

sioners (and therefore federal officials not of the executive branch) must be free from executive control.

Chapter 5

1. It is possible that the public esteem for the judiciary remains stronger than that for the legislative and executive branches because real public knowledge of court decisions and activities is low. Part of the blame can be attributed to the episodic and generally superficial media coverage of courts.

2. *Zenith Radio Corp. v. United States* (1978, 450) is the only case decided by the Supreme Court since 1978 that deals with the subsidization of imports by foreign countries. In this case, the Treasury Department secretary's interpretation of what constituted a "bounty or a grant" as required by trade statutes was challenged. After examining the legislative history, the Court sided with the secretary's interpretation as being reasonable and within the meaning of the statute.

3. Supreme Court decisions repugnant to the legislature and the states can be overturned with a constitutional amendment. In U.S. constitutional history, however, it has been incredibly difficult and rare for Supreme Court decisions to be overturned by a constitutional amendment. So far only four constitutional amendments have been enacted to overturn Supreme Court precedents. These are the Eleventh (protects states from lawsuits by citizens of other states), Fourteenth (conferred citizenship to all persons born or naturalized in the United States and overturned *Dred Scott v. Sanford* [1857]), Sixteenth (legalized income tax), and Twenty-sixth (lowered voting age to 18) (see Epstein and Walker 1992, 10).

Chapter 6

1. This is a gatekeeping power requiring that any four of the nine justices must vote to hear a case before it can be heard.

2. I was unable to gather the industry data for the cases of unfair practices in import trade (Section 337) and so these data are not included in the regression models reported in chapter 8. While the data are limited in this sense, the few Section 337 variables that I do have will complement the analysis I seek to make. Section 337 cases usually concern infringement of intellectual property rights of citizens and corporations, and only the ITC is responsible for conducting investigations to determine whether such infringement exists and issuing a policy recommendation to the president. Section 337 determinations are subject to judicial review, not in the Court of International Trade but in the Federal Circuit, with possible appeal to the Supreme Court.

3. A key piece of evidence concerning GATT's success in promoting freer trade around the world is that among the industrial countries alone, average tariff levels declined from a high of 10 percent in the 1950s to less than 5 percent in 1990 (see Yoffie 1993, xii).

4. My discussion with court staff suggests that judges very rarely issue unpublished opinions and that when they do, the matters involved are usually trivial and nondispositive.

5. See Committee on Use of Appellate Court Energies, Advisory Council for Appellate Justice, *Standards for Publication of Judicial Opinions,* Federal Judicial Center Research Series, no. 73–2 (Washington, DC: 1973); see also Hoffman (1981).

6. This valuable database was produced by Professor Harold J. Spaeth of Michigan State University and in 1991 published by the Inter-University Consortium for Political and Social Research (ICPSR) as data set no. 9422.

7. This database was produced in 1990 by Professor C.K. Rowland of the University of Kansas. The data are unpublished civil cases filed and terminated in the three federal district courts and are available from the ICPSR (no. 9367).

8. Under the constitutional facts doctrine, however, a reviewing court may scrutinize the trial court's finding of facts when that finding is deemed clearly erroneous and deprives a litigant of due process rights (*Fiske v. Kansas* 1927). But in recent years, the Supreme Court has moved to discourage this practice in order to "preserve the respect due trial judges by minimizing appellate court interference with numerous decisions they must make in the prejudgment stages of litigation [and] to promote the efficient administration of justice" (*Firestone Tire & Rubber Co v. Risjord* 1981, 374).

9. Oftentimes when Federal Circuit judges issue their opinions, their discussion of the case facts is truncated for reasons of judicial economy. It is not uncommon for the Federal Circuit to adopt the opinion of the lower court as its own and to refer readers interested in getting background information on the case to the lower court's opinion. See, for example, *Bantam Travelware Div. of Peter's Bag Corp. v. United States* (1988).

10. Wood and Waterman (1991) provide a good analysis of the behavior of regulatory agencies and the importance of institutional structure in the responsiveness to political control. They find, for example, that executive branch agencies are more responsive to executive political influence than are independent regulatory agencies.

11. I thank Wendy L. Hansen for making these data available to me.

12. The cost of pursuing an international trade case is enormous. The expense starts at the agency level. According to the General Accounting Office, the average cost of pursuing an international trade remedy runs from $150,000 to $555,000 for antidumping cases, plus $50,000 to $85,000 to appeal the case to the Court of International Trade (U.S. General Accounting Office 1988).

13. Litigants frequently need access to past judicial dispositions or other court information that can be relevant to their case preparations. In the Court of International Trade in New York City, where most trade hearings are held, it cost 50 cents per page to photocopy documents in 1997, and by court rule, court documents cannot be removed from the courthouse.

Chapter 7

1. *Cumulation* is the aggregation of volume and price information with respect to imports from two or more countries for the purposes of the ITC's material injury determination. The aggregation of supposedly dumped or supposedly subsidized imports from two or more countries for the purposes of volume and price

analyses is termed *cross-cumulation.* See the opinion of Judge Oscar Davis in *Bing-ham & Taylor Division, Virginia Industries, Inc. v. United States* (1987).

2. The calculation for this test is $C = -2 *$ (Log-likelihood ratio$_{\text{restricted model}} -$ Log-likelihood ratio$_{\text{unrestricted model}}$), with degrees of freedom equal to the number of restrictions in the constrained model. C is the nested chi-square value. For the models in table 10, $C = 18.06$, which is significant only at the 20 percent level with 13 degrees of freedom. (For more information on the nested chi-square test, see Aldrich and Nelson 1984, 59).

3. This variable was initially coded trichotomously as 0 = domestic firm, 1 = foreign firm, 2 = both. From these three categories, I constructed two dummy vari-ables using the "both" category as the base category to isolate the independent effects of domestic and foreign firms.

4. I do not consider certain political and economic factors in this model because doing so would defy the logic of the model, which is to explain whether the Court of International Trade is likely to affirm or reverse a regulatory decision. For example, if the model were to include a variable such as concentration ratio, a significant and positive coefficient would mean that the court is likely to affirm a protectionist regulatory decision and a nonprotectionist decision simultaneously when the domestic industry is highly concentrated. That would make the most sense if the protectionist cases were separated from the nonprotectionist ones. In subsequent models, I separate the cases so as to determine the directional impact of the variables.

5. The analysis reported here builds on work reported in my 1995 article with Wendy L. Hansen and Renée J. Johnson published in the *American Journal of Political Science.* The choice variable in the present discussion focuses on the *pol-icy* decisions of the court above and beyond judicial deference, which is the focus of the cases we used in the models reported in our article to explain the dynamics of specialized court-agency interactions.

6. In addition, I examined whether Democratic judges as a group were more protectionist or less protectionist than Republican judges as a group, using the appointing president's party as the control variable. No clear pattern emerges to suggest that party affiliation plays a decisive role in whether the court would award regulatory protection to domestic firms. As indicated earlier, the unrestricted model is more representative of CIT decision making. Hence, the outcome of the unrestricted model is discussed. The restricted model, however, is incomplete; the significant showing of the political affiliation of the judges in the restricted model in table 11 is therefore unimportant.

7. My figures are from the 1988 GAO report on the pursuit of trade remedies by small business. On average, an additional $42,000 to $168,000 is required to successfully pursue an administrative review whereby administrative agencies determine whether to continue, alter, or terminate the remedies being provided to an industry by the government (U.S. General Accounting Office 1988).

Chapter 8

1. This information was obtained by fax from the Clerk of the Court of Appeals for the Federal Circuit, March 29, 1995.

2. The substantive results of the logit and WLS methods were similar in terms of the their coefficients and variables that reached statistical significance. But because the distribution of the dependent variable is skewed, with a mean of .71, weighted least squares predicted only 30 percent of the cases within the .8 and 1.0 range and one case to be 1.20, which proves that a linear estimator is inappropriate to explain binary choice situations (Aldrich and Nelson 1984). And so, for theoretical reasons, the logit results are reported and discussed.

3. The calculation for AIC is given by the equation: AIC $= -2*(\text{LLR} + K)$, where K is the number of variables to be estimated.

4. Excerpted from January 21, 1994, letter of Judge Giles Sutherland Rich to author and used here by permission of Judge Rich. (Full text of the letter appears in appendix A4.)

Chapter 9

1. In antidumping and countervailing duty cases, the European Community, Australia, Canada, and developing countries are also very active. But the United States is the undisputed leader of the pack (see Nivola 1993, 72; Boltuck and Litan 1991, 5).

References

Aberbach, Joel D., and Bert A. Rockman. 1976. "Clashing Beliefs Within the Executive Branch." *American Political Science Review* 70:456–68.

Abraham, Henry J. 1986. "Contemporary Judicial Processes and a Democratic Society." *Political Science Quarterly* 101:277–88.

Abraham, Henry J. 1988. *Freedom and the Court,* 5th ed. New York: Oxford University Press.

Abraham, Henry J., Griffin B. Bell, Charles E. Grassley, Eugene W. Hickok, John W. Kern, Stephan J. Markman, and Wm. Bradford Reynolds, eds. 1990. *Judicial Selection, Merit, Ideology and Politics.* Washington, DC: National Center for the Public Interest.

Administrative Office of the United States Courts. 1994. *Report of the Director, L. Ralph Mecham: Judicial Business of the United States Courts.* Washington DC.

Alchian, Armen A. 1950. "Uncertainty, Evolution, and Economic Theory." *Journal of Political Economy* 58:211–21.

Alchian, Armen A., and Harold Demsetz. 1972. "Production, Information Cost, and Economic Organization." *American Economic Review* 62:777–95.

Aldrich, John H., and Forrest D. Nelson. 1984. *Linear Probability, Logit, and Probit Models.* Newbury Park: Sage Publications.

Allison, Graham T. 1971. *The Essence of Decision.* Boston: Little, Brown.

Almanac of the Federal Judiciary. 1996. Vols. 1 and 2. New York: Aspen Law and Business Publishers.

Amemiya, Takeshi. 1980. "Selection of Regressors." *International Economic Review* 21:331–54.

Anderson, Keith B. 1993. "Agency Discretion or Statutory Direction: Decision Making at the U.S. International Trade Commission." *Journal of Law and Economics* 36:915–35.

Arnold, Douglas R. 1987. "Political Control of Administrative Officials." *Journal of Law, Economics, and Organization* 3:279–86.

Arthurs, Rich. 1986. "ITC's Liebeler: Tough Enough to Advance to the Federal Circuit?" *Legal Times,* 30 June.

Baldwin, Robert. 1985. *Political Economy of U.S. Import Policy.* Cambridge: MIT Press.

Ball, Howard. 1987. *Courts and Politics: The Federal Judicial System.* Englewood Cliffs, NJ: Prentice Hall.

Bardach, Eugene, and Robert A. Kagan. 1982. *Going by the Book: The Problem of Regulatory Unreasonableness.* Philadelphia: Temple University Press.

Barshefsky, Charlene, and Michael J. Firth. 1988. "International Trade Decisions of the United States Court of Appeals for the Federal Circuit during the Year 1987." *American University Law Review* 37:1167–1206.

Barringer, William H., and Christopher A. Dunn. 1979. "Antidumping and Countervailing Duty Investigations under the Trade Agreements Act of 1979." *The Journal of International Law and Economics* 14:1–37.

Barrow, Deborah, Gary Zuk, and Gerard S. Gryski. 1996. *The Federal Judiciary and Institutional Change.* Ann Arbor: University of Michigan Press.

Bauer, Raymond A., Ithiel De Sola Pool, and Lewis A. Dexter. 1963. *American Business and Public Policy: The Politics of Foreign Trade.* New York: Antherton Press.

Baum, Lawrence. 1977. "Judicial Specialization, Litigant Influence, and Substantive Policy: The Court of Customs and Patent Appeals." *Law and Society Review* 11:823–50.

Baum, Lawrence. 1982. "The Influences of Legislative and Appellate Courts Over the Policy Implementation Process." In *Cases in Public Policy-Making,* 2d ed., ed. James E. Anderson. New York: Holt/Rinehart/Winston Press.

Baum, Lawrence. 1990. *American Courts: Policy and Process,* 2d ed. Boston: Houghton Mifflin.

Baum, Lawrence. 1991. "Specializing the Federal Courts: Neutral Reforms or Efforts to Shape Judicial Policy?" *Judicature* 74:217–24.

Baum, Lawrence. 1994a. "Specialization and Authority Acceptance: The Supreme Court and Lower Federal Courts." *Political Research Quarterly* 47:693–703.

Baum, Lawrence. 1994b. "What Judges Want: Judges' Goals and Judicial Behavior." *Political Research Quarterly* 47:749–68.

Baumgartner, Frank R., and Bryan D. Jones. 1993. *Agendas and Instability in American Politics.* Chicago: University of Chicago Press.

Bawn, Kathleen. 1995. "Political Control Versus Expertise: Congressional Choices about Administrative Procedures." *American Political Science Review* 89:62–73.

Becker, Gary S. 1983. "A Theory of Competition among Pressure Groups for Political Influence." *Quarterly Journal of Economics* 98:371–400.

Becker, Gary S. 1985. "Public Policies, Pressure Groups, and Dead Weight Costs." *Journal of Public Economics* 28:329–47.

Bendor, Jonathan, Serge Taylor, and Roland Van Gaalen. 1985. "Bureaucratic Expertise Versus Legislative Authority: A Model of Deception and Monitoring in Budgeting." *American Political Science Review* 79:1041–60.

Bennett, Marion T. 1991. *The United States Court of Appeals for the Federal Circuit—A History (1982–1990).* Published by Authorization of the United States Judicial Conference Committee on the Bicentennial of the Constitution of the United States.

Bentley, Arthur. 1908. *The Process of Government.* Chicago: University of Chicago Press.

Bernstein, Marver H. 1955. *Regulating Business by Independent Regulatory Commission.* Princeton: Princeton University Press.

Berry, Jeffrey M. 1977. *Lobbying for the People.* Princeton: Princeton University Press.

Berry, Kristine R. 1989. "IMPORTS—Cumulation and Unfair Trade Competition—Cumulation Deemed Proper When a 'Reasonable Overlap' of Competition Exists."*Georgia Journal of Comparative and International Law* 19: 653–64.

Bhagwati, Jagdish. 1988. *Protectionism.* Cambridge: MIT Press.

Biskupic, Joan. 1989. "Justice Department and ABA Settle Their Differences." *Congressional Quarterly Weekly Report* 47:1327.

Biskupic, Joan. 1992. "Bush Treads Well-Worn Path in Building Federal Bench." *Congressional Quarterly Weekly Report* 50:111–13.

Boltuck, Richard, and Robert E. Litan, eds. 1991. *Down in the Dumps: Administration of the Unfair Trade Laws.* Washington, DC: Brookings Institution.

Bond, Jon R. 1980. "The Politics of Court Structure." *Law and Policy Quarterly* 2:181–88.

Brenner, Saul. 1984. "Issue Specialization as a Variable in Opinion Assignment on the U.S. Supreme Court." *Journal of Politics* 46:1217–25.

Brown, Roger G. 1982. "Party and Bureaucracy: From Kennedy to Reagan." *Political Science Quarterly* 97:279–94.

Bruff, Harold H.1991. "Specialized Courts in Administrative Law." *Administrative Law Review* 43:329–66.

Budget of the United States Government, 1980–1987.

Caldeira, Gregory A. 1985. "The Transmission of Legal Precedent: A Study of State Supreme Courts." *American Political Science Review* 79:178–93.

Caldeira, Gregory A. 1986. "Neither the Purse nor the Sword: Dynamics of Public Confidence in the Supreme Court." *American Political Science Review* 80: 1209–26.

Caldeira, Gregory A. 1987. "Public Opinion and the Supreme Court: FDR's Court-Packing Plan." *American Political Science Review* 81:1139–53.

Caldeira, Gregory A., and John Wright. 1995. "Lobbying for Justice: The Rise of Organized Conflict in the Politics of Federal Judgeships." In *Contemplating Courts,* ed. Lee Epstein. Washington, DC: CQ Press.

Calvert, Randall, Mark J. Moran, and Barry Weingast. 1987. "Congressional Influence Over Policy Making: The Case of the FTC." In *Congress: Structure and Policy,* ed. Matthew McCubbins and Terry Sullivan. New York: Cambridge University Press.

Canon, Bradley C. 1991. "Courts and Policy: Compliance, Implementation, and Impact." In *The American Courts: A Critical Assessment,* ed. John B. Gates and Charles A. Johnson. Washington, DC: CQ Press.

Cannon, James R. 1991. "Should the Federal Circuit Take a 'Hard Look' at International Trade Cases in the 1990s?" *American University Law Review* 40: 1093–1115.

Carp, Robert A., and C. K. Rowland. 1983. *Policy-Making and Politics in the Federal District Courts.* Knoxville: University of Tennessee Press.

Carp, Robert A., and Ronald Stidham. 1996. *Judicial Process in America,* 3d ed. Washington, DC: CQ Press.

Chase, Harold W. 1972. *Federal Judges: The Appointing Process.* Minneapolis: University of Minnesota Press.

Cheyes, Abram. 1976. "The Role of the Judge in Public Law Litigation." *Harvard Law Review* 89:1281–1316.

Chubb, John E. 1985. "The Political Economy of Federalism." *American Political Science Review.* 79:994–1015.

Coase, Ronald. 1937. "The Nature of the Firm." *Econometrica* 4:386–405.

Cofer, Donna Price. 1986. "The Question of Independence Continues: Administrative Law Judges within the Social Security Administration." *Judicature* 69:228–35.

Cohen, David M. 1981. "The 'Residual Jurisdiction' of the Court of International Trade under the Customs Court Act of 1980." *New York Law School Law Review* 26:471–503.

Cohen, David M. 1990. "International Trade Decisions of the United States Court of Appeals for the Federal Circuit During 1989." *American University Law Review* 39:1171–1231.

Cohen, Mark A. 1992. "The Motives of Judges: Empirical Evidence from Antitrust Sentencing." *International Review of Law and Economics* 12:13–30.

Cohen, Michael D., James G. March, and Johan P. Olsen. 1972. "A Garbage Can Model of Organizational Choice." *Administrative Science Quarterly* 17:1–25.

Cohodas, Nadine. 1988. "Trade Views Imperil Reagan Judicial Nominee." *Congressional Quarterly Weekly Report* 46:675–76.

Coleman, John J., and David B. Yoffie. 1990. "Institutional Incentives for Protection: The American Use of Voluntary Export Restraints." In *International Trade: The Changing Role of the United States,* ed. Frank J. Macchiarola. New York: Academy of Political Science.

Cook, Brian J., and B. Dan Wood. 1989. "Principal-Agent Models of Political Control of Bureaucracy." *American Political Science Review* 83:965–78.

Cooper, Richard N. 1987. "Trade Policy as Foreign Policy." In *U.S. Trade Policies in a Changing World Economy,* ed. Robert M. Stern. Cambridge: MIT Press.

Cramton, Roger C. 1976. "Judicial Lawmaking and Administration." *Public Administration Review* 36:551–62.

Crowley, Donald W. 1987."Judicial Review of Administrative Agencies: Does the Type of Agency Matter?" *Western Political Quarterly* 40:265–83.

Currie, David P., and Frank I. Goodman. 1975. "Judicial Review of Federal Administrative Action: Quest for the Optimum Forum." *Columbia Law Review* 75:1–85.

Dahl, Robert A. 1957. "Decision-Making in a Democracy: The Supreme Court as a National Policymaker." *Journal of Public Law* 6:279–95.

Davis, Otto A., M. A. H. Dempster, and Aaron Wildavsky. 1966. "A Theory of the Budgetary Process." *American Political Science Review* 60:529–47.

Denzau, Arthur T., and Michael C. Munger. 1986. "Legislators and Interest Groups: How Unorganized Interests Get Represented." *American Political Science Review* 80:89–106.

Derthick, Martha. 1990. *Agency Under Stress: The Social Security Administration in American Politics.* Washington, DC: Brookings Institution.

Derthick, Martha, and Paul J. Quirk. 1985. *The Politics of Deregulation.* Washington, DC: Brookings Institution.

Destler, I. M. 1986. "Protecting Congress or Protecting Trade?" *Foreign Policy* 62:96–107.

Destler, I. M. 1992. *American Trade Politics,* 2d ed. Washington, DC: Institute for International Economics.

Destler, I. M., and John S. Odell. 1987. *Anti-Protection: Changing Forces in United States Trade Politics.* Washington, DC: Institute for International Economics Press.

DeWitt, Benjamin Parke. 1915. *The Progressive Movement: A Non-Partisan, Comprehensive Discussion of Current Tendencies in American Politics.* New York: Macmillan Press.

Dilulio, John J., Jr. 1987. *Governing Prisons: A Comparative Study of Correctional Management.* New York: Free Press.

Dix, George E. 1964. "The Death of the Commerce Court: A Study in Institutional Weakness." *American Journal of Legal History* 8:238–60.

Dobson, John M. 1976. *Two Centuries of Tariffs: The Background and Emergence of the U.S. International Trade Commission.* Washington, DC: U.S. Government Printing Office.

Downs, Anthony. 1967. *Inside Bureaucracy.* Boston: Little, Brown.

Ducat, Craig R., and Robert L. Dudley. 1989. "Federal District Judges and Presidential Power During the Postwar Era." *Journal of Politics* 51:98–118.

Dunner, Donald R. 1992. "Federal Circuit Bar Association and American Bar Association Tenth Anniversary Celebration of the United States Court of Appeals for the Federal Circuit." *Federal Circuit Bar Journal* 2:297–301.

Dutt, Jill. 1993. "NAFTA Passes: House OKs Trade Pact, 234–200, after Heated Debate." *Newsday,* 18 November.

Eavey, Cheryl L., and Gary J. Miller. 1984. "Bureaucratic Agenda Control: Imposition or Bargaining?" *American Political Science Review* 78:719–33.

Eggertsson, Thrainn. 1990. *Economic Behavior and Institutions.* New York: Cambridge University Press.

Ehrenhaft, Peter D. 1981. "The 'Judicialization' of Trade Law." *Notre Dame Lawyer* 56:595–613.

Eichengreen, Barry. 1988. "Did International Economic Forces Cause the Great Depression?" *Contemporary Policy Issues* 6:92–114.

Eisner, Marc A. 1991. *Antitrust and the Triumph of Economics: Institutions, Expertise, and Policy Change.* Chapel Hill: University of North Carolina Press.

Eisner, Marc A., and Kenneth Meier. 1990. "Presidential Control versus Bureaucratic Power: Explaining the Reagan Revolution in Antitrust." *American Journal of Political Science* 34:269–87.

Elhauge, Einer R. 1991. "Does Interest Group Theory Justify More Intrusive Judicial Review?" *Yale Law Journal* 101:31–110.

Epstein, David, and Sharyn O'Halloran. 1994. "Administrative Procedures, Information, and Agency Discretion." *American Journal of Political Science* 38:697–722.

Epstein, Lee, and C. K. Rowland. 1991. "Debunking the Myth of Interest Group Invincibility in the Courts." *American Political Science Review* 85:205–17.

Epstein, Lee, Jeffrey A. Segal, Harold J. Spaeth, and Thomas G. Walker. 1994. *The Supreme Court Compendium: Data, Decisions, and Developments.* Washington, DC: CQ Press.

Epstein, Lee, and Thomas G. Walker. 1992. *Constitutional Law for a Changing America: Rights, Liberties, and Justice.* Washington, DC: CQ Press.

Epstein, Lee, Thomas G. Walker, and William J. Dixon. 1989. "The Supreme Court and Criminal Justice Disputes: A Neo-Institutional Perspective." *American Journal of Political Science* 33:825–41.

Estreicher, Samuel, and Richard L. Revesz. 1989. "Nonacquiescence by Federal Administrative Agencies." *Yale Law Journal* 98:679–710.

Fama, Eugene F. 1980. "Agency Problem and the Theory of the Firm." *Journal of Political Economy* 88:288–307.

Farber, Daniel A., and Philip P. Frickey. 1993. *Law and Public Choice: A Critical Introduction.* Chicago: University of Chicago Press.

Farber, Daniel A., and Suzanna Sherry. 1990. *A History of the American Constitution.* St Paul, MN: West Publishing Press.

Farish, Stephen E. 1984. "IT Dumping Guidelines." *Georgia Journal of International and Comparative Law* 14:597–612.

Fenno, Richard F. 1959.*The President's Cabinet.* Cambridge: Harvard University Press.

Fenno, Richard F. 1973. *Congressmen in Committees.* Boston: Little, Brown.

Ferejohn, John, and Charles Shipan. 1990. "Congressional Influence on Bureaucracy." *Journal of Law, Economics, and Organization* 6:1–20.

Finger, J. M., Keith Hall, and Douglas Nelson. 1982. "The Political Economy of Administered Protection." *American Economic Review* 82:452–66.

Fiorina, Morris. 1981. *Congress: Keystone of the Washington Establishment,* 2d ed. New Haven, CT: Yale University Press.

Frankfurter, Felix, and James M. Landis. 1928. *The Business of the Supreme Court: A Study in the Federal Judicial System.* New York: Macmillan Press.

Friedman, Milton. 1962. *Capitalism and Freedom.* Chicago: University of Chicago Press.

Galanter, Marc. 1974. "Why the Haves Come Out Ahead: Speculations on the Limits of Legal Change." *Law and Society Review* 9:95–160.

Gambitta, Richard A. L., Marlynn L. May, and James C. Foster, eds. 1981. *Governing Through Courts.* Beverly Hills, CA: Sage Publications.

George, Tracy E., and Lee Epstein. 1992. "On the Nature of Supreme Court Decision Making." *American Political Science Review* 86:323–37.

Gerhart, Peter M. 1977. "Judicial Review of Customs Service Actions." *Law and Policy in International Business* 9:1101–89.

Gibson, James L. 1978. "Judges' Role Orientations, Attitudes, and Decisions." *American Political Science Review* 72:911–24.

Gibson, James L. 1981. "Personality and Elite Political Behavior: The Influence of Self-Esteem on Judicial Decision-Making." *Journal of Politics* 43:104–25.

Giles, Michael W., and Thomas G. Walker. 1975. "Judicial Policy-Making and Southern Social Segregation." *Journal of Politics* 37:917–36.

Gillen, Mark. 1991. "Countervailing Duties: Efficiency and Public Choice." *Ottawa Law Review* 23:1–34.

Gizzi, Michael C. 1993. "Examining the Crisis of Volume in the U.S. Courts of Appeals." *Judicature* 77:96–103.

Glazer, Nathan. 1975. "Towards an Imperial Judiciary." *Public Interest* 41: 104–23.

Glazer, Nathan. 1978. "Should Judges Administer Social Services?" *Public Interest* 50:65–80.

Goldberger, Arthur S. 1964. *Econometric Theory.* New York: John Wiley and Sons.

Goldman, Sheldon. 1991. "The Bush Imprint on the Judiciary: Carrying on a Tradition." In *Judicial Politics: Readings from Judicature,* ed. Elliot E. Slotnick. Chicago: American Judicature Society.

Goldman, Sheldon. 1993. "Bush's Judicial Legacy: The Final Imprint." *Judicature* 76:282–97.

Goldstein, Judith. 1986. "The Political Economy of Trade: Institutions of Protection." *American Political Science Review* 80:161–84.

Goldstein, Judith. 1993. *Ideas, Interest, and American Trade Policy.* Ithaca, NY: Cornell University Press.

Goodnow, Frank J. 1900. *Politics and Administration: A Study in Government.* New York: Russel and Russel.

Goodsell, Charles T. 1985. *The Case for Bureaucracy.* Chatham, NJ: Chatham House.

Gormley, William T. 1979. "A Test of the Revolving Door Hypothesis at the FCC." *American Journal of Political Science* 23:665–83.

Gormley, William T. 1986. "Regulatory Issue Networks in a Federal System." *Polity* 18 (summer).

Gormley, William T. 1989. *Taming the Bureaucracy.* Princeton: Princeton University Press.

Gormley, William T., John Hoadley, and Charles Williams. 1983. "Potential Responsiveness in the Bureaucracy: Views of Public Utility Regulation." *American Political Science Review* 77:704–17.

Gourevitch, Peter Alexis. 1991. "International Trade, Domestic Coalitions, and Liberty: Comparative Responses to the Crises of 1873–1896." In *International Political Economy: Perspectives on Global Power and Wealth,* 2d ed., ed. Jeffry A. Frieden and David A. Lake. New York: St. Martin Press.

Graglia, Lino. 1982. "In Defense of Judicial Restraint." In *Supreme Court Activism and Restraint,* ed. Stephen C. Halpern and Charles M. Lamb. Lexington, MA: D. C. Heath.

Granovetter, Mark. 1985. "Economic Action and Social Structures: The Problem of Embeddedness." *American Journal of Sociology* 91:481–510.

Gray, Virginia, and David Lowery. 1996. *The Population Ecology of Interest Representation.* Ann Arbor: University of Michigan Press.

Greene, William H. 1993. *Econometric Analysis.* New York: Macmillan.

Grier, Kevin B., Michael C. Munger, and Brian E. Roberts. 1994. "The Determinants of Industry Political Activity." *American Political Science Review* 88:911–26.

Grossman Joel B., Herbert M. Kritzer, Kristin Bumiller, and Stephen McDougal. 1981. "Measuring the Pace of Civil Litigation in Federal and State Trial Courts." *Judicature* 65:86–113.

Gujarati, Damodar N. 1988. *Basic Econometrics.* New York: McGraw-Hill.

Handberg, Roger. 1979. "The Supreme Court and Administrative Agencies: 1965–1978." *Journal of Contemporary Law* 6:161–76.

Halpern, Stephen C., and Charles M. Lamb, eds. 1982. *Supreme Court Activism and Restraint.* Lexington, MA: D. C. Heath.

Hansen, Wendy L. 1990. "The International Trade Commission and the Politics of Protectionism." *American Political Science Review* 84:21–46.

Hansen, Wendy L., Renée J. Johnson, and Isaac Unah. 1995. "Specialized Courts, Bureaucratic Agencies, and the Politics of U.S. Trade Policy." *American Journal of Political Science* 39:529–57.

Hansen, Wendy L., and Keeok Park. 1995. "Nation-State and Pluralistic Decision Making in Trade Policy: The Case of the International Trade Administration." *International Studies Quarterly* 39:181–211.

Hansen, Wendy L., and Thomas J. Prusa. 1993a. "Does Administrative Protection Protect?" *Regulation: Cato Review of Business & Government* 16:35–43.

Hansen, Wendy L., and Thomas J. Prusa. 1993b. "Congressional Decision-Making and the Rise of Delegation: An Application to Trade Policy." Paper presented at the annual meeting of the American Political Science Association, September 2–5, Washington, DC.

Hansen, Wendy L., and Thomas J. Prusa. 1996. "Cumulation and ITC Decision-Making: The Sum of the Parts Is Greater than the Whole." *Economic Inquiry* 34:746–69.

Harriman, Linda, and Jeffrey D. Straussman. 1983. "Do Judges Determine Budget Decisions? Federal Court Decisions in Prison Reform and State Spending for Corrections." *Public Administration Review* 43:343–51.

Heclo, Hugh. 1978. "Issue Networks and the Presidential Establishment." In *The 'New' American Political System,* ed. Anthony King. Washington, DC: American Enterprise Institute for Public Policy Research.

Hibbing, John R. 1991. *Congressional Careers: Contours of Life in the U.S. House of Representatives.* Chapel Hill: University of North Carolina Press.

Hoffman, Daniel N. 1981. "Nonpublication of Federal Appellate Court Opinions." *Legal System Journal* 6:405–34.

Holmstrom, B. R. 1979. "Moral Hazard and Observability." *Bell Journal of Economics* 10:7–91.

Horgan, J. Kevin. 1988. "The Impact of Interlocutory Judicial Decisions upon Antidumping and Countervailing Duty Proceedings." *Florida International Law Journal* 3:187–205.

Horlick, Gary N., and Geoffrey D. Oliver. 1989. "Antidumping and Countervailing Duty Law Provisions of the Omnibus Trade and Competitive Act of 1988." *Journal of World Trade* 23:5–49.

Horowitz, Donald L. 1977. *The Courts and Social Policy.* Washington, DC: Brookings Institution.

Howard, J. Woodward, Jr. 1981. *Courts of Appeals and the Federal Judicial System.* Princeton: Princeton University Press.

Ikenberry, John G. 1988. "Conclusion: An Institutional Approach to American Foreign Economic Policy." *International Economics* 42 (winter).

Jackson, John E. 1991. *The World Trading System.* Cambridge: MIT Press.

Jameson, Paul W. 1986. "Recent International Trade Commission Practice Regarding the Material Injury Standard: A Critique." *Law and Policy in International Business* 18:517–77.

Johnson, Charles A. 1987a. "Law, Politics, and Judicial Decision-Making: Lower Federal Court Uses of Supreme Court Decisions." *Law and Society Review* 21:325–42.

Johnson, Charles A. 1987b. "Content-Analytic Techniques and Judicial Research." *American Politics Quarterly* 15:169–97.

Johnson, Charles, and Bradley C. Canon. 1984. *Judicial Policies: Implementation and Impact.* Washington, DC: CQ Press.

Jones, Bryan D., Frank R. Baumgartner, and Jeffery C. Talbert. 1993. "The Destruction of Issue Monopolies in Congress." *American Political Science Review* 87:657–71.

Jordan, Ellen R. 1981. "Specialized Courts: A Choice?" *Northwestern University Law Review* 76:745–85.

Kaplan, Seth. 1991. "Injury and Causation in USITC Antidumping Determinations: Five Recent Approaches." In *Policy Implications of Antidumping Measures,* ed. P. K. M. Tharakan. Amsterdam, North-Holland: Elsevier Science Publishers.

Katzmann, Robert A. 1988. *Judges and Legislators: Toward Institutional Comity.* Washington, DC: Brookings Institution.

Kaufman, Herbert. 1956. "Emerging Conflicts in the Doctrines of Public Administration." *American Political Science Review* 50:1057–73.

Keech, William R., and Kyoungsan Pak. 1995. "Partisanship, Institutions, and Change in American Trade Politics." *Journal of Politics* 57:1130–42.

Kelly, Michael J. 1996. *The Lives of Lawyers: Journeys in the Organization and Practice.* Ann Arbor: University of Michigan Press.

Kelman, Steven. 1990. "Congress and Public Spirit: A Commentary." In *Beyond Self-Interest,* ed. Jane Mansbridge. Chicago: University of Chicago Press.

Keohane, Robert O., and Joseph S. Nye. 1989. *Power and Interdependence.* New York: Harper-Collins.

Khademian, Anne M. 1992. *The SEC and Capital Market Regulation: The Politics of Expertise.* Pittsburgh: University of Pittsburgh Press.

Kingdon, John W. 1984. *Agendas, Alternatives and Public Policies.* Boston: Little, Brown.

Knoll, Michael S. 1989. "An Economic Approach to the Determination of Injury under United States Antidumping and Countervailing Duty Law." *New York University Journal of International Law and Politics* 22:37–116.

Knott, Jack H., and Gary J. Miller. 1987. *Reforming Bureaucracy: The Politics of Institutional Choice.* Englewood Cliffs, NJ: Prentice-Hall.

Koch, Charles H. 1986. "Judicial Review of Administrative Discretion." *George Washington Law Review* 54:469–511.

Kort, Fred. 1966. "Quantitative Analysis of Fact Patterns in Cases and Their Impact on Judicial Decision." *Harvard Law Review* 79:1595–1603.

Krasner, Stephen. 1976. "State Power and the Structure of International Trade." *World Politics* 28:317–47.

Kreps, David M. 1990. "Corporate Culture and Economic Theory." In *Perspectives on Positive Political Economy,* ed. James E. Alt and Kenneth A. Shepsle. New York: Cambridge University Press.

Krippendorff, Klaus. 1980. *Content Analysis: An Introduction to Its Methodology.* Newbury Park: Sage.

Krugman, Paul R. 1987. "Is Free Trade Passé?" *Economic Perspectives* 1:131–44.

Kuhn, Perla M. 1986. "International Trade Law Developments in the United States Court of Appeals for the Federal Circuit during the Year 1985." *American University Law Review* 35:1073–96.

Kuklinski, James H., and John E. Stanga. 1979. "Political Participation and Government Responsiveness: The Behavior of California Superior Courts." *American Political Science Review* 73:1090–99.

Landau, Martin. 1969. "Redundancy, Rationality, and the Problem of Duplication and Overlap." *Public Administration Review* 29:346–58.

Landes, William M., and Richard A. Posner. 1975. "The Independent Judiciary in an Interest-Group Perspective." *Journal of Law and Economics* 18:875–901.

Liao, Tim Futing. 1994. "Interpreting Probability Models: Logit, Probit, and Other Generalized Linear Models." Thousand Oaks, CA: Sage.

Lindbloom, Charles. 1959. "The Science of 'Muddling Through.'" *Public Administration Review* 19:79–88.

Lindbloom, Charles. 1977. *Politics and Markets.* New York: Basic Books.

Litan, Robert E. 1989. "Speeding Up Civil Justice." *Judicature* 73:162–67.

Lorch, Robert S. 1967. "The Administrative Court Idea before Congress." *Western Political Quarterly* 20:65–81.

Lowi, Theodore. 1964. "American Business, Public Policy, Case Studies, and Political Theory." *World Politics* 16:677–716.

Lowi, Theodore J. 1969. *The End of Liberalism: Ideology, Policy, and the Crisis of Authority.* New York: Norton Press.

Lowi, Theodore J. 1984. "The New Public Philosophy: Interest-Group Liberalism." In *The Political Economy: Readings in the Politics and Economics of American Public Policy,* ed.Thomas Ferguson and Joel Rogers. Armonk, NY: M. E. Sharpe.

Madison, James, Alexander Hamilton, and John Jay. [1788] 1987. *The Federalist Papers,* ed. Isaac Kramnick. New York: Penguin Books.

Markey, Howard T. 1992. "The Federal Circuit and Congressional Intent."*American University Law Review* 41:577–79.

Marshall, Thomas R. 1989. *Public Opinion and the Supreme Court.* Boston: Unwin Hyman.

Mashaw, Jerry. 1985. "Prodelegation: Why Administrators Should Make Political Decisions." *Journal of Law, Economics and Organization.* 1:81–100.

McCraw, Thomas K. 1984. *Prophets of Regulation.* Cambridge: Harvard University Press.

McCubbins, Matthew D., Roger Noll, and Barry Weingast. 1987. "Administrative Procedures as Instruments of Political Control." *Journal of Law, Economics and Organization* 3:243–77.

McCubbins, Matthew D., Roger Noll, and Barry Weingast. 1989."Structure and Process, Politics and Policy: Administrative Arrangements and the Political Control of Agencies." *Virginia Law Review* 75:431–82.

McCubbins, Matthew D., and Talbot Page. 1987. "A Theory of Congressional Delegation." In *Congress: Structure and Policy,* ed. Matthew D. McCubbins and Terry Sullivan. Cambridge: Cambridge University Press.

McCubbins, Matthew D., and Thomas Schwartz. 1984. "Congressional Oversight Overlooked: Police Patrol versus Fire Alarms." *American Journal of Political Science* 28:165–79.

McCubbins, Matthew D., and Terry Sullivan. 1987. *Congress: Structure and Policy.* New York: Cambridge University Press.

McFeeley, Neil D. 1987. *Appointment of Judges: The Johnson Presidency.* Austin: University of Texas Press.

McGraw, Kathleen M. 1991. "Managing Blame: An Experimental Test of the Effects of Political Accounts." *American Political Science Review* 85:1133–57.

McGuire, Kevin T. 1995. Capital Investments in the U.S. Supreme Court: Winning with Washington Representation." In *Contemplating Courts,* ed. Lee Epstein. Washington, DC: CQ Press.

McIntosh, Wayne. 1983. "Private Use of a Public Forum: A Long Range View of the Dispute Processing Role of Courts." *American Political Science Review* 77:991–1010.

McKeown, Timothy. 1984. "Firms and Tariff Regime: Explaining the Demand for Protection." *World Politics* 36:215–33.

Meador, Daniel J. 1983. "An Appellate Court Dilemma and a Solution through Subject Matter Organization." *Journal of Law Reform* 16:471–92.

Meador, Daniel J. 1992. "The Origin of the Federal Circuit: A Personal Account." *American University Law Review* 41:581–620.

Meier, Kenneth J. 1985. *Regulation: Politics, Bureaucracy, and Economics.* New York: St. Martin Press.

Melnick, R. Shep. 1983. *Regulation and the Courts.* Washington, DC: Brookings Institution.

Melnick, R. Shep. 1985. "The Politics of Partnership." *Public Administration Review* 45:653–60.

Middleton, Martha. 1983. "Specialty Courts: Two More Justices Speak Out." *American Bar Association Journal* (January) 69: 23.

Middleton, Martha. 1984. "Federal Circuit Asks Bar: 'Help Define Our Work.'" *National Law Journal* (May 7).

Miller, Arthur, and Terry M. Moe. 1983. "Bureaucrats, Legislators and the Size of Government." *American Political Science Review* 77:297–322.

Milner, Helen. 1993. "Maintaining International Commitments in Trade Policy." In *Do Institutions Matter?* ed. R. Kent Weaver and Bert A. Rockman. Washington, DC: Brookings Institution.

Miner, Roger J. 1993. "Federal Court Reform Should Start at the Top." *Judicature* 77:104–8.

Mitchell, William C. 1990. "Interest Groups: Economic Perspectives and Contributions." *Journal of Theoretical Politics* 2 (1): 85–108.

Mitchell, William C., and Michael C. Munger. 1991. "Economic Models of Interest Groups: An Introductory Survey." *American Journal of Political Science* 35:512–46.

Mock, William B. T., Jr. 1986. "Cumulation of Import Statistics in Injury Investigations before the International Trade Commission." *Northwestern Journal of International Law and Business* 7:433–79.

Moe, Terry M. 1982. "Regulatory Performance and Presidential Administration." *American Journal of Political Science* 26:197–224.

Moe, Terry M. 1984. "The New Economics of Organization." *American Journal of Political Science* 28: 739–77.

Moe, Terry M. 1985. "Control and Feedback in Economic Regulation: The Case of the NLRB." *American Political Science Review* 1094–1116.

Moe, Terry M. 1987. "An Assessment of the Positive Theory of Congressional Dominance." *Legislative Studies Quarterly* 4:475–521.

Moe, Terry M. 1989. "The Politics of Bureaucratic Structure." In *Can Government Govern?* ed. John E. Chubb and Paul E. Paterson. Washington DC: Brookings Institution.

Moore, Michael O. 1992. "Rules or Politics?: An Empirical Analysis of IT Anti-Dumping Decisions." *Economic Inquiry* 30:449–66.

Morrison, Samuel E., Henry Steel Commager, and William E. Leuchtenburg. 1977. *A Concise History of the American Republic,* vol. 2. New York: Oxford University Press.

Mueller, John E. 1970. "Presidential Popularity from Truman to Johnson." *American Political Science Review* 64:18–34.

Murphy, Walter F. 1964. *Elements of Judicial Strategy.* Chicago: University of Chicago Press.

Murray, Tracy. 1991. "The Administration of the Antidumping Duty Law by the Department of Commerce." In *Down in the Dumps: The Administration of the Unfair Trade Laws,* ed. Richard Boltuck and Robert T. Litan. Washington, DC: Brookings Institution.

Nagel, Stuart S. 1961. "Political Party Affiliations and Judges' Decisions." *American Political Science Review* 55:843–50.

Nathan, Richard P. 1986. "The Administrative Presidency." In *Bureaucratic Power in National Policy Making,* 4th ed., ed. Francis E. Rourke. Boston: Little, Brown.

Neustadt, Richard E. 1990. *Presidential Power and the Modern Presidents.* New York: Free Press.

Niskanen, William. 1971. *Bureaucracy and Representative Government:* New York: Aldine-Atherton.

Nivola, Pietro S. 1986. "The New Protectionism: U.S. Trade Policy in Historical Perspective." *Political Science Quarterly* 101:577–600.

Nivola, Pietro S. 1990. "Trade Policy: Refereeing the Playing Field." In *A Question of Balance: The President, Congress, and Foreign Policy,* ed. Thomas E. Mann. Washington, DC: Brookings Institution.

Nivola, Pietro S. 1993. *Regulating Unfair Trade.* Washington, DC: Brookings Institution.

Noll, Roger G., and Bruce Owen, eds. 1983. *The Politics of Deregulation.* Washington, DC: American Enterprise Institute.

North, Douglass. 1990. "Institutions and a Transaction Cost Theory of Exchange." In *Perspectives on Positive Political Economy,* ed. James E. Alt and Kenneth A. Shepsle. New York: Cambridge University Press.

O'Brien. David M. 1993. *Storm Center: The Supreme Court in American Politics,* New York: W. W. Norton.

Ogul, Morris S. 1981. "Congressional Oversight: Structure and Incentives." In *Congress Reconsidered,* 2d ed., ed. Lawrence C. Dodd and Bruce I. Oppenheimer. Washington, DC: CQ Press.

Olson, Mancur. 1965. *The Logic of Collective Action.* Cambridge: Harvard University Press.

Ostrom, Charles W., and Dennis M. Simon. 1988. "The President's Public." *American Journal of Political Science* 32:1096–1119.

Pacelle, Richard L., and Lawrence Baum. 1992. "Supreme Court Authority in the Judiciary." *American Politics Quarterly* 20:169–91.

Passell, Peter. 1993. "U.S.'s Tough Trade Enforcement." *New York Times,* 20 July.

Pastor, Robert. 1983. "The Cry-and-Sigh Syndrome: Congress and Trade Policy." In *Making Economic Policy in Congress,* ed. Allen Schick. Washington, DC: American Enterprise Institute for Public Policy.

Peltason, Jack W. 1955. *Federal Courts in the Political Process.* New York: Random House.

Peltzman, Sam. 1976. "Toward a More General Theory of Regulation." *Journal of Law and Economics* 19:211–48.

Peltzman, Sam. 1989. "The Economic Theory of Regulation after a Decade of Deregulation." *Brookings Papers on Economic Activity* (Microeconomics): 1–41.

Pertschuk, Michael. 1982. *Revolt against Regulation.* Berkeley: University of California Press.

Pierce, Richard J., Sidney A. Shapiro, and Paul A. Verkuil. 1992. *Administrative Law and Process,* 2d ed. Westbury, NY: Foundation Press.

Porter, Michael E. 1985. *Competitive Advantage: Creating and Sustaining Superior Performance.* New York: Free Press.

Posner, Richard A. 1983. "Will the Federal Courts of Appeals Survive Until 1984?: An Essay on Delegation and Specialization of the Judicial Function." *Southern California Law Review* 56:761–91.

Posner, Richard A. 1985. *Federal Courts: Crisis and Reform.* Cambridge: Harvard University Press.

Pratt, John W., and Richard J. Zeckhauser. 1985. *Principals and Agents: The Structure of Business.* Boston: Harvard School of Business Press.

Pressman, Jeffrey L., and Aaron Wildavsky. 1973. *Implementation.* Berkeley: University of California Press.

Prestowitz, Clyde V. 1988. *Trading Places: How We Are Giving Our Future to Japan and How to Reclaim It.* New York: Basic Books.

Pritchett, C. Herman. 1948. *The Roosevelt Court: A Study in Judicial Politics and Values, 1937–1947.* New York: Macmillan.

Quirk, Paul. 1990. "Deregulation and the Politics of Ideas in Congress." In *Beyond Self-Interest,* ed. Jane Mansbridge. Chicago: University of Chicago Press.

Rapkin, Jeremy. 1989. *Judicial Compulsion: How Public Law Distorts Public Policy.* New York: Basic Books.

Ray, Edward J. 1989. *U.S. Protectionism and the World Debt Crisis.* New York: Quorum Books.

Re, Edward D. 1981. "Litigation before the United States Court of International Trade." *New York Law School Law Review* 26:437–58.

Redden, Kenneth R. 1982. *Federal Special Court Litigation.* Charlottesville, VA: Michie Company.

Redford, Emmette S. 1969. *Democracy in the Administrative State.* New York: Oxford University Press.

Reed, Patrick C. 1996. *The Role of Federal Courts in U.S. Customs and International Trade Law.* New York: Oceana Publications.

Restani, Jane A. 1988. "Judicial Review in International Trade: Its Role in the Balance between Delegation by Congress and Limitation of Executive Discretion." *American University Law Review* 37:1075–86.

Revesz, Richard L. 1990. "Specialized Courts and the Administrative Lawmaking System." *University of Pennsylvania Law Review* 138:1111–74.

Rhoads, Steven E. 1985. *The Economist's View of the World: Government, Markets, and Public Policy.* New York: Cambridge University Press.

Richardson, Richard J., and Kenneth N. Vines. 1967. "Review, Dissent, and the Appellate Process: A Political Interpretation." *Journal of Politics* 29:597–616.

Rifkind, Simon. 1951. "A Special Court for Patent Litigation? The Danger of a Specialized Judiciary." *American Bar Association Journal* 37:425–30.

Riker, William, and Barry Weingast. 1988. "Constitutional Regulation of Legislative Choice: The Political Consequences of Judicial Deference to Legislatures." *Virginia Law Review* 74:373–402.

Robyn, Dorothy. 1987. *Breaking the Special Interests: Trucking Deregulation and the Politics of Policy Reform.* Chicago: University of Chicago Press.

Rodgers, William H., Jr. 1979. "A Hard Look at Vermont Yankee: Environmental Law under Close Scrutiny." *Georgetown Law Review* 67:699–727.

Rodgers, Harrell, Jr., and Charles S. Bullock III. 1976. *Coercion to Compliance.* Lexington, MA.: D. C. Heath.

Rohde, David, and Harold J. Spaeth. 1976. *Supreme Court Decision Making.* San Francisco: W. H. Freeman Press.

Rosenberg, Gerald N. 1991. *The Hollow Hope: Can Courts Bring about Social Change?* Chicago: University of Chicago Press.

Rosenberg, Gerald N. 1995. "The Real World of Constitutional Rights: The Supreme Court and the Implementation of the Abortion Decisions. In *Contemplating Courts,* ed. Lee Epstein. Washington, DC: CQ Press.

Rosenbloom, David H. 1981. "Judicial Response to the Rise of the American Administrative State." *American Review of Public Administration* 50:29–51.

Rosenswein, Rifka. 1991. "Trade Court: Life in the Shadows." *Manhattan Lawyer* (March) Lexis/Nexis.

Rourke, Francis E. 1984. *Bureaucracy, Politics, and Public Policy,* 3d ed. New York: Harper Collins.

Rourke, Francis E. 1992. "Responsiveness and Neutral Competence in American Bureaucracy." *Public Administration Review* 52:539–46.

Sabatier, Paul A. 1988. "An Advocacy Coalition Framework of Policy Change and the Role of Policy-Oriented Learning Therein." *Policy Studies* 21:129–68.

Salamon, Lester M., and John J. Siegfried. 1977. "Economic Power and Political Influence: The Impact of Industry Structure on Policy." *American Political Science Review* 71:1026–43.

Sarat, Austin. 1977. "Surveying American Legal Culture: An Assessment of Survey Evidence." *Law and Society Review* 11:427–88.

Scalia, Antonin. 1989. "Judicial Deference to Administrative Interpretations of Law." *Duke Law Journal* 1989:511–21.

Schattsneider, E. E. 1935. *Politics, Pressure Groups and the Tariff.* New York: Prentice Hall.

Schneider, Mark, and Paul Teske. 1995. *Public Entrepreneurs: Identifying Agents for Change in the Local Market for Public Goods.* Princeton: Princeton University Press.

Scholz, John T., and Fend-Heng Wei. 1986. "Regulatory Enforcement in a Federalist System." *American Political Science Review* 80:1249–70.

Sears, David O., and Carolyn L. Funk. 1990. "Self-Interest in Americans' Political Opinion." In *Beyond Self-Interest,* ed. Jane J. Mansbridge. Chicago: University of Chicago Press.

Segal, Jeffrey A. 1984. "Predicting Supreme Court Cases Probablistically: The Search and Seizure Cases, 1962–1981." *American Political Science Review* 78:891–900.

Segal, Jeffrey A. 1986. "Supreme Court Justices as Human Decision Makers: An Individual-Level Analysis of Search and Seizure Cases." *Journal of Politics* 48:938–55.

Segal, Jeffrey A. 1987. "Senate Confirmation of Supreme Court Justices: Partisan and Institutional Politics." *Journal of Politics* 49:998–1015.

Segal, Jeffrey A., Charles Cameron, and Albert Cover. 1992. "A Spatial Model of Roll Call Voting: Senators, Constituents, Presidents, and Interest Groups in Supreme Court Confirmations." *American Journal of Political Science* 36:96–121.

Segal, Jeffrey A., and Albert D. Cover. 1989. "Ideological Values and the Votes of Supreme Court Justices." *American Political Science Review* 83:557–65.

Segal, Jeffrey A., and Harold J. Spaeth. 1993. *The Supreme Court and the Attitudinal Model.* New York: Cambridge University Press.

Shapiro, Martin. 1968. *The Supreme Court and Administrative Agencies.* New York: Free Press.

Shapiro, Martin. 1981. *Courts: A Comparative and Political Analysis.* Chicago: University of Chicago Press.

Shapiro, Martin. 1988. *Who Guards the Guardian? Judicial Control of Administration.* Athens: University of Georgia Press.

Sheehan, Reginald S. 1992. "Federal Agencies and the Supreme Court: An Analysis of Litigation Outcomes, 1953–1988." *American Politics Quarterly* 20: 478–500.

Sheehan, Reginald S., William Mishler, and Donald R. Songer. 1992. "Ideology, Status, and Differential Success of Direct Parties before the Supreme Court." *American Political Science Review* 86:475–86.

Shepsle, Kenneth A. 1979. "Institutional Arrangements and Equilibrium in Multidimensional Voting Models." *American Journal of Political Science* 23:27–60.

Shepsle, Kenneth. 1982. Review of *The Politics of Regulation,* by James Q. Wilson. *Journal of Political Economy* 90:216–21.

Shepsle, Kenneth A. 1989. "Studying Institutions: Some Lessons from the Rational Choice Approach." *Journal of Theoretical Politics* 1:131–47.

Shepsle, Kenneth A. 1992. "Congress is a 'They' Not an 'It': Legislative Intent as Oxymoron." *International Review of Law and Economics* 12:239–56.

Shughart, William E., and Robert D. Tollison. 1985. "The Cyclical Character of Regulatory Activity." *Public Choice* 45:303–11.

Simon, Herbert A. 1957. *Administrative Behavior: A Study of Decision-Making Processes in Administrative Organizations,* 2d ed. New York: Free Press.

Slotnick, Elliot E. 1984. "Judicial Selection Systems and Nomination Outcomes: Does the Process Make a Difference?" *American Politics Quarterly* 12:225.

Smith, Steven S., and Christopher J. Deering. 1984. *Committees in Congress.* Washington, DC: CQ Press.

Songer, Donald R. 1979. "The Relevance of Values for the Confirmation of Supreme Court Nominees." *Law and Society Review* 13:927–48.

Songer, Donald R. 1987. "The Impact of the Supreme Court on Trends in Economic Policy Making in the United States Court of Appeals." *Journal of Politics* 49:831–41.

Songer, Donald R., and Susan Haire. 1992. "Integrating Alternative Approaches to the Study of Judicial Voting: Obscenity Cases in the U.S. Courts of Appeals." *American Journal of Political Science* 36:963–82.

Songer, Donald R., Jeffrey A. Segal, and Charles M. Cameron. 1994. "The Hierarchy of Justice: Testing a Principal-Agent Model of Supreme Court–Circuit Court Interactions." American Journal of Political Science 38:673–96.

Songer, Donald R., and Reginald S. Sheehan. 1992. "Who Wins on Appeal? Upperdogs and Underdogs in the United States Courts of Appeals." *American Journal of Political Science* 36:235–58.

Spaeth, Harold J., and Stuart H. Teger. 1982. "Activism and Restraint: A Cloak for the Justices' Policy Preferences." In *Supreme Court Activism and Restraint,* ed. Stephen C. Halpern and Charles M. Lamb. Lexington, MA: D. C. Heath.

Spiller, Pablo T., and Rafael Gely. 1992. "Congressional Control or Judicial Independence: The Determinants of U.S. Supreme Court Labor-Relations Decisions, 1949–1988." *RAND Journal of Economics* 23:463–92.

Spriggs, James F. II. 1996. "The Supreme Court and Federal Administrative Agencies: A Resource-Based Theory and Analysis of Judicial Impact." *American Journal of Political Science* 40:1122–51.

Stanfield, Rochelle L. 1986. "Resolving Disputes." *National Journal* (November): 2764–68.

Stewart, Richard B. 1975. The Reformation of American Administrative Law." *Harvard Law Review* 88:1667–1711.

Stidham, Ronald, and Robert A. Carp. 1987. "Judges, Presidents, and Policy Choices: Exploring the Linkage." *Social Science Quarterly* 68:395–404.

Stigler, George J. 1971. "The Theory of Economic Regulation." *Bell Journal of Economics and Management Science* 2:3–21.

Strover, Robert V., and Don W. Brown. 1975. "Understanding Compliance and Noncompliance with Law: The Contributions of Utility Theory." *Social Science Quarterly* 56:363–75.

Takacs, Wendy E. 1981. "Pressures for Protectionism: An Empirical Analysis." *Economic Inquiry* 19:687–93.

Tate, C. Neal. 1981. "Personal Attribute Models of the Voting Behavior of U.S. Supreme Court Justices: Liberalism in Civil Liberties and Economic Decisions, 1946–1978." *American Political Science Review* 75:355–67.

Teske, Paul. 1991. "Interests and Institutions in State Regulation." *American Journal of Political Science* 35:139–54.

Truman, David B. 1959. *The Governmental Process.* New York: Alfred A. Knopf.

Tyler, Tom R. 1990. *Why People Obey the Law.* New Haven, CT: Yale University Press.

Ulmer, Sidney. 1973. "Social Background as an Indicator of the Votes of Supreme Court Justices." *American Journal of Political Science* 17:622–30.

Unah, Isaac. 1995. "Taming the Shrewd through Judgment: Judicial Influence over U.S. Trade Policy Implementation." Paper presented at annual meeting of the Midwest Political Science Association, April 6–8, Chicago.

Unah, Isaac. 1997. "Specialized Courts of Appeals' Review of Bureaucratic Actions and the Politics of Protectionism." *Political Research Quarterly* 50:851–78.

U.S. Department of Commerce. Bureau of the Census. 1974–90. *Annual Survey of Manufactures.* Washington, DC: GPO.

U.S. Department of Commerce. Bureau of the Census. 1980–90. *Census of Manufactures, Subject Statistics.* Washington, DC: GPO.

U.S. Department of Commerce. Bureau of the Census. 1980–90. *Current Industrial Reports: Survey of Plant Capacity.* Washington, DC:GPO.

U.S. Department of Commerce. Bureau of the Census. 1979–90. *United States Exports of Domestic Merchandise, SIC-based Products by World Areas.* Washington, DC: GPO.

U.S. Department of Commerce. Bureau of the Census. 1980–90. *United States Imports for Consumption, SIC-based Products by World Areas.* Washington, DC: GPO.

U.S. General Accounting Office. 1988. *Pursuit of Trade Law Remedies by Small Business.* Report no. GAO/NSIAD-89-69BR. Washington, DC: GPO.

U.S. International Trade Commission. 1978–94. *Annual Reports.* Washington, DC: GPO.

U.S. International Trade Commission. 1986. *Certain Fresh Atlantic Groundfish from Canada.* Publication no. 1844. Washington DC.

U.S. International Trade Commission. 1992. *Minivans from Japan.* Publication no. 2529. Washington DC.

U.S. Trade Representative. 1978–88. *Annual Report of the President of the United States on the Trade Agreements Program.* Washington DC: GPO.

Vance, Andrew P. 1981. "Judicial Review of Antidumping Orders in the United States and European Economic Community." *New York Law School Law Review* 26:577–607.

Waldo, Dwight. 1948. *The Administrative State.* New York: Ronald Press.

Wasby, Stephen L. 1970. *The Impact of the United States Supreme Court: Some Perspectives.* Homewood, IL: Dorsey Press.

Wasby, Stephen L. 1981. "Arrogation of Power: Judicial 'Imperialism' Revisited." *Judicature* 65:208–19.

Waterman, Richard W. 1989. *Presidential Influence and the Administrative State.* Knoxville: University of Tennessee Press.

Weaver, R. Kent. 1986. "The Politics of Blame Avoidance." *Journal of Public Policy* 6:371–98.

Weber, Max. 1946. *Essays in Sociology.* New York: Oxford University Press.

Weber, Robert Philip. 1990. *Basic Content Analysis.* Newbury Park, CA: Sage.

Weingast, Barry. 1984. "The Congressional-Bureaucratic System: A Principal-Agent Perspective (With Application to the SEC)." *Public Choice* 44:147–95.

Weingast, Barry R., and Mark J. Moran. 1983. "Bureaucratic Discretion or Congressional Control? Regulatory Policymaking by the Federal Trade Commission." *Journal of Political Economy* 91:765–800.

White, Leonard D. 1927. *The City Manager.* Chicago: University of Chicago Press.

Whitney, Scott S. 1973a. "The Case for Creating a Special Environmental Court System." *William and Mary Law Review* 14:473.

Whitney, Scott S. 1973b. "The Case for Creating a Special Environmental Court System—A Further Comment." *William and Mary Law Review* 15:33.

Wildavsky, Aaron. 1984. *The Politics of the Budgetary Process,* 4th ed. Boston: Little, Brown.

Wildavsky, Ben. 1995. "Cracking Up." *National Journal* 27:2636–40.

Williamson, Oliver. 1975. *Markets and Hierarchies.* New York: Free Press.

Williamson, Oliver. 1991. "Economic Institutions: Spontaneous and Intentional Governance." *Journal of Law, Economics, and Organization* 7:159–87.

Willison, David H. 1986. "Judicial Review of Administrative Decisions: Agency

Cases before the Court of Appeals for the District of Columbia, 1981–1984." *American Politics Quarterly* 14:317–27.

Wilson, Graham K. 1985. *The Politics of Safety and Health.* Oxford: Clarendon Press of the Oxford University Press.

Wilson, James Q. 1980. *The Politics of Regulation.* New York: Basic Books.

Wilson, James Q. 1989. *Bureaucracy: What Governments Do and Why They Do It.* New York: Basic Books.

Wilson, Woodrow. [1887] 1978. "The Study of Administration." In *The Administrative Process and Democratic Theory,* ed. Louis C. Gawthrop. Boston: Houghton Mifflin.

Wolf, Charles, Jr. 1988. *Markets or Governments: Choosing Between Imperfect Alternatives.* Cambridge: MIT Press.

Wolfe, Christopher. 1994. *The Rise of Modern Judicial Review: From Constitutional Interpretation to Judge-Made Law.* Lanham, MD: Rowman and Littlefield.

Wood, B. Dan, and James E. Anderson. 1993. "The Politics of U.S. Antitrust Regulation." *American Journal of Political Science* 73:1–39.

Wood, B. Dan, and Richard W. Waterman. 1991. "The Dynamics of Political Control over Bureaucracy." *American Political Science Review* 85:801–28.

Wood, B. Dan, and Richard W. Waterman. 1994. *Bureaucratic Dynamics: The Role of Bureaucracy in a Democracy.* Boulder, CO: Westview Press.

Yankelovich, Daniel, and I. M. Destler, eds. 1994. *Beyond the Beltway: Engaging the Public in U.S. Foreign Policy.* New York: W. W. Norton.

Yarbrough, Beth V., and Robert M. Yarbrough. 1991. *The World Economy: Trade and Finance,* 2d ed. Chicago: Dryden Press.

Yarbrough, Tinsley. 1982. "The Judge as Manager: The Case of Judge Frank Johnson." *Journal of Policy Analysis and Management* 1:386–400.

Yates, Douglas. 1982. *Bureaucratic Democracy.* Cambridge: Harvard University Press.

Yoffie, David B. 1993. *Beyond Free Trade: Firms, Governments, and Global Competition.* Boston: Harvard Business School Press.

Zeman, Frances Kahn. 1983. "Legal Mobilization: The Neglected Role of the Law in the Political System." *American Political Science Review* 77:690–703.

Cases Cited

Alberta Pork Producers' Marketing Board v. United States, 11 CIT 563 (1987)
American Lamb Co. v. United States, 4 Fed. Cir. (T) 47 (1986)
Bantam Travelware Div. of Peter's Bag Corp. v. United States, 857 F.2d 742 (1988)
Bingham and Taylor Division, Virginia Industries, Inc. v. United States, 5 Fed. Cir. (T) 90 (1987)
Brown v. Board of Education of Topeka I, 347 U.S. 483 (1954)
Bureau of Alcohol v. Federal Labor Relations Authority, 464 U.S. 89 (1983)
Cabot Corp. v. United States, 9 CIT 489 (1985)
Calabrian Corp. v. U.S. International Trade Commission, 16 CIT 342 (1992)
Canadian Meat Council v. United States, 11 CIT 362 (1987)
Carter v. Carter Coal Co. 298 U.S. 238 (1936)
Chevron, U.S.A. Inc. v. National Resources Defense Council, 467 U.S. 837 (1984)
Copperweld Corp. v. United States, 12 CIT 148 (1988)
Dred Scott v. Sanford, 19 Howard 393 (1857)
Environmental Defense Fund v. Ruckelshaus, 439 F.2d 584 (D.C. Cir. 1971)
Firestone Tire & Rubber Co. v. Risjord, 449 U.S. 368 (1981)
Fiske v. Kansas, 274 U.S. 380 (1927)
Fundicao Tupy S.A. v. United States, 11 CIT 23 (1987)
Fundicao Tupy S.A. v. United States, 6 Fed. Cir. (T) 106 (1988)
Granges Metallverken, AB v. United States, 13 CIT 147 (1989)
Humphrey's Executor v. United States, 295 U.S. 602 (1935)
Hyundai Pipe Co., Ltd. v. U.S. International Trade Commission, 11 CIT 117 (1987)
Lochner v. New York, 198 U.S. 45 (1905)
Lopez v. Heckler, 725 F.2d 1489 (9th Cir. 1984)
Marbury v. Madison, 5 U.S. (1 Cranch) 137 (1803)
Marubeni America Corp. v. United States, 17 CIT 360 (1993)
Olympic Adhesives Inc. v. United States, 13 CIT 145 (1989)
Parke-Davis & Co. v. H. K. Mulford Co., 189 F.95 115 (S.D.N.Y. 1911)
Roe v. Wade, 410 U.S.113 (1973)
Roquette Freres v. United States 6 CIT 293 (1983)
Schechter Poultry Corp. v. United States, 295 U.S. 495 (1935)
Udall v. Tallman, 329 U.S. 143 (1965)
United States v. Curtiss-Wright Corp., 299 U.S. 304 (1936)
West Coast Hotel Co. v. Parish, 300 U.S. 379 (1937)
Zenith Radio Corp. v. United States, 437 U.S. 443 (1978)

Name Index

223

Subject Index